Computer Studies a first course

Computer Studies a first course

John Shelley and Roger Hunt

Imperial College Computer Centre

Pitman

PITMAN PUBLISHING LIMITED
39 Parker Street, London WC2B 5PB

Associated Companies

Copp Clark Pitman, Toronto
Fearon Pitman Publishers Inc, Belmont, California
Pitman Publishing New Zealand Ltd, Wellington
Pitman Publishing Pty Ltd, Melbourne

© J Shelley & R Hunt 1980

First published in Great Britain 1980

ISBN 0 273 01272 X

Typeset at The Universities Press (Belfast) Limited and reproduced
and printed by photolithography and bound in
Great Britain at The Pitman Press, Bath.

Contents

Preface

With technology continually changing, computing has never remained static ever since the first days of the early 1940s and this is perhaps never more true than today with the rapid advances taking place in micro-electronics. However, the fundamentals are less prone to change, and computing syllabuses by their very procedure must remain constant for at least several years.

Having worked within computing in an educational environment for many years and, as a consequence, having become deeply involved in secondary level computer education in a variety of forms, the authors have always been surprised to find that so few texts exist for students of Computer Studies. This text is offered, therefore, to students at the Certificate of Secondary Education, GCE Ordinary and GCE Alternate Ordinary levels as they exist in the United Kingdom, as well as to students outside the UK studying similar courses.

Although syllabuses abound, there is a body of material which is common to all. It is this core material with suitable extensions which the authors have attempted to provide. It is left to the teachers to guide their pupils to those parts of the book which are appropriate to an individual syllabus.

It remains for us to acknowledge: the kind assistance of John Cushion of Pitman Publishing Limited; the keen appraisal of this text by John Hill of Chatham House Boys Grammar School in Ramsgate; and the generous permission of the Hampshire Education Committee and Tony Rackham for allowing much of their Time Chart to be reflected in Chapter 8.

J. S. & R. H. 1979

Dedication
To the inheritors of the
information society,
especially
MARI-ELENA & RICHARD JAMES

Introduction

The text comprises ten main sections including an introductory chapter and a main appendix devoted to binary arithmetic. The material has been organised so as to permit the flexibility required to accommodate the natural desire of many teachers to design their own Computer Studies courses. Some begin with programming, others with a description of the main components of a computer; others, again, start off with an historical summary or with an introduction to binary arithmetic. The order of the chapters is not intended, therefore, to be followed slavishly. An individual student may begin to read any chapter and by means of cross-referencing be referred to more detailed information contained in some other chapter. This has resulted in some overlap of material especially in Chapters 5 and 7, where the topics discussed are, respectively, applications of computers and their social implications.

Exercises, many taken from past examination papers, are to be found at the end of each major section. Hints to some of the solutions have been collected together in Appendix 2. There is a notable paucity of questions relating to social implications. In part, this results from the difficulty of marking such answers, and, in part, is due to the practice of many teachers to set course work or project essays upon this subject.

A list of the more important words and terms used in each section has been provided at the end of relevant chapters and may be found again in the Glossary for ease of reference. As far as possible, the terms as defined in the Glossary are taken from the British Computer Society publication *A Glossary of Computing Terms* which is becoming the accepted standard in the United Kingdom.

Examination Boards

AEB	The Associated Examining Board
UCLES	University of Cambridge Local Examinations Syndicate
EAEB	East Anglian Examinations Board
EMREB	East Midlands Regional Examinations Board
JMB	Joint Matriculation Board
MREB	Metropolitan Regional Examinations Board
OLE	Oxford Local Examinations
SREB	Southern Regional Examinations Board
SWEB	South Western Examinations Board
WJEC	Welsh Joint Education Committee
WMEB	West Midlands Examinations Board
YREB	Yorkshire Regional Examinations Board

Acronyms

Hardware	CPU	central processing unit
	ALU	arithmetic and logic unit
	CU	control unit
	PC	program counter
	IR	instruction register
	IAS (IAM)	immediate access store (memory)
	BIT	binary digit
	K	kilo; in binary 1024 (2^{10})
Input/Output	CRT	cathode ray tube
Devices	COM	computer output microfilm
	MICR	magnetic ink character recognition
	OCR	optical character recognition
	VDU	visual display unit
Languages	APL	a programming language
	ALGOL	algorithmic language
	BASIC	beginners all purpose symbolic instruction code
	COBOL	common business oriented language
	FORTRAN	formula translator
	PL/1	programming language 1
Computers	ENIAC	electronic numerical integrator and calculator
	EDSAC	electronic delay storage automatic calculator
	EDVAC	electronic discrete variable automatic computer
	LEO	Lyons electronic office
	UNIVAC	universal automatic computer
Companies	IBM	International Business Machines
	CDC	Control Data Corporation
	ICL	International Computers Limited
	CAL (CAI)	computer-assisted learning (instruction)
	CML	computer-managed learning

Introduction to Computers

Most people today have heard about computers. They appear in films and on television. They are reported in newspapers. No self-respecting science-fiction story can ignore them any longer. Many people's working lives are at least indirectly geared towards computers, and most people's domestic lives are somehow affected if only by paying bills generated by computers. Yet, few people could either describe or define a computer.

Definition

Many dictionaries define a computer as "an electronic machine designed for calculating". We shall suggest a totally different one. A computer is **an electronic machine designed to process information**. Both are true but the dictionary definition is more appropriate to the very early machines, whereas our definition is more appropriate for today's computers. The former definition is derived from the very word "compute" which means to "reckon" or "calculate", and indeed the very first computers were built to perform calculations for producing gun-firing tables and navigation tables. But from 1955, about ten years after the first computers were built, the commercial world began to make serious use of computers to process information, so that today more than 80% of the world's computers are used for commercial applications. However, before going too far, we shall need to ask what *type* of computer we are referring to. Is it an analogue or a digital computer?

Analogue and Digital Computers

An **analogue computer** is able to act upon information which is of a physical nature, not unlike the way that a *thermometer* will sense the temperature or a *barometer* will sense changes in the surrounding atmosphere. Analogue computers can be used in aeroplanes to process many different physical forms of information. When linked, for example, to the fuel-level indicator, the altimeter, the flight-speed indicator and to the various electrical circuits, the analogue computer can "report" on the behaviour or the mis-behaviour of all the readings so that the pilot has an up-to-date picture at any given moment of all flight controls. Thermometers, altimeters and barometers are all examples of analogue devices capable of sensing physical information such as pressure or temperature. This kind of physical information is a continuous unbroken flow of information, and the measuring instruments simply have to respond accordingly to this continuous flow and the changes in its intensity.

On the other hand, **digital computers** interpret information which is of a broken or discontinuous nature. The term **discrete information** is used in computing terminology. An ordinary light switch can be either on or off. Each situation is quite distinct, and in fact they are the only possible situations. There can be no situation in between on and off, that is there are no continuous changes in intensity. In practice, digital computers interpret electrical pulses which, like the light bulb, can be in one of only two possible states. Either a pulse is present or it is absent. Depending upon the computer manufacturer, the pulse is either a positive or a negative voltage. It is customary for programmers and most other computer users to represent this two-state information by the binary numbers zero and one (0, 1). (Binary is derived from the Latin word bi, meaning two.)

In this text, we are going to concentrate on digital computers, the type of computer people refer to when they talk about computers.

Processing Information

By "processing information" we mean that computers can record, manipulate and reproduce everyday information.

Recording Information

Letters of the alphabet, numbers, and other symbols in common use such as the comma, the full-stop, the sterling or dollar sign, open and closed brackets, mathematical and logic symbols, etc, must all be recorded or translated into electrical pulses before the computer can recognise them (see Chapter 1 for further details). Special recording devices translate the everyday characters into electrical pulses. They are called **input devices** and are discussed in Chapter 3. Characters may be typed at a device similar to a typewriter but called a **teletypewriter** or *teletype*, or punched as holes onto special cards or rolls of paper-tape. Some input devices can read our handwriting or even in a few limited instances understand the human voice. The main purpose of these input units then is to act as a *translator* between the computer and the information as it exists in the world outside.

Manipulating Information

It is only when information has been recorded by the input device that the main computer can do something with it, to process or manipulate that information. We shall see in Chapter 1 that computers can perform, surprisingly, only a few basic internal operations. These are so basic

however that they can be applied to an enormous variety of applications.

Reproducing Information

Once the main computer has manipulated information, we would like to be able to see the results. These will be in an electrical form inside the computer, which is not convenient for human beings to understand. Consequently, **output devices** exist to perform the opposite of the input devices, namely to convert or translate electrical pulses into our everyday characters. These characters may appear on a device similar to our domestic television screens (called visual display units, VDUs) but, as with things seen on television, they do not stay there permanently. Therefore, if we need a permanent copy of the results we can have it printed onto paper. Teletypewriters have such printing facilities, but other special printing devices also exist for *computer output* and, since they build up a line of print at a time, they are called **line printers**. The advantage is that they are much faster than the printing devices of teletypes.

It is also possible to have results displayed in graphical form by **graph plotters**. Some other output devices can even generate the human voice so that we can *hear* the results. These and other devices are discussed in Chapter 3.

Hardware

From the above section, it is clear that a computer must consist of at least three distinct units, an input device, a processor, and an output device, as shown in the Figure 1. These separate units are called **hardware** and, when linked together into a working system, are called the computer system hardware. Depending on the computer manufacturer, these pieces of equipment vary in size and shape and in colour,

Fig. 1

as do the various motor cars from different manufacturers. Electric cables link the various units so that the electrical pulses can travel from machine to machine. The cables are usually run underneath a false floor several centimetres in depth in the computer room. The lengths of the cables are often required to be exact to a fraction of a centimetre otherwise the speed with which the pulses travel can impair the speed of the processor unit.

Processor Unit

We shall discuss the processor unit in detail in Chapter 1 but a few words now are in order. It is not just one unit as implied in Figure 1 but really three units all working together in harmony. Its more formal title is the **central processing unit** (CPU). One of the units is a memory in which information to be processed is stored. However, the **memory unit** or store is very expensive and, therefore, limited in size. In turn, this affects the amount of information which can be stored. For a very large volume of information as in a payroll application, it will be necessary to have additional and less expensive storage facilities. These are magnetic devices and are able to retain the electrical information as held in the main memory of the CPU.

Chapter 3 discusses these additional or **auxiliary storage devices**, which are similar to our own domestic tape cassettes and record discs. Figure 2 illustrates their connection to the main central memory. Information has to pass from the auxiliary devices into the main central memory for processing.

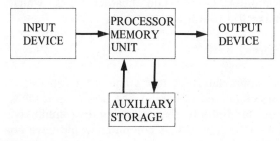

Fig. 2

Software

A computer has no knowledge of what to do unless a human being tells it *exactly* what to do. Computers as yet do not understand the human language except in a very limited way and, consequently, we have to instruct them in specialised computer languages called **programming languages**. A programmer is someone skilled in the art of instructing computers to perform some duty. He or she does so by writing down instructions in sequence, using many of the everyday symbols we are familiar with, and then having these converted into electrical pulses by an input device. The sequence of instructions written in a programming language is called a **program.**

Some programs will tell a computer how to perform such tasks as performing a payroll application, stock-taking, traffic control, calculating a mathematical formula, etc., and are known as **computer application programs**. But other more specialised programs are needed to tell the various hardware units which make up a computer system how to work together. These are called **computer systems programs**. Both types are frequently referred to as **software** or *software programs* to distinguish them from the hardware. Without computer systems software, the hardware units could not function.

A few examples will make this point clear. An electric light bulb cannot work by itself unless electricity is present. The switch and bulb can be likened to the computer hardware and the power supplied by the electricity to the software. A television set without any power to drive the units is again like the hardware. A motor-car by itself is just hardware, but with petrol, oil and water and, of course, a driver, the hardware can function and the car move from place to place. So it is with computers. The hardware units by themselves do nothing, but with software they can be made to function as a unit and to perform useful tasks.

The systems programs provide the software necessary to drive the computer hardware and the application programs make the computer perform some useful work.

Programs and Data

Application programs by themselves are only a set of instructions. Something else is needed for these instructions to work on. In a payroll program, the instructions will tell a computer how to produce all the weekly salary slips, but the details of each employee, his or her name, number of hours worked during the week, rate of pay per hour, tax to be deducted, etc., must also exist. These are the details upon which the payroll program will work and are called **data**. (The word "data" is the Latin word for "facts" and is plural. The singular word is *datum*. Throughout this text we shall use the word "data" to mean both the singular and the plural. Although this is grammatically incorrect, this usage has become customary.)

Programming Languages

A programming language by comparison with our natural languages is very restricted. A language such as Fortran has a vocabulary of only 18 words. Today there are many programming languages available. Fortran was the first of the so-called **high-level languages** (see Chapter 2) and was designed primarily to solve mathematical problems. Its main use is for scientific problems, whereas Cobol was designed to solve commercial-type problems and is commonly used for business applications. Basic, the most recent of the three, is closely related to Fortran and is used within the educational environment. In Figure 3 some of the more common programming languages are described but there are many more which we have not included.

Why are there so many languages and do we really need all of them? In fact, most practising programmers will often use only one language, although they may be familiar with one or two more. So in practice we do not need to know more than one language. However, not every computer is able to understand all available languages (discussed in Chapter 2) and, consequently, when a programmer is writing programs for a particular computer, he will have only a limited choice of available languages. Most computers can be made to understand Fortran and Cobol and this is one of the reasons for their popularity, but PL/1, for example, can only be understood by computers made by International Business Machines (IBM).

Some of the more common languages are not adequate enough for solving *all* types of problem and programmers working in specialised areas have to make use of specialised languages. Snobol is such an example and was designed for analysing sentences and text. Being a specialised language however, it is not a convenient language for solving problems in science or commerce. APL is an example of a language developed for use with a particular computer system, namely a time-sharing environment (see Chapter 6). APT is an example of a language developed for numerically controlled machine tools, hence its name Automatically Programmed Tools.

When existing languages prove to be unsuitable for a given application or computer system, someone develops another new language for that purpose. Hence the reason for so many languages. However, the more common languages of Figure 3 are those used by the majority of programmers and can solve most types of problems.

The Characteristics of Computers

Our friends and members of our families have certain characteristics. They may be fat or thin, short or tall, have a cheerful or gloomy personality, be serious or frivolous in temperament. A computer has certain characteristics which make it a useful tool for man.

Speed

To appreciate how fast a computer can calculate compared with man, see how long it takes you to multiply the following two numbers: $245\,678 \times 876\,534$. A computer would have no trouble in performing thousands of such calcu-

Language	Date	Meaning	Developed by	Application area
FORTRAN	1956	Formula Translator	IBM	Scientific
COBOL	1958	Common Business Oriented Language	US Dept. of Defense	Commercial
ALGOL	1958	Algorithmic Language	International Committee	Scientific
RPG	1961	Report Generator	IBM	Commercial
APL	1962	A Programming Language	K. Iverson	Time-sharing system
PL/1	1963	Programming Language 1	IBM	Scientific & commercial systems
BASIC	1965	Beginners All-purpose Symbolic Instruction Code	Kemeny & Kurtz	Teaching
Pascal	1968	named after the French philosopher	N. Wirth	Teaching

Fig. 3

lations, and in very fast machines even millions, in the space of *one second!* So fast are the arithmetical processes of computers within one second that computer people have to talk in terms of milliseconds, microseconds, nanoseconds, and even picoseconds (Figure 4). Not only can a computer calculate very quickly but it can process information at speeds far beyond the capabilities of human beings.

Storage Ability

Unlimited amounts of information can be held in a computer system due to the auxiliary storage devices. Any piece of this information can be quickly retrieved and placed in the main memory of the CPU. Without the ability to store vast quantities of data and to access that data quickly, computers would be of little use in commercial applications.

One interesting point is that once a piece of information has been recorded and stored in the auxiliary device, it will never be "forgotten" by the computer unless it is deliberately

Millisecond	=	one thousandth of a second
Microsecond	=	a millionth of a second
Nanosecond	=	a thousand-millionth of a second
Picosecond	=	a million-millionth of a second

Fig. 4

changed or removed. In this sense, computers are superior to human memories which frequently "forget" information as we all know when sitting for examinations or answering general knowledge questions.

Consistent Performance

As human beings we all have our "bad days" when we are not at our best. Computers on the other hand do not have any "off days" (except,

5

SPEED Computers work at incredible speeds, performing hundreds, thousands and even millions of calculations in a second.

STORAGE Unlimited quantities of data can be stored in auxiliary memory devices. Once recorded, a piece of information can never be forgotten.

CONSISTENT Unlike human beings, computers do not become bored or tired when performing many thousands of calculations. They are ideal machines for carrying out work of a highly repetitive nature.

ACCURATE Computers are very reliable. It is the programs or data which can lead to inaccurate results. Therefore do not believe everything which comes from a computer.

Fig. 5

perhaps, when they break down) and, unlike human beings, they are consistent in their performance. For example, if a computer is told to calculate a series of numbers a thousand times, it would calculate the 987th with exactly the same care and attention as it would the first. This could not be said for human beings. We lose concentration, easily become tired and bored. A computer does not show any of these traits and is, therefore, ideal for performing tasks which have a repetitive nature.

Accuracy

It is very unlikely today that incorrect results can be produced by computers without the user being given some kind of warning. If the hardware should mis-behave whilst processing information, or if the information being passed from one unit to another becomes altered (*corrupted*), computers are able to report such occurrences.

Being machines, computers perform what is called *finite arithmetic* (see Chapter 1), i.e. the actual numbers which are used are precise to only a given extent. In practice, these approximations cause no real problems to the scientific user because there are ways of overcoming any restrictions.

If results are produced which are incorrect, they usually occur because of a *human* error and not as a consequence of any deficiency in the computer itself. Either, the *application program* contains a wrong instruction which will be obeyed by a computer in the same way that it will obey a correct instruction (i.e. the computer itself cannot know whether an instruction is correct or not); or the *data* which the computer is told to process is incorrect; or, perhaps, the *systems programs* are wrong. Thus, although we say that the computer itself is a highly accurate and reliable machine, we must not necessarily believe that every result it produces is correct.

What Computers Cannot Do

By now we should have a clear idea that computers are electronic machines and as such do not possess all the qualities and characteristics of human beings. Computers may add up very quickly and may never get tired of repeating the same things over and over again but they cannot do many things we as human beings take for granted. A computer could not, for example, look at a painting by one artist and compare it with one by another artist. They are not able to make a value judgement of such qualities as the use of colour and tone, the style of the paintings, etc.

A computer, it is true, can be programmed to generate "poetry" (although whether this could be classified as a work of art is debatable) but it cannot appraise what it "writes". It can make no distinction between what is complete rubbish and what some would call "poetry". It can be programmed to produce pretty designs but it must be left to human beings to decide which is good and which is bad.

Computers have no feelings so they cannot be sad or happy, or, in fact, tired or hot. They can overheat and then not function correctly but so can the engine of a motor-car and we do not pretend that engines *feel* hot. It is human beings who have emotions and feelings, not computers.

A computer, as yet, could not make up a joke or appreciate a joke. It could only "tell" a joke if someone had previously written the joke and programmed the computer to output that joke in some form, perhaps onto printed paper or even "spoken" from a tape cassette or via a computer voice-synthesizer.

In summary, computers have no ability to make value judgements about art, people or politics. They have no emotions and no physical feelings, thus they cannot fall in love, cry because they are unhappy, laugh at jokes, or indeed appreciate the use of the English language by famous writers. On the other hand, they cannot feel cold and will never have a nervous breakdown or feel the sensation of pain. They might break down and not function but this will be due to some mechanical or electronic fault which can be repaired by a maintenance engineer. Whatever it does it can only do because some human programmer has instructed it in the first place.

In this Introduction many points have been raised but few answered in any detail. This will be the purpose of the following chapters.

Chapter 1 discusses the technicalities of the computer as an electronic digital machine. It has been structured in two parts. Part 1 provides a brief introduction, Part 2 provides a closer look at some of the more technical aspects. This can be a difficult chapter for the beginner and Part 2 is only recommended once a degree of familiarity with computers has been achieved, perhaps via programming or after some of the other chapters have been digested.

Chapter 2 looks at the types of programming languages but there is no attempt to "teach" programming. That is the responsibility of a teacher or, at second best, the subject of an entire book, not the subject of one chapter.

Chapter 3 discusses the input, output and auxiliary storage devices.

Chapters 4 *and* 5 cover many of the concepts used in commercial data processing and look at some of the applications to which computers are put.

Chapter 6 investigates the reasons for the development of computer systems such as batch processing and time-sharing, and discusses the purpose of systems software.

Chapter 7 raises some of the problems society faces through the use of computers. Many issues are discussed but their importance should be further investigated by students with their teachers.

Chapter 8 provides an historical survey of computers and their technology within the larger context of a brief history of Information Processing. Although some computer educationists spend a great deal of their time telling people to ignore the history of computers, some of us do like to make this choice for ourselves. It is included here for those who like to know something about the history of the subject they are studying.

Following Chapter 8 is a set of general questions.

Appendix 1 provides a simple introduction to number systems and in particular to the binary system, for those who have not studied this area before or who have forgotten some aspects.

Appendix 2 provides hints and answers to some of the exercises set at the end of each chapter.

Important Words and Terms in this Introduction

digital computers
discrete information

analogue computers
continuous information
physical information·

processing information
   recording, processing and reproducing information

hardware
input devices
   teletypewriters
output devices
   graph plotters
   line printers

central processing unit
memory unit
auxiliary storage devices

computer output
software
programming languages
program
data
computer application programs
computer systems programs
high-level languages
finite arithmetic

Exercises

1 If the following pulse train represents the binary number 100110, draw a pulse train for the binary number 1110010.

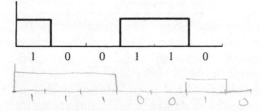

| 1 | 0 | 0 | 1 | 1 | 0 |

2 Why do electronic computers use binary representation? (*EAEB* 1977) *base two (High or low)*

3 Which of the following is *not* an analogue device? *a)* a petrol gauge *b)* a cash register *c)* a thermometer *d)* an altimeter *e)* a slide rule (*EMREB* 1977) *(b) CASH REGISTER*

4 Discuss briefly the differences between analogue and digital computers. *Analog - measure; digital - count*

5 Define a digital computer. *This uses binary notation and counts but cannot measure. (Processor)*

6 Which best completes the sentence? "A computer processes information..." *a)* very seldom *b)* automatically *c)* at once *d)* eventually *e)* by truncating (*EMREB* 1977) *(b) automatically*

7 Describe at least three characteristics of a computer. *① accurate, ② does not forget ③ does not become bored & too weary.*

8 Describe the four main hardware components of a computer as outlined in this Introduction. Explain the purpose of auxiliary storage devices. *Input, Processing, auxiliary storage and output.*

9 Name three common high-level languages stating the general application area for which each was designed. *Fortran - Scientific; Cobol - Commercial; Algal - Scientific*

10 What is the purpose of computer system software? *To instruct the hardware what to do*

11 Is it true that computers can do almost anything that a human being can do? Support your answer with examples. *No. They can't think or move, or sleep.*

1 Computing Machines

Many of the topics you will learn about in computing are directly affected by the fundamental structure of the *central processing unit*, the CPU for short. For example, what computers can do (their applications), how they are "programmed", why data files are organised in particular ways, the types of input/output devices, all are a direct result of the way in which the CPU is arranged. For this reason, in the first major chapter of this text, we shall concentrate on the central processing unit. The chapter is divided into two parts. If you master the first part, much of the material in subsequent chapters will be more readily understood. The second part provides more detail and may be read now or left until some later stage.

Part 1   The Structure of the Central Processing Unit (CPU)

In this section, we shall take an overall look (overview) at the CPU. It essentially consists of three sections: a memory unit, an arithmetic/logic unit, and a control unit. Each of these will be described in this chapter but we will first look at "information" in terms of the computer.

Forms of Information

You have probably heard that computers are called *electronic digital* machines. Both these terms really refer to the way in which computing machines work, that is, how they "handle information". Let us first, however, see how a human being will "handle" the following piece of information: the decimal integer number ten

(10). It is in itself only one piece of information but refers to ten individual units. This quantity can be expressed in several ways:

ten	expressed as an English word
10	expressed in the base ten (denary)
1010	expressed in the base two (binary)
12	expressed in the base eight (octal)
A	expressed in the base sixteen (hexadecimal)
X	expressed in the Roman numbering system.

All these forms or expressions refer to the same thing—the quantity ten. More than one form is used everyday by most people in the Western world. In contrast, a computer is restricted to just one means of expression, namely by electrical pulses and must use only one form of expression. An electrical pulse exists or it does not exist, rather like an electric light bulb being either *on* or *off*. Within a computer, these pulses may exist in a variety of ways; for example, they may be present or absent, or of positive or negative voltage, or at either of two voltage levels. The actual method chosen will depend upon some design feature of the computer itself and does not concern the ordinary user of the computer. The important point to appreciate is that information within a computer can be most easily represented in two states.

Computer people find it convenient to use binary to represent the "electrical pulse information". Binary form has therefore only two digits; they are zero and one (see Appendix 1). Thus the binary 1 may be represented by the presence of a pulse or the positive voltage or the higher of two positive pulses, whilst the binary zero may be represented by the absence of a pulse or the negative voltage or the lower of two voltages. Figure 1.1 illustrates this. Although computer people frequently talk about

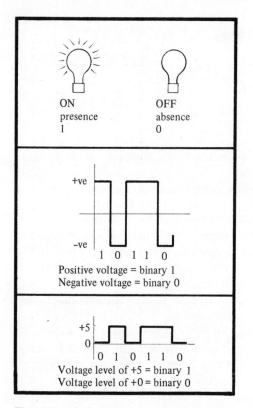

ON
presence
1

OFF
absence
0

+ve

-ve

1 0 1 1 0

Positive voltage = binary 1
Negative voltage = binary 0

+5
0

0 1 0 1 1 0

Voltage level of +5 = binary 1
Voltage level of +0 = binary 0

Fig. 1.1   Methods of representing binary zero
and one by voltage levels in electronic devices

However, computers are used to express more than just the two numbers 1 and 0. In our everyday world, we have letters of the alphabet (A–Z), digits 0 to 9 (base ten), and a variety of other symbols such as the full-stop, the comma, open and closed brackets, the sterling symbol (£), etc. Consequently, the binary digits will have to be organised in some way so that at least many of our everyday symbols can be represented within the computer.

A group of three bits can give a maximum of eight unique patterns (see Figure 1.2). If we arrange that one of the patterns, say the 000, represents the letter A, then the remaining

1)	000	A
2)	001	B
3)	010	C
4)	011	D
5)	100	E
6)	101	F
7)	110	G
8)	111	H

Fig. 1.2   Possible binary patterns to represent
the letters A-H

binary digits being inside the CPU, we must remember that there are only electrical pulses, each one being in one of two possible states. From a design point of view, it is a much simpler task to design an electronic computer with only two states than to build one with ten states and ten differring voltage levels. This is why binary is preferred rather than our everyday denary system.

Organisation of Binary Patterns

For the rest of this chapter and in many other sections of this text, we shall adopt the common and more convenient method of referring to the electrical pulses as binary digits or its shorter form **bits**, where a bit will be one of the two binary digits 0, 1.

seven other patterns represent the letters B, C, D, E, F, G and H. Since we need to represent, at a minimum, twenty-six capital letters, the ten decimal digits, and at least eleven of the more common special symbols, then at least 47 unique patterns are required! Five bits will allow only 2^5 (i.e. 32) unique patterns and so will not be sufficient. But six bits will permit 2^6 or 64 patterns, enough for our 47 characters with 17 spare.

Thus, if in our design of a CPU we group a series of six bits together, then it is possible to translate our basic set of 47 characters into 47 individual and unique binary patterns. It is a common practice, therefore, for computer designers to arrange the bits (remember, electrical pulses) into groups of six or even eight bits. These groups are often referred to as **bytes**. Eight bits will allow for 256 (2^8) unique patterns and is very common especially with

Character Description	Printed Symbol	Machine Code		Character Description	Printed Symbol	Machine Code	
		Zone	Numeric			Zone	Numeric
Zero	0	00	0000	At	@	10	0000
One	1	00	0001		A	10	0001
Two	2	00	0010		B	10	0010
Three	3	00	0011		C	10	0011
Four	4	00	0100		D	10	0100
Five	5	00	0101		E	10	0101
Six	6	00	0110		F	10	0110
Seven	7	00	0111		G	10	0111
Eight	8	00	1000		H	10	1000
Nine	9	00	1001		I	10	1001
Colon	:	00	1010		J	10	1010
Semi-colon	;	00	1011		K	10	1011
Less than	<	00	1100		L	10	1100
Equals	=	00	1101		M	10	1101
Greater than	>	00	1110		N	10	1110
Question mark	?	00	1111		O	10	1111
Space		01	0000		P	11	0000
Exclamation	!	01	0001		Q	11	0001
Quotes	"	01	0010		R	11	0010
Hash mark	#	01	0011		S	11	0011
Pound	£	01	0100		T	11	0100
Percentage	%	01	0101		U	11	0101
Ampersand	&	01	0110		V	11	0110
Apostrophe	'	01	0111		W	11	0111
Left Parenthesis	(	01	1000		X	11	1000
Right Parenthesis	)	01	1001		Y	11	1001
Asterisk	*	01	1010		Z	11	1010
Plus	+	01	1011	L.H. Bracket	[	11	1011
Comma	,	01	1100	Dollar	$	11	1100
Hyphen/Minus	−	01	1101	R.H. Bracket	]	11	1101
Stop	.	01	1110		↑	11	1110
Solidus	/	01	1111		↓	11	1111

An example of a 64-character set, using 6 bits to determine each character

microcomputers. It permits small as well as capital letters to be represented and many more of the special symbols. In this way, by organising bits into groups, our everyday symbols can be represented internally within the CPU, as patterns of binary digits, or, more accurately, patterns of electrical pulses, with each pulse being in one of two possible states. We shall have more to say about this in Part 2 of this chapter.

How To Represent Numbers

So far we have seen that a computer is an electronic machine which contains information in the form of electrical pulses and that for us it is easier to think of these pulses in terms of binary digits. Furthermore, by grouping these bits together, many of our everyday characters can be represented or expressed as binary patterns. However, computers have more to do than simply handle characters, they also perform arithmetic upon numbers. With as small a group as six bits, the range of whole (integer) numbers which can be held inside a computer will only be 0 to 63 numerals (or, with an eight-bit group, a range from 0 to 255). These are only the positive numbers, what about negative ones? There are several methods.

The simplest is the so called **sign-and-magnitude (sign-and-modulus)** approach whereby one of the bits in a group, usually the leftmost bit, is used to indicate the sign of the number. Normally, zero sign bit represents the plus or positive sign, a one bit the negative. (See Figure 1.3.) Consequently, in a six-bit word where one bit is used as a sign bit, only five bits remain for the number itself. 2^5 will provide a range now of −31 to +31. This method was used on a second generation machine, the IBM 7094, but today it is more common to use "complementation" to represent negative numbers. (This is discussed in detail in Part 2.) For the moment you should be clear that, with a six or eight bit group, no practical arithmetic can be performed. Consequently, most computers have a much larger grouping of bits, such as 12, 24, 32, 36 or even 60 bits. Let us now relate these points to one of the three main components of the CPU, namely the central memory (CM).

Central Memory (CM)

So far we have shown that a necessary approach to the design of a central memory is to have large groups of bits, certainly many more than six or eight. These larger groups vary in size, typically from 12 or 32 to even 60 bits, according to the computer manufacturer. The Control Data Corporation (CDC) Cyber range of computers have 60 bits which allows an extremely large spread of integer numbers to be handled. Thus, the type of problem to be solved on such a computer would be essentially of a mathematical nature. A typical 16-bit computer, on the other hand, such as the PDP 11/04, would be more appropriate for business/

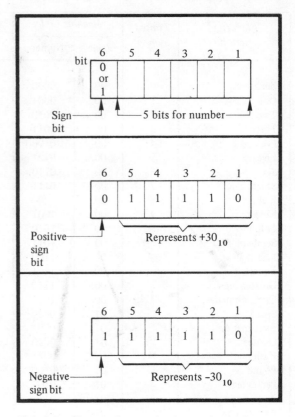

Fig. 1.3 Sign-and-magnitude method of representing positive and negative numbers

commercial applications where the emphasis is not on mathematics but on data which does not normally involve numbers of extreme size.

These groups of bits, from 12 to 60, are frequently called **words** and a central memory consists of many thousands of such groupings or words. Thus, the Cyber range of computers may have as many as $128\,K \times 60$ bit words. The K stands for the "binary kilo or thousand", which is 1024 (i.e. 2^{10}). Figure 1.4 shows the number of bits and words, etc. for both the Cyber and the PDP 11/04 computers.

We have now seen that, to represent a character, six or even eight bits are required, but that to perform arithmetic on numbers of any practical size then more bits are required. A sixteen-bit word is often the minimum length for commercial applications, and, for computers

12

specifically designed for numerical work, up to sixty bits is not unusual. Since computers have to handle both characters and numbers, the common approach is to have word lengths greater than six or eight bits but to allow each word to store more than one character. For example, the Cyber range with its sixty-bit word length uses six bits to represent a character. Thus one word may hold either a very large number or up to ten characters ($6 \times 10 = 60$ bits).

Each word then is a **storage location** for holding information in the form of characters or numbers, and we shall see in Chapter 2 that central memory words or locations can also store program instructions. Furthermore, each word has a unique address numbered from zero up to the maximum address (for a 32K store that would be 32 767), so that when required any individual location may be accessed.

Since the CM locations are very expensive, there is a limit to the number that any computer will have. Thus, material which has to be retained is held on a cheaper and much larger form of storage device. These additional devices (called **secondary** or **auxiliary**) are magnetic tapes and magnetic discs. (See Chapter 3 for details.)

The CM then is a unit of the CPU which is capable only of storing or holding information. No computation can take place in this storage area. This activity is reserved for another unit.

128K	=	128 x 1024
	=	131 072 words
	=	7 864 320 bits
for a 60-bit word		

32K	=	32 x 1024
	=	32 768 words
	=	524 288 bits
for a 16-bit word		

Fig. 1.4 Comparison of bits in a Cyber and PDP 11 computer

The Arithmetic/Logic Unit (ALU)

The four basic arithmetic operations of addition, subtraction, multiplication, and division take place in the second main unit, separate from the central memory. The circuitry of CM is designed to *hold* or *store* information. The circuitry of this second unit must be designed to perform arithmetic operations on the information. It is therefore known as the arithmetic and logic unit, since it performs both arithmetic and logic operations. We shall refer to it as the ALU for short.

Those computers designed especially for mathematical problems (such as the Cyber 170 series) have much more highly developed, complex circuitry in their ALU than those designed for commercial problems.

One of the main components of the ALU is the **accumulator** which is used when the unit is performing arithmetic. An accumulator is similar to a CM storage location and is capable of storing the same number of bits as are held in a word of central memory. But in addition to holding information it also possesses associated circuitry to carry out arithmetical processes. We shall discuss the logic circuitry in Part 2.

The Control Unit (CU)

Let us take the simple example of adding together two numbers, and in this way discuss the role of the third unit of the CPU, the control unit (the CU). The process of adding two numbers together requires three things. First, the *two numbers* to be added, which are stored in two separate locations in CM; secondly, an *instruction* informing the computer that two numbers have to be added (as opposed to being multiplied or divided); and, finally, some section or *unit* which will be able to obey the "adding instruction" by taking both of the numbers from the CM, placing them in the arithmetic unit, and then passing on a signal to the ALU so that the addition can take place. This is the purpose of the CU. Not only must it decode (interpret, obey) a given instruction,

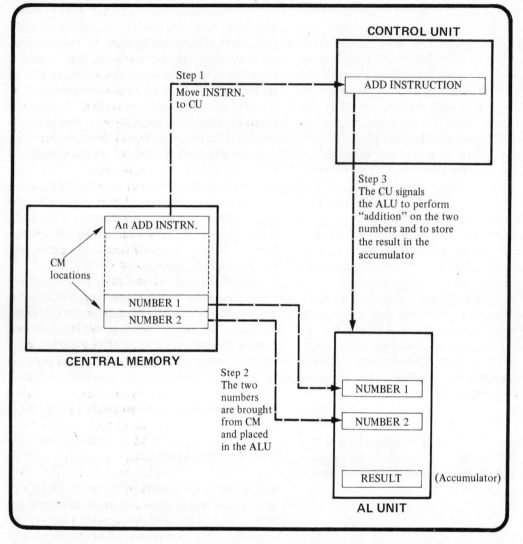

CONTROL UNIT

ADD INSTRUCTION

Step 1
Move INSTRN.
to CU

Step 3
The CU signals
the ALU to perform
"addition" on the two
numbers and to store
the result in the
accumulator

An ADD INSTRN.

CM
locations

NUMBER 1
NUMBER 2

CENTRAL MEMORY

Step 2
The two
numbers
are brought
from CM
and placed
in the ALU

NUMBER 1

NUMBER 2

RESULT   (Accumulator)

AL UNIT

Fig. 1.5 Three steps involved in the execution of an instruction by the CU (Note that the "ADD instruction" must contain the addresses of the numbers to be added)

but it must also move data from the CM to the ALU. Chapter 2 discusses this aspect in much more detail but Figure 1.5 illustrates the process. Computer people often talk about the CU "executing" instructions. This has nothing to do with chopping off heads but of obeying a given **program instruction**. (Instructions other than "adding" are discussed in Chapter 2.)

If we wish to know the result of the above addition which has taken place and then been stored in the accumulator, it will be necessary to inform the CU through yet another program instruction: "place the result of the addition in one of the CM storage locations". Thus, we can see that the function of the CU is to obey instructions (as presented by a programmer) and to place data (either characters or numbers) from the CM into the ALU and vice versa.

The Work of a Computer

We have seen that a computer consists essentially of an ALU, a CU and a CM which collectively are known as the CPU. Furthermore, in order to get information into the CM to begin with, some form of input device is required and, in order to get information out of the CM, some output device is necessary. We can now summarise all the basic operations or functions which a computer can perform. The interesting thing here is that there are very few basic operations, indeed only four!

1) Input/output operations
2) Arithmetical operations
3) Logic and comparison operations
4) Movement of data to and from and within the CM.

Secondary or Auxiliary Storage

We have already pointed out that a program, or the data which a program works on, must be in central memory, otherwise the computer cannot recognise its existence. This is rather like our own memories. Having information on a piece of paper (i.e. outside our memory) is no good when it comes to having to remember the information (as we have to do in examinations), then it has to be inside our heads. We can retain only so much information in our own memory and likewise for the computer. It can hold only so much information in its CM. The actual amount will depend on the size (capacity) of the CM. We have already quoted two sizes of CM, the $128K \times 60$ bit word length for the CDC Cyber 174 and the PDP 11/04 with its $32K \times 16$ bit word length. The former has 131 072 locations and the latter 32 768. Although these numbers may appear to be quite large, we have to remember that the program must be present in CM as well as data. In Chapter 6 we shall also see that certain other programs, which control the operation of the computer, must be resident in CM as well. Consequently, not all CM locations are available for data. Typical commercial applications such as a payroll program may have to work on

several hundred thousand data items. Clearly, the CM cannot contain *all* this data at one time.

It is not possible to increase the size of the CM without increasing considerably the overall cost of the computer itself, since CM locations are expensive and form a major proportion of the cost of a computer. Therefore, other and cheaper methods of retaining large volumes of data have to be used. During the first generation of computers (see Chapter 8) data was held on **punched cards** or **paper tape**. When required, the information was read into CM via a card or paper tape reader. But this proved to be a slow process and became even less satisfactory as the volume of data increased. Other methods were investigated and the second generation began to make use of **magnetic tape**. In situations in which all the data could not be contained in the CM at one time, data was arranged on the magnetic tape in convenient **blocks**. One block would be read into the CM and, once processed by the program, the next block would be read in. (See also Chapters 3 and 4.)

Other devices for storing information outside the main memory were **magnetic drums** and **magnetic discs**, which were capable of transferring information into CM at a faster rate but were much more expensive. Today, there are a number of other, smaller disc devices, such as the "floppy disc", which are attracting a great deal of attention, particularly in smaller computer systems as frequently used by small business and commercial concerns, as well as in the microcomputer field.

All we are saying at this stage is that central memory is the main or *primary* storage area of any computer. It is of limited capacity but is the only store which can be used directly by the CPU during the execution of a program. Then there are the *secondary* storage devices made up of one or more of the devices already mentioned and which can be of unlimited size. Information from these secondary or backing stores must be passed into the main memory before the CPU can perform any operations upon it.

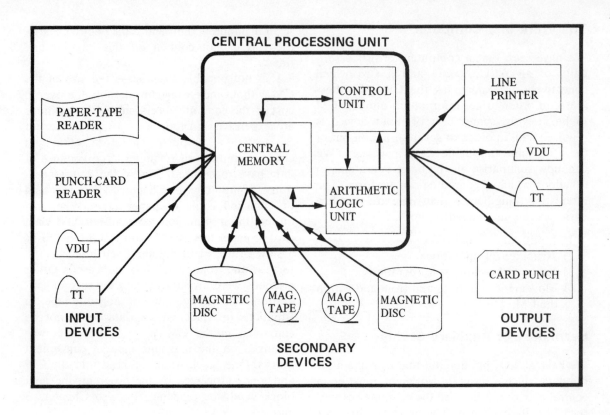

Fig. 1.6 Computer system hardware
(TT = teletype terminal, VDU = visual display unit)

Figure 1.6 illustrates a typical computer hardware system, showing the actual machines which make up the computer system.

Part 2 The Operation of the Central Processing Unit

Many people of the world belong to an industrial society, since the way in which their society is organised and the way in which they lead their everyday lives is a result of their dependence upon industry. In Britain, for example, people have been dependent upon industry for several centuries. The way in which an industry such as a coal mine, a chemical plant and a steel mill performs its work depends upon technology. Coal has been brought to the surface for many centuries but the techniques or the technology for doing so have changed from time to time. Water, steam and electricity have all been used to drive the machines which aid the coal miner. In the field of computing, the technology for designing computers has changed many times since the first computer was built some 35 years ago. A brief account of these changes can be found in the chapter on the historical developments of computers. What we shall look at in this second part of this chapter is more of the technical details of the electronic circuitry which go to make up the CPU. If we want to know something about the way in which computers work then we must study the technology which underlies them. Fortunately, we need not delve too deeply into this area but some understanding will help to make us aware of why programs have to be written in certain ways.

Two-state Components

Computers evolved as a direct result of electronics. We have already seen that it is easier to design electrical components which are capable of being in one of two possible states rather than being in one of ten possible states. Hence, binary is used frequently to represent these two possible states. There are many components which operate in a two-state manner:

an electric bulb may be *on* or *off*

a magnet may be magnetised in one direction or the opposite direction

a relay can be on or off

a transistor can conduct or not conduct (and, as a result, it behaves like a switch)

a voltage level may be zero or +5 volts.

We need not be concerned with which method may be employed in a given computer; it only concerns those specialising in computer design. All we need to be aware of is that electronics allows a fast and easy way of representing binary digits (bits).

The Central Memory (CM)

The CM is the simplest unit to consider first. It is purely a unit for holding or storing program instructions or information, which consist of a certain number of binary digits grouped together into words or locations. The electronic storage media used in these main memories vary. But each element must be capable of being switched into one of two states such that each element can effectively store a binary zero or a binary one. Over the past fifteen to twenty years, these elements (which can still be found in many computers) have been magnetic ferrite (iron) rings called **cores** (see Figure 1.7), about the size of a pinhead.

The present trend is towards semiconductor memories, where each element consists of a transistor capable of representing either one of the two binary bits. These elements were introduced by IBM in 1971. They are smaller and faster than cores but are more expensive. They have the disadvantage of losing or having their contents "destroyed" if the power supply is

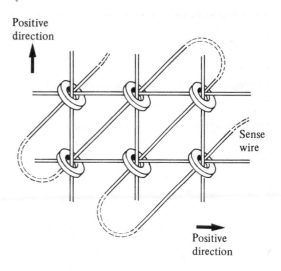

Positive direction

Sense wire

Positive direction

Fig. 1.7 Magnetic core memory

switched off. This type of storage is said to be *impermanent* or **volatile** as opposed to *core* storage which is *permanent* or **non-volatile**.

From Figure 1.7, we can see three wires passing through each core. Two are used to magnetise the core in one direction, thus establishing the presence of a binary bit. A clockwise direction is considered to represent a 1, whilst an anti-clockwise direction represents a 0. The third wire known as a *sense wire* is used to detect whether it is a nought or a one that is represented.

Usually, it is convenient to arrange the storage elements into a series of planes (layers). The number of planes will depend upon the number of bits in a word. Thus, a sixteen-bit word will have a series of sixteen planes. The actual number of elements in each plane will depend upon the CM size of the computer.

Because the CMs were made of magnetic cores for nearly twenty years, the term *core store* is often used today to refer to central memory even though the actual storage elements are not cores. Another common name for this CM is the **immediate access store** (IAS).

Information is stored as binary patterns in the words of the CM for use at some time by the CU. In order to access or "get at" the information in a particular location, the CU must know the **address** of that location. Thus,

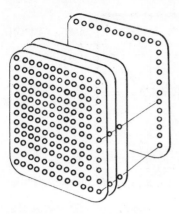

Fig. 1.8 Set of core planes

in a 32K central memory, each location will have a unique address in the range 0 to 32 767 Do not confuse the *address* of a location with the *contents* or information stored in the location. (This is further discussed in Chapter 2.) The time required, usually measured in millionths of a second (microseconds), for the CU to obtain the information in a word is called the **access time**.

When a piece of information is stored or placed in a location, we say that information is **written to** a memory location; whereas, when information is retrieved from a CM location we say that information is **read from** a location.

The type of computer we have been discussing has a word length of a particular size and each word in CM has the same number of bits. This is called a **fixed word length** computer. Other types of computer allow the number of bits per word to vary and are called **variable word length** computers. This latter method helps to store information in a more compact manner.

The Control Unit (CU)

The control unit consists of specialised electronic circuitry designed to decode program instructions held in central memory. Each instruction is read from CM into a register called the **instruction register** (IR). The process of

reading an instruction from CM into the IR, and then of decoding or executing that instruction, is often referred to as the **fetch-execute** process.

The instructions which collectively form a program are stored one after the other, with each instruction occupying one word of CM. The binary patterns into which each instruction is translated (see Chapter 2) is read from a location by the CU into the IR (the fetch cycle). Once it is in the IR, then the execute cycle takes place whereby the instruction is obeyed. The binary patterns of a given instruction will be used to operate electronic circuits designed to accomplish the purpose of the instruction. (Chapter 2 discusses in detail these various types of instructions.)

If arithmetic is to be performed upon two numbers, then, clearly, an instruction must not only specify which of the four arithmetical processes to carry out but also the addresses in CM of the numbers involved. Thus, a second function of the CU is to read data from CM into the ALU which is designed to perform the calculations. We shall see in Chapter 2 that many instructions consist of two parts. One part indicates the actual operation to be performed; the second part indicates the address in CM of the data upon which the operation is performed. Figure 1.9 illustrates this.

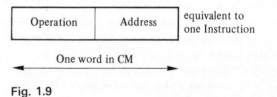

Fig. 1.9

For those who are used to a high-level language such as Basic or Fortran, this style of program instruction may appear unusual. Chapter 2 will explain why and how a program written in a high-level language will eventually end up in the above format when the program is placed into locations of central memory. Usually, one instruction will occupy one CM word, but in some machines where the word length is longer than in others, it is a common practice to put two or more instructions in one word. However, this need not really concern us unless we want to write highly specialised programs for operating computer hardware (system programs).

At this stage, we are simply stating that a program instruction, in whatever language it is written, will eventually become a series of binary digits, with an operation part and an address portion. The IR is designed to obey the operation and if any data is required by the operation then the CU will read that data from CM. Some instructions wish to place data into CM, i.e. to write data to CM, as opposed to reading from CM. This process will also involve the CU.

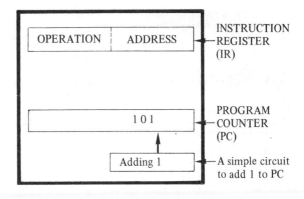

Fig. 1.10 Control unit circuitry

The CU and Program Instructions

How does the CU know where to find the next instruction (or the first for that matter)? In other words, how do program instructions get into the IR one after the other in the sequence proposed by the programmer? Fortunately, matters are arranged to make this process quite simple. Once a program has been written, each instruction can be stored in consecutive (following) locations within the CM. In most computers, the first instruction of any program is placed in one particular location. This means that the CU will always know where to find the first instruction.

Just before any program is obeyed, the address of this particular location is placed in a register called the **program counter** or PC (Figure 1.10). Thus, if the starting address is always 101 (i.e. 101_{10}) for instance, then, before the program is due to be executed, the address of the CM location 101, which contains the first instruction of the program, will be placed in the program counter. Since all the other instructions are placed one after the other in sequence, the second instruction will be found in location 102, the third in location 103, etc. In other words the original address in the PC is simply incremented (i.e. increased) by one each time an instruction is executed, thereby always

pointing to the *next* instruction to be "fetched" from CM.

All that is needed therefore is a simple set of circuits which will increment the PC by one every time an instruction is executed. In fact the PC is normally incremented by one just before the current instruction is decoded so that, *after* the execution of an instruction, the PC is always pointing to the next instruction to be obeyed. This process continues until one of the instructions eventually informs the CU to STOP the execution of the entire program. Thus, program instructions are normally executed one after the other in strict sequence as written down by the programmer.

A program consisting of twenty instructions will have the first instruction placed in address location 101 and the last instruction in address location 120. All the other instructions will occupy locations 102–119. (See Figure 1.11.) Note that instruction 8 (locn. 108) points back towards instruction 4 (locn. 104).

If you have written any programs you will know about the common and useful instruction which enables programmers to go backwards or forwards in a program, and execute some other instruction *instead* of the next instruction in sequence. This allows a programmer to *repeat* a series of instructions without having to rewrite those instructions time and time again. How does the CU cope with this situation?

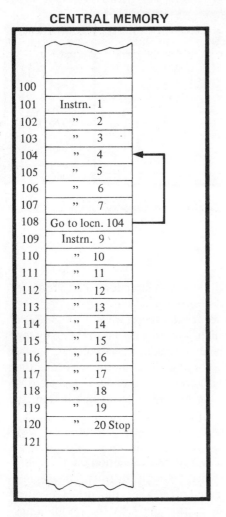

CENTRAL MEMORY

100	
101	Instrn. 1
102	" 2
103	" 3
104	" 4
105	" 5
106	" 6
107	" 7
108	Go to locn. 104
109	Instrn. 9
110	" 10
111	" 11
112	" 12
113	" 13
114	" 14
115	" 15
116	" 16
117	" 17
118	" 18
119	" 19
120	" 20 Stop
121	

Fig. 1.11 Program with 20 instructions in locations 101 to 120

The CU and Jump Instructions

Taking the example in Figure 1.11, when instruction 7 is being executed, the PC will point towards address 108, i.e. the address of the next instruction to be executed. When instruction 7 has been completed, therefore, the CU will inspect the PC to find the address of the next instruction to be fetched from CM and to be placed in the IR. In this case, the address is 108. Thus, the instruction from location 108 will be read from CM into the IR. The PC will

now be incremented automatically by one, so that it will be pointing to the next address in sequence, that is 109. However, instruction eight will say "GO TO instruction 4 at address 104 and execute that instruction next, instead of whatever address is given in the PC". Clearly, what needs to happen is that, by executing this instruction, the contents of the PC will change from 109 to the address of instruction 4, i.e. 104. The circuits operated by the GO TO instruction will cause this to happen.

After instruction 8 has been executed, the CU will again inspect the contents of the PC in order to find the address of the next instruction to read into the IR. It will now find the address 104 rather than 109. Consequently, the instruction at address 104 will be read into the IR next. Obviously, we can now see why it is so important for a programmer to make GO TO or Jump instructions point to the correct instruction. The computer does not care about what instruction it next executes. Since it is so easy to make a wrong transfer by the use of GO TO instructions, a language which reduces their need, such as Pascal, also reduces the source of such potential errors.

To summarise the circuitry of the CU, we see that two registers are needed, the Instruction Register which decodes program instructions and the Program Counter which keeps account of the address of the next instruction. The IR has associated circuitry to read from or write to locations in CM, as well as the ability to signal to the ALU which arithmetical or logical operation to perform. Figure 1.12 summarises the interaction of the CU with the CM and the ALU. Let us now move on to a discussion about the arithmetic and logical unit.

The Arithmetic and Logical Unit (ALU)

The ALU has specialised circuitry capable of carrying out arithmetical and logical operations. The arithmetical operations are of two sorts: basic operations and comparisons.

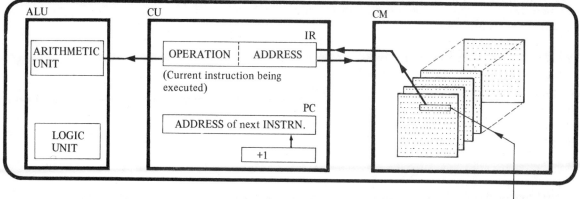

ALU   CU   CM

IR

ARITHMETIC UNIT

OPERATION | ADDRESS

(Current instruction being executed)

PC

ADDRESS of next INSTRN.

+1

LOGIC UNIT

Series of bits in CM holding an instruction or item of data

Fig. 1.12 Interaction of the control unit with the central memory and the arithmetic/logic unit

The basic operations involve:
    addition, subtraction, multiplication, and division

Comparison operations involve:
    greater than, *less than*, *equal to*, *less than or equal to*, *greater than or equal to*, and *not equal to* operations

Logical operations involve:
    NOT, AND, OR, NAND, NOR.
The ALU is operated by the CU which, because it has the task of decoding a given instruction, can pass a signal informing the ALU which operation to perform. The CU also has to pass to the ALU the data upon which the operation is to be performed. Let us now take each of the basic types of operations in turn and look at the details more closely.

Arithmetic Operations

ADDITION   The four basic arithmetical operations involve working on at least two numbers. As an example of how the ALU works, let us suppose that two numbers have to be added together. One of these numbers will be stored in a specific storage location called the **accumulator register**. The other number will be read from CM under the control of the CU into another register within the ALU. The CU will signal that addition is to be performed and the result or answer of the addition of the two separate numbers will be totalled or accumulated in the accumulator register, hence its name. In this way, the accumulator is similar to the display panel of a pocket calculator which acts as a totaliser or accumulator of the numbers operated upon.

What if three numbers are to be added together? Here we become involved in programming concepts. This is discussed in Chapter 2 but the point we need to make here is that computers work in the following way. Of the three numbers to be added, the first two are dealt with in the way already described. This partial result will be left in the accumulator and the third number is then read from CM into the other storage register of the ALU and then their addition performed. Consequently, only two numbers are actually added at one time.

21

SUBTRACTION Computers perform subtraction by a method of addition known as **"complementation"**. Now, this is not so strange as it sounds since many shopkeepers adopt a similar method many times each day.

Suppose that we wish to purchase an item worth 57p and hand over a one pound note (equivalent to 100 pence). The shopkeeper does not bother to subtract 57 from 100, rather he opens the till and then complements the 57 pence up to 100. The amount of money he takes from the till is what he gives us. Thus, he will take out a one-penny piece and will add it to the original 57 to make 58. Then a two-penny piece is extracted and added to the 58 to make 60 pence. A ten-penny piece is next taken out, now the total is 70; a further ten-penny piece makes the total 80; two more ten-penny pieces will now add up to 100. Thus, the

   1 penny
   2 penny piece
   4×10 penny pieces

will amount to 43 pennies, namely our change. But note how all this was achieved by a method of addition and *not* subtraction. Computers work in the same way and binary complementation is discussed more fully in Appendix 1. Thus, by a method of complementation, most commonly the so-called **twos complement** method, computers are able to perform subtraction.

MULTIPLICATION The process of multiplication for computers can be reduced to a very simple procedure but, before we can appreciate this, let us first look at how multiplication is frequently carried out by people using the decimal system. For example, suppose we wish to multiply 123 by 204.

123	Multiplicand (MD)
×204	Multiplier (MR)
492	i.e. multiply 123 by 4—the least significant digit of the MR (204).
000	000—but shift one place towards the left.
246	Multiply 123 by 2 and shift result one place further towards the left.
25092	Total by addition.

Some people prefer to begin with the most significant digit (MSD) of the multiplier and to shift towards the right, thus:

123 MD
204 MR
———
246 i.e. multiply the MD (123) by the MSD of the MR (2).
000 i.e. multiply by zero and shift one place towards the right.
492 i.e. multiply by 4 and shift one further place towards the right.
———
25092 Total arrived at by addition.

This procedure involves a knowledge of multiplication in denary and, of course, the process of shifting to the left (if multiplying first by the LSD of the multiplier) or to the right (if multiplying first by the MSD of the multiplier). This could be easily adapted for binary since binary multiplication involves fewer rules. We repeat them here for convenience (but see Appendix 1).

$1 \times 1 = 1$
$0 \times 1 = 0$
$1 \times 0 = 0$
$0 \times 0 = 0$

Let us see how to multiply 111_2 by 100_2 (i.e. 7 by 4), beginning with the LSD of the multiplier and therefore shifting left:

111 MD
100 MR
———
000 ⎫
000 ⎬ partial results
111 ⎭
———
11100 i.e. $16 + 8 + 4 = 28_{10}$

COMPUTER MULTIPLICATION It is inconvenient in terms of computer circuitry to have to store partial results and then finally add together the partial results, as we have done above. Therefore, as the partial results are generated, they tend to be totalled together in the accumulator. Furthermore, it becomes easier to shift partial results to the right rather than to shift the multiplicand to the left. Thus, by a combination of adding and shifting, computers perform multiplication. Let us see this process in operation using the following examples.

Example 1

     10_2 MD   2 in denary
   $\times 11_2$ MR   3 in denary

i.e. multiply 2 by 3.

   The usual starting point for computers is with the least significant *bit* (LSB).

a) 10   MD
     11   MR
     $\overline{10}$ i.e. the MD is added to the accumulator
          cleared at the start of the process to zero.
     010   Now shift one place to right.

b) 110   The MD is added to the acc. $010+10=110$
     0110   Shift one place to the right.
     end of operation

     $0110_2 = 6_{10}$ i.e. $10_2 \times 11_2$

Example 2

Multiply 7 by 5, i.e. 111_2 by 101_2.

a) 111   MD
     101   MR
     $\overline{111}$ Add MD to acc. (cleared to zero first).
     0111   Shift one place to the right.

b) 0111   Since the MR contains 0, there is no change
               in acc. contents but...
     00111   Shift one place to the right.

c) 100011   Add MD to acc.   00111
                                $+111$
                              $\overline{100011}$

     0100011   Shift to right
     end of operation

$0100011_2 = 35_{10}$ i.e. $111_2 \times 101_2$

THE SHIFT REGISTER   The **shift register** is capable of shifting its binary contents one digit at a time to the right, and in more sophisticated machines to the left as well. We have already seen how it is used to perform multiplication in the ALU, but it has many other more technical applications within the electronics of the computer hardware, as well as being used by programmers working in low-level languages.

DIVISION Division becomes a more complicated process, better discussed in a more advanced course, but we can note here for the sake of completeness that, through complementation and shifting, division is achieved quickly by the circuitry of the ALU.

Comparison Operations

Little need be said about the circuitry used for comparison functions since, like division, it is more appropriate for an electronics course. The main emphasis in this text is that these operations are of value to programmers. The six comparison operations already listed (p. 21) operate upon two data values. Thus, programmers find them useful tools when it becomes necessary for their program to compare two numbers, x and y, and then, depending upon the result, to perform one of two possible actions.

The result of the comparison test will be either True or False. Thus, at a given time if $x = 3$ and $y = 4$, then the six comparison tests will yield the results given in Figure 1.13.

X		Operation	Y	Result
3	=	equal to	4	F
3	≠	not equal to	4	T
3	>	greater than	4	F
3	<	less than	4	T
3	≥	greater than or equal to	4	F
3	≤	less than or equal to	4	T

Fig. 1.13

Logical Operations

We turn to the logical operations and discuss these in some detail, after which we shall be in a position to show how they can be used in one application, namely as a signal device between the CU and the ALU. Fortunately, logical operations are simple to understand. The actual electronic circuits will produce an output depending upon the input presented to them. The inputs to these electronic circuits are of course electrical pulses, which for simplicity are referred to as binary digits. The NOT circuit has only one input, whereas all the others may have two or more. However, all circuits produce only one output. These electronic circuits are more commonly known as **logic gates**.

NOT or INVERTER Function

This is very simple; the input is merely reversed or *inverted* by the circuit so that the output becomes the opposite of the input. Thus, a 1 input will become a 0 output, whilst a 0 input will become a 1 output (Figure 1.14). In terms

Input A	Output
1	0
0	1

Fig. 1.14

of voltages, if zero volts represents the binary zero and +5 volts the binary 1, then a zero voltage input will become a +5 volt on output.

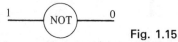

Fig. 1.15

We can represent these circuits diagrammatically (Figure 1.15). The circle represents the circuitry and the particular type of function performed is written inside. The one or more inputs to the circle are represented by lines on the left-hand side, the one output by a line on the right-hand side of the circle. If it becomes necessary to denote which binary digit the input is and which the output is, these can be written next to the line.

The two possible outputs of the NOT circuit may also be represented in a tabular form by what is called a **truth table**. By tradition the inputs are placed on the left-hand side of the double lines and the output on the right-hand side (Figure 1.14).

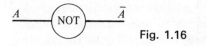

Fig. 1.16

In the case of the NOT function there is also a special way of representing the output. If A is the input which can take either a zero or a one, then $\bar{A}$ represents the output (Figure 1.16). We call this "A bar" since it has a bar above it, or sometimes "not A" . It simply means the reverse of what was the input.

AND Function

If we look at the truth table for the AND function (shown with only two inputs, Figure 1.17), we see that a positive 1 output results only when *both* (or *all* if more than two inputs) are also 1. All other possible combinations produce a zero or negative result. Figure 1.18

Input A	Input B	Output
0	0	0
0	1	0
1	0	0
1	1	1

Fig. 1.17   AND truth table: output is 1 only when both inputs are 1

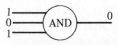

Fig. 1.18   Output is 0 since only two of the three inputs are 1

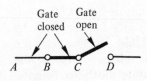

Fig. 1.19

shows a symbolic diagram with three inputs. This particular gate function can also be represented as shown in Figure 1.19 with three inputs. For the current to flow from the input side A via B and C all the way through to the output D, all three gates or switches must be closed (i.e. have a binary 1 pulse). The illustration has the third (C) gate open (i.e. presence of a zero) and so the current cannot pass along to the output D.

OR or INCLUSIVE-OR Function

The truth table for the OR function (Figure 1.20) shows that a result of 1 is always obtained except where *all* inputs are zeros. Thus if *any* of the inputs are 1, the output will be 1. Figure 1.21 shows how the circuit is represented for two inputs.

A	B	C	Output
0	0	0	0
0	0	1	1
0	1	0	1
0	1	1	1
1	0	0	1
1	0	1	1
1	1	0	1
1	1	1	1

Fig. 1.20   Inclusive-OR truth table

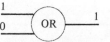

Fig. 1.21   Two-input OR function

One point to note is that, when every input is a 1, the output is still a 1. Because of this, the OR function is sometimes referred to as the *inclusive*-OR function. There is another type of OR function which excludes this situation and is therefore referred to as the *exclusive*-OR

A	B	C	Output
0	0	0	0
0	0	1	1
0	1	0	1
0	1	1	1
1	0	0	1
1	0	1	1
1	1	0	1
1	1	1	0

Fig. 1.22   Exclusive-OR truth table

A	B	OR	NOT
0	0	0	1
0	1	1	0
1	0	1	0
1	1	1	0

A	B	Output
0	0	1
0	1	0
1	0	0
1	1	0

Fig. 1.24   NOR truth table

Fig. 1.25   OR-NOT gates form the NOR function

function (Figure 1.22). In all other respects the inclusive-OR and the exclusive-OR work in the same way.

Figure 1.23 shows a third way of representing the OR gate. If either gate is down, then the current can flow through to the output.

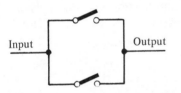

Fig. 1.23   Gate diagram for OR function

The other two logic functions which we next describe consist of two of the gates already outlined.

NOR Function

This is the inclusive-OR function with the output from the OR inverted by the NOT function, hence the term NOR. For a two-input NOR function, for example, the truth table is shown in two ways (Figure 1.24). The first gives an OR followed by the NOT: the second shows the NOR as a combination of both functions. Figure 1.25 shows the circuit representation.

NAND Function

This involves an AND and a NOT sequence. Like the NOR function, the result of the AND operation is passed to an inverter circuit to form the output from a NAND circuit. We show this as one step in the NAND truth table (Figure 1.26). Figure 1.27 shows the circuit representation.

A	B	Output
0	0	1
0	1	1
1	0	1
1	1	0

Fig. 1.26   NAND truth table

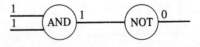

Fig. 1.27   AND-NOT gates form the NAND function

The Usefulness of Logic Gates

We know that computers are electronic machines which consist of a very large number of electronic circuits interconnected in often highly complex ways. The five basic logic circuits (the logic gates) are the basic elements which go to make up these more complex electronic systems. These gates are at the heart of computer circuitry and provide control of information flow, perform arithmetic and logic functions, help to store information, and even provide the timing circuitry necessary to synchronise the working of the whole computer.

For example, the exclusive-OR function (Figure 1.22) can be used to detect the not-equal (non-equivalence) state since it will produce an output only when both inputs are *not* the same. Again, by combining four AND gates in the CU, it is possible to detect which arithmetic operation is being requested by a program instruction. Let us assume that the following binary patterns are used by a given computer to indicate the four arithmetic operations:

00 indicates addition
01 indicates subtraction
10 indicates multiplication
11 indicates division

One of the four possible two-bit function codes is placed in the Instruction Register (IR), in bit position 1 and in bit position 2. The circuitry is so designed that each bit position can produce two outputs—the original bit value itself together with its inversion. Thus the original two bits of the function code generate four outputs. These four outputs pass through a set of four AND gates, each one equivalent to one of the four arithmetic operations. By the arrangement of the circuits, only one of the four AND gates can receive two positive inputs, thus generating an output (see Figure 1.28) which corresponds to one arithmetic operation.

Let us take the example of where a multiplication instruction (10) is placed in the IR. The binary pattern 10 corresponding to the multiplication operation will be placed in bit positions 1 and 2, with bit position 1 containing zero, and bit position 2 containing 1. As a result, bit 1 will generate a one (positive) pulse via the NOT gate to both the addition and the multiplication AND gates. Bit 2 will generate a positive pulse (not via the NOT gate but because it is a one bit) to both the multiplication and the division AND gates. You can now see that of the four AND gates, only the multiplication gate re-

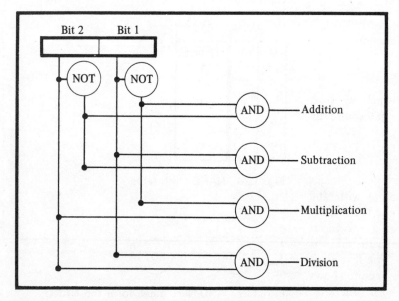

Fig. 1.28 Instruction decoder for arithmetic operations

ceives two positive pulses and, therefore, only the multiplication control signal will be stimulated. Work through Figure 1.28 to satisfy yourself that this is so.

In this way, the decoding of the original binary pattern will operate only one of the four gates at any one time. It is this method by which the CU can inform the ALU which of the four arithmetical processes to carry out. Try the other three possible two-bit binary patterns in the IR to prove what has been described.

Hopefully, you can now begin to appreciate the manner in which the CU "informs" the ALU which operation to perform by combining four AND gates. The entire computer circuitry is built up on a similar principle. It does become much more complex, however, than the simple case of arithmetic illustrated. For instance, the CU must be able to decode not only the four basic arithmetical procedures but also input and output operations, logical and comparison operations, etc. Thus the binary patterns must increase from two to perhaps six or even eight. In consequence the instruction decoder contains many more circuits. This is what we mean by complexity. Some computers have 30 or 40 instructions which they are capable of carrying out or have been designed to decode. Others may have as many as 200 or so. Nevertheless, the principle demonstrated remains the same whether the instruction or operation bits number two or eight. The greater the number of instructions a computer can decode, the more complex the instruction decoder becomes and therefore the more expensive the computer itself.

Another factor which can increase the overall cost of the machine is the type of electronic circuits used. Some are faster than others. The CDC Cyber range of machines designed to perform arithmetic (principally involving only addition and shifting) very quickly is an expensive machine and it has an instruction set of over 200. It is the same with motor cars. A sports model is more expensive than the normal family saloon since, because it can travel at higher speeds, its engine is more complicated.

So far we have discussed the electronic circuitry of the CM, the CU and the ALU. Figure 1.29 combines all three units of the CPU to show their interconnections.

We are now in a better position to discuss one final point, namely, the accuracy of computer arithmetic.

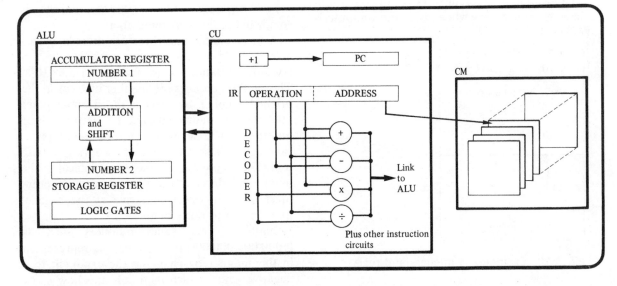

Fig. 1.29 Interconnections between the various units of the CPU (The CU shows only the four arithmetical instructions)

Accuracy of Computer Arithmetic

It often comes as a surprise to mathematicians and scientists to discover that arithmetic as performed by computers is often limited and not 100% accurate. Let us take one example first and then discuss the reasons. If we were to calculate the following problem using pen and paper, we would get an answer of 1·0.

$$(1·0 \div 3·0) \times 3·0$$

However a computer, or a pocket calculator for that matter, is likely to produce 0·99999 . . . ! The main reason for this is the way in which computers store numbers in central memory.

Certain large computers and the more expensive pocket calculators will provide an answer of 1·0 due to a more sophisticated rounding circuitry.

Storage of Numbers

There are two basic types of number: those without a decimal point (called **integer** or whole numbers) and those with a decimal point (**real** or *floating point* numbers). Figure 1.30 illustrates various examples. Both types are stored in a location in different ways but of course will have to be in binary when inside the computer's memory.

1.0	Real
1.23	numbers
0.34	Decimal
.92	points
0.0	
1	Integer
123	numbers
0	No decimal
	points

Fig. 1.30   Examples of integers and reals

STORAGE OF INTEGER NUMBERS   Let us take an example of an eight-bit word and see how integer numbers are stored. Following the

common approach, we shall use the leftmost bit to indicate the sign of the number, i.e. bit 8, thereby leaving seven bits for the actual number itself. Consequently, with an eight-bit word we can store positive numbers up to the range of +127, i.e. $(2^7 - 1)$. Applying twos complement method to represent negative numbers, the same word can now represent integers within the range of −128 to +127. The formula for arriving at the range is given in Appendix 1 but is repeated here for convenience; n gives the number of bits in a word.

The formula is

$$-2^{n-1} \leqslant N \leqslant 2^{n-1} - 1 \quad \text{twos complement}$$

Thus our 8-bit word, according to the formula, is

$$-2^{8-1} \leqslant N \leqslant 2^{8-1} - 1 = -128 \text{ to } +127$$

whereas a 12-bit word would allow a range of −2048 to +2047:

$$-2^{12-1} \leqslant N \leqslant 2^{12-1} - 1 = -2048 \text{ to } +2047$$

REAL NUMBERS   Real numbers are stored in a different way. Often scientists work with very large or very small numbers which make their representation in the standard decimal notation rather clumsy.

For example, 123 000 000 000 000·00 is somewhat difficult to remember.

A more simple and therefore more manageable way to represent the same number in scientific notation is as follows: $1·23 \times 10^{14}$. This method reduces the number of zeros in the original number by placing the decimal point after the first significant digit (i.e. between the 1 and the 2). The decimal 10 after the multiplication sign indicates that we are working in base ten. The exponent of the base indicates the number of places to the *right* the decimal point must move in order to arrive at the original number, 14 in our example.

Similarly, very small numbers such as 0·000 000 000 000 162 can also be represented in this manner by changing the exponent to a negative value, which then indicates how many places to the *left* the decimal point must move in order to arrive at the original number, giving $1·62 \times 10^{-13}$.

Computers use a similar but slightly different form called **normalisation**, whereby the decimal point is placed in front of the first significant digit. Thus the above two numbers become

$$0 \cdot 123 \times 10^{+15}$$
$$0 \cdot 162 \times 10^{-12}$$

Note that, with this normalised notation, zeros cannot lie immediately after the decimal point. Furthermore, by removing unwanted zeros, this method can compact the number into a smaller space, thus saving storage inside the computer. Seventeen decimal characters would be required to store the smaller of the two numbers, whereas only eleven are required in normalised form.

In our computer experience within this book, we shall not have to deal with numbers of such extreme range but knowing how they are stored will help you to appreciate more about the way in which computers work. A few examples may help you to become more familiar with normalised notation.

Example 1. The number +1.52 is written in normalised format as $0 \cdot 152 \times 10^{+1}$. Here the decimal point has been shifted from between the digits 1 and 5 to the beginning (the left) of digit 1. The exponent +1 tells us how many places to the *right* we must move the point to arrive at the original number.

Example 2. The number +152·0 becomes $0 \cdot 152 \times 10^{+3}$. Here the exponent +3 tells us to move the decimal point 3 places to the right.

Example 3. The number +5671·0 becomes $0 \cdot 5671 \times 10^{+4}$.

But suppose the original number was +0·005 671. Now the decimal point has to shift to the *left*, which is signified by a *negative* exponent to regain the original number, thus: $0 \cdot 5671 \times 10^{-2}$.

Example 4. The number 0·0321 becomes $0 \cdot 321 \times 10^{-1}$ in normalised form.

Example 5. The number 0·000 0014 becomes $0 \cdot 14 \times 10^{-5}$.

If the orginal number is already in a normalised form, 0·123, then this is represented as: $0 \cdot 123 \times 10^{0}$. Note that the fraction part is *not* the number (except in the one case where the number is already normalised), it only provides the significant digits of the number. The exponent is there to show where the decimal point has to be placed in order to arrive back at the original number.

Thus, we see that normalisation as used in computers involves two parts to a number. The first part holds the significant digits and is called the **fraction** or **mantissa**; and the second part the **exponent** or **characteristic** (Figure 1.31). A closer look at Example 4 where the original

Mantissa	Exponent

Fig. 1.31 Memory location divided into mantissa and exponent for storing a real number

number was +0·0321 shows that six pieces of information are necessary when the number is normalised. Thus, $+0 \cdot 321 \times 10^{-1}$ requires

1) the plus sign indicating a positive real number
2) the real number itself, 0·321, in normalised form
3) the multiplication sign
4) the base of the real number, i.e. 10 (ten)
5) the sign for the exponent
6) the actual exponent i.e. integer 1.

Binary Floating Point Numbers

Using the above six pieces of information, let us see how binary real numbers are represented.

$+6 \cdot 0_{10}$ becomes $+110 \cdot 0_{2}$ in binary. In normalised form this becomes

Sign of number	Binary digits	Mult. sign	Base	Sign of exponent	Exponent
+	0·1100	×	10	+	11

i.e. $0 \cdot 110_{2} \times 10_{2}^{+11_{2}}$

$0 \cdot 25_{10}$ becomes 0·01 in binary and, when normalised, becomes $0 \cdot 10 \times 10^{-1}$.

Storage of Real Numbers

Having already seen that a computer word is a group of so many bits, how can real numbers be stored in a group of eight bits? In practice each computer manufacturer can adopt one of several methods. We shall describe only one possible method in any detail but the essential principle is the same for whichever actual method is employed on a given computer.

The word is divided into two parts. We shall allocate five bits for the fraction (mantissa) and three for the exponent (characteristic). We

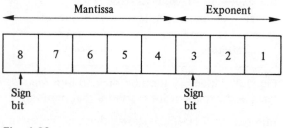

Mantissa   Exponent

| 8 | 7 | 6 | 5 | 4 | 3 | 2 | 1 |

Sign bit (bit 8)   Sign bit (bit 3)

Fig. 1.32

know that both of these may be either positive or negative and therefore each part must have a sign bit. Figure 1.32 illustrates this: bit 8 is used as the sign for the mantissa and bit 3 as the sign for the exponent. Thus we have provided four out of the six pieces of information. We do not need to represent the other two pieces since the base is known to be binary and the multiplica-

tion sign can be implied as existing between bits four and three.

The IBM 370 series and the CDC Cyber series reduce the information to three by storing the exponent in a particular way, but this method need not concern us.

Figure 1.33 shows how the positive binary number $110 \cdot 0$ (or $+6_{10}$) and the negative binary $-0 \cdot 01$ (or $-0 \cdot 25_{10}$) are stored in eight-bit words. The decimal point is implied between bits 8 and 7. We have adopted the common method of storing, in twos complement form, the mantissa and the exponent in the second example.

Having seen how both integer and real numbers are stored in a computer word, we may now return to the question of accuracy. The range of *integer* numbers in an eight-bit word, using twos complement for negative numbers, is -128 to $+127$.

Suppose a certain multiplication or a series of additions were to go outside of the range, then what would happen? Clearly, that number cannot be represented in the given number of bits. Take the example of the eight-bit word. A multiplication of $10_{10} \times 13_{10}$ yields a product of 130_{10}. But the maximum integer positive number in an eight-bit word is 127. In this case an eight-bit word computer cannot represent 130 since it exceeds the range. This condition is known as **overflow** since the extra bits "spill out of the word" and are lost. Some computers will

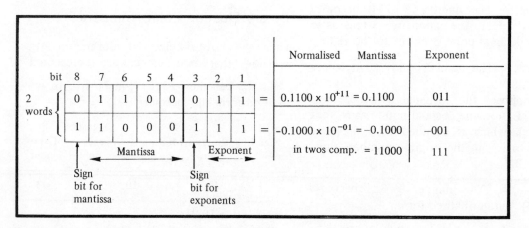

bit 8 7 6 5 4 3 2 1		Normalised Mantissa	Exponent
0 1 1 0 0 0 1 1	=	$0.1100 \times 10^{+11} = 0.1100$	011
1 1 0 0 0 1 1 1	=	$-0.1000 \times 10^{-01} = -0.1000$ in twos comp. $= 11000$	-001 111

2 words

Mantissa   Exponent

Sign bit for mantissa   Sign bit for exponents

Fig. 1.33

32

stop execution of a program if overflow occurs, others do not. In the latter case, the programmer may be totally unaware that his results are incorrect.

In the case of real numbers, overflow occurs if the range of the *exponent* is exceeded. Thus with our three-bit exponent, the range is -4 to $+3$. Thus if we exceed $+3$, then overflow results, and similarly, if an exponent is smaller than -4, a condition known as **underflow** occurs.

Clearly, the size of a computer word (that is the number of bits it contains) is limited; some have 8, some 12, others 16, 32, 36 or even 60. In this sense we say that computers have a *finite* number of bits and therefore the range of their numbers must also be finite or limited. Naturally, an eight-bit word is very limiting for arithmetic, and computers designed for use by mathematicians or scientists have much larger word lengths. Machines which do have only eight bits have facilities for grouping two or more words together in order to extend their arithmetical capability.

Again, it is not always possible to exactly represent a decimal fraction in binary. For example, 0.2 cannot be exactly represented in binary. The nearest we can get to it with ten binary digits is

$$0.0011001100(0.19921875_{10})$$

Thus if we multiply 1.2 by 10.0 in binary, the result is always something less than 12.0. We can get very near to it but never actually achieve a result of twelve. Furthermore, the actual precision of the result will depend totally upon the number of binary bits in the word of the computer we are using. So as a consequence of having a finite word length, and the inability of binary to exactly represent certain decimal fractions, computer arithmetic is limited or finite. It cannot be a hundred percent accurate. What can be done? First, since we live and work in a finite world, every practical scientist is willing to accept something less than absolute accuracy. This means that computers can be used to produce results that are as near to absolute accuracy as a given task requires. Human beings are used to accepting or tolerating something less than perfection.

In certain cases where greater precision is required than that offered by one computer word, certain programming languages such as Fortran permit two words to be used. Here the second word can be linked to the first such that, in effect, the word length is doubled. Hence the term Double Precision as used in Fortran.

Important Words and Terms in Chapter 1

Central memory CM (immediate access memory, IAS, primary, main storage, core storage)
words, locations
word length
byte
bits

Storage
secondary storage (auxiliary, backing stores)
magnetic tape
magnetic disc
magnetic drum

Arithmetic/logic unit ALU
accumulator
shift register

Control unit CU
instruction register IR
program counter PC
instruction decoder
fetch-execute cycle

Finite arithmetic
twos complement
integer numbers and overflow
real numbers and overflow, underflow
binary floating point
mantissa, fraction
exponent, characteristic
base two, base ten
truth table
sign and modulus, sign and
    magnitude
program instruction

Exercises 1

1 What do the following stand for: ALU, CPU, CU, K?

2 Which computer can store more binary digits, a 16K 32-bit machine or a 32K 16-bit machine?

3 Explain the terms: bit, byte, word, word length.

4 What do all these have in common: IAS, central memory, store unit?

5 How many bits are required to represent a character set containing 48 characters?

6 State briefly how our everyday information is stored in computers?

7 A name or number used to identify a storage location is called (select one answer from the list below):
a) a byte *b*) a carry bit *c*) a record *d*) an address *e*) a file

8 What are the main functions of the *central processer* of a computing system? (*OLE* 1978)

9 What are the three main components of a CPU? Discuss their activities.

10 What features would you expect to find in a computer especially designed for numerical work?

11 What is the purpose of the accumulator register in the ALU?

12 What registers would you expect to find in the CU and what are their functions?

13 What is the central memory (immediate access memory) of a computer used for?

14 What types of number do computers have to handle? Briefly describe how each one is stored in the main memory.

15 Draw a truth table for the NOR function; the inclusive-OR function; the AND function.

16 What is the difference between the inclusive-OR function and the exclusive-OR function? Illustrate your answer by means of truth tables.

17 Which is the best description of a NOT gate? (*EMREB* 1977)

a) If the input bit is 1, the result is 0; if the input bit is 0, the result is 1.
b) If the input bit is 1 or 0, the result is 1.
c) If the input bit is 1, the result is 1; if the input bit is 0, the result is 0.
d) The result is always 0.
e) The result is 1, only if the input bit is 1.

18 What is the output of the following circuit when

a) $A = 0$; $B = 1$
b) $A = 1$; $B = 0$

(*OLE* 1978)

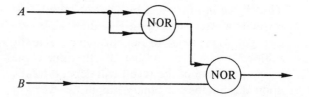

19 Which logic gate does the following truth table represent? (*AEB* spec.)

Inputs		Output
A	*B*	*C*
0	0	0
0	1	1
1	0	1
1	1	1

20 From the logic function shown, state the value of C if

a) A is 1, B is 0
b) A is 0, B is 1
c) A is 1, B is 1

(*JMB* spec. 1978)

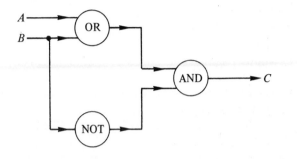

21 Give a truth table for the logic function below, i.e. what is the output at C, D and E for the four possible inputs at A and B.

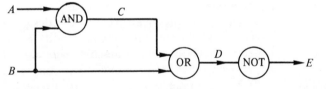

22 Copy and complete the truth table for the logical circuit below. (*SWEB* 1977)

A	B	C	D
0		0	
0		1	
0	1		
0	1		
1		0	
	0	1	
	1		
	1		

23 The diagram below shows a simple piece of decoding logic. Complete the table shown, in order to find the value of H for each of the inputs listed. (*AEB* spec.)

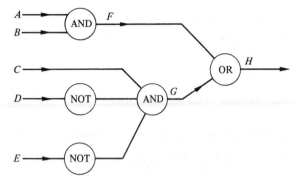

A	B	C	D	E	F	G	H
1	1	0	1	1			
0	1	1	0	0			
0	0	1	0	1			
1	1	1	1	1			
1	0	0	1	1			
1	1	1	0	0			

24 "Overflow" may occur when two numbers are multiplied together within a digital computer. State clearly what you understand by this statement. (*UCLES* 1977)

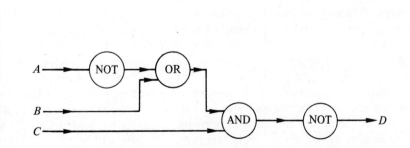

2 Principles and Techniques of Programming

Introduction

A language such as English or French is rich in vocabulary. This means that the many thoughts and ideas which we human beings have, can be expressed in these natural languages. On the other hand, a programming language has a very small vocabulary, much smaller than that of a young child. An average seven year old has a vocabulary of over 2000 words; whereas programming languages such as "standard" Fortran and Basic have around 20. This could make us think that nothing much can be done or said in a computer language. In one sense, this is perfectly true. It has already been shown (page 15) that any computer, no matter how expensive or sophisticated, is, after all, capable of performing only four basic operations:

1) Input/output operations
2) Arithmetic operations
3) Comparison/logical operations
4) Movement/structuring of data.

Therefore, there is no need for a computer language to have a rich vocabulary. It is we who need large vocabularies because as human beings we have to express a much wider variety of operations which need to take into account our emotions, intellect and judgements. A computer cannot love or hate anything or anyone; a computer cannot look at a painting and form any concept of beauty; a computer cannot hear two pieces of music and form a judgement as to which it prefers; a computer cannot look at a scene of Nature and be moved to express its feelings in terms of poetry. It is true that "poetry" can be generated by a computer; however that computer cannot appraise its own "work". All the computer can do is to perform its four basic operations, but at a very fast rate, much more quickly than we humans could perform them. If a computer has such a limited range of operations, why are there so many computer languages, and why are some called low level and others high level?

Evolution of Languages

There are two major types of computer or programming languages—*low-level* and *high-level*. As shown in Figure 2.1, the low-level languages can be further divided into *machine code* and *assembly languages.*

When a computer is being designed, it will be constructed to understand (obey) just one language. This may come as a complete surprise to those who are used to seeing "their" computer apparently understanding and obeying programs written in several different languages. But it is a fact that any given computer is designed to understand only one language and this is called its **machine code** or **machine language**. If a program is written in any other language, then that program will have to be translated into the machine language of the computer, but more of this later.

When the machine code instructions are in the central memory of the computer, they will be, of course, in numerical form, in certain binary patterns since this is the natural number system of digital computers. We human beings are more at home with the decimal number system. Consequently, machine code programmers tend to write computer instructions in decimal and let the input device convert these to binary before they are placed in central memory. Thus, to the programmer a decimal number may well represent a machine function, e.g. 01 could mean "add", 02 could mean "subtract".

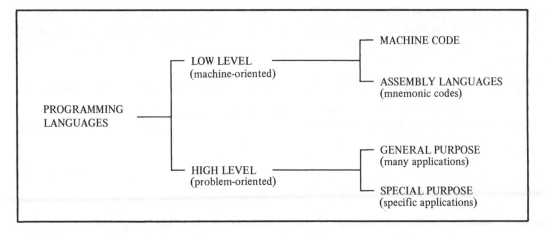

Fig. 2.1 Levels of programming languages

In the early days of computers, it was easier for programmers to write machine code programs, because they were the very people who had created the language when designing the machine. Indeed, some of these first programmers actually wrote in binary itself, claiming that, since this was the natural language of a computer, then humans had to learn it too if they wanted to communicate with the machine. Fortunately, this attitude did not last very long simply because it proved too tedious for human beings to think in binary numbers. Writing instructions in decimal numbers is difficult enough because it means constantly having to remember which number means which operation. Since human beings prefer to use words, a new type of language evolved, based on the machine code, which used letters instead of decimal numbers to represent computer operations, e.g. 01 would become ADD, 02 SUBTRACT. However, "subtract" is a long word to keep writing down in full and so a shorthand form or mnemonic (pronounced "neh-mon-ik" and derived from the Greek word "memory") was used, namely, SUB. Both ADD and SUB are symbolic names to represent the addition and subtraction operations of a computer. The computer cannot understand the symbols ADD, in the same way that computers do not understand decimal numbers. All the computer understands, or, rather, has been specifically designed to understand, is that when it comes across the binary pattern 0001 (decimal 01) as part of an instruction, the electrical pulses which are represented by the binary pattern will activate the addition operation in the arithmetic logic unit. These symbols or mnemonic type languages are known as **assembly level languages**.

Both machine and assembly languages are called "low level". The term "low" does not mean "inferior" in any sense, but rather "closeness" to the way in which the machine has been built. We saw in Chapter 1 that a word or location in central memory can contain either a piece of data or an instruction. The format of a computer instruction is basic (primitive) and consists of only two parts, a verb (or function) and an object (or address), so that the only style of "sentence" one can have in a low-level language program is "perform this operation using this address".

High-level Languages

One disadvantage with a low-level language is that because of the primitive sentence structure it takes many such instructions to perform even a simple task. For example, to add three numbers together involves at least four instructions, whereas in everyday arithmetic this can be achieved with merely one, e.g. $x = a + b + c$.

Another class of language developed which took more account of the type of *problem* to be solved rather than any account of how a computer was designed. Since the early problems for computer solution were of a mathematical and scientific nature, it is not surprising to find that the new class of programming languages were designed to solve mathematical and scientific problems. Fortran and Algol are such examples. These languages which are aimed at the problem to be solved are called **problem-oriented** high-level languages. In Fortran it is possible to say in just one instruction, and not four as in the case of low-level languages, that three numbers are to be added together. Yet the term "high" must not be confused with any meaning of superiority. It simply means pointing or oriented towards the problem to be solved and not towards the structure of the machine.

High-level languages such as Fortran, Algol, Basic can be used by an individual programmer to solve many different types of problem. In this sense, they are called *general purpose languages*, the one language being used to solve many classes of problems. There is another type of high-level language which is known as a *special purpose language* and which is designed to help a programmer solve one class of problem. Snobol is such a language and is used to solve textual problems; RPG is another, and is used in the commercial world to generate business reports. However, neither of these languages could be used to solve any problem other than the type it was specially designed to solve. It is possible to use Basic to generate reports (or to handle text) but for a programmer who has to write *many* report-generating (or text-handling) programs, it is easier to use RPG (or Snobol).

In conclusion, machine code languages were the earliest (1940s) computer languages, but are still being created every time a new make of computer is introduced; assembly level languages first began to appear in the early 1950s; and high-level languages were not introduced until 1958. Remember, it is only the machine language that is dependent upon a particular

computer; assembly and high-level languages can be used with any computer, provided that the computer has some means of translating the program into its own language.

Low-level Language Principles

In this section we shall take a look at some principles of low-level languages. It has already been stated that a low-level language is oriented towards the design features of a computer, i.e. it is a **machine-oriented** language, whereas a high-level language is *problem-oriented*.

A Simple Computer

In order to appreciate this point, let us first "define" part of a simple computer. It will have 1024 locations (words) of central memory, with each word containing 12 binary digits. We already know that one word can contain a piece of information or one instruction but we shall now look at instructions in more detail.

Instruction Formats

Instructions consist of two parts (we can extend this to three later on), and may be thought of as simple sentences consisting of a verb and an object. From now on we will call the verb an *operation* or *function* code (i.e. "do something"), and the object an *address* (i.e. the location in central memory which is used by the operation code). Furthermore, we will allocate 4 bits for the function codes and 8 bits for the address portion. Figure 2.2 shows bits 1–8 used for the address and bits 9–12 used for the function code. From our knowledge of binary (Appendix 1) we know that 4 bits can have up to 16 different binary patterns ($2^4 = 2 \times 2 \times 2 \times 2 = 16$) whilst 8 bits allow for 256. Thus our 12-bit word can allow up to 16 different function codes and can address any of the first 256 locations in memory. We shall see later on how to address the remaining locations.

12	11	10	9	8	7	6	5	4	3	2	1
Function				Address							

Fig. 2.2 Basic instruction format

Having thought out the basic word design of our machine and the size of central memory, we can now begin to think about the actual machine code it will use. Since computers can perform only four basic types of operations (input/output, arithmetic, comparison, and movement of data), we can arrange for the basic arithmetic operations of addition, subtraction, multiplication and division to be given the four binary patterns which are equivalent to the first four decimal numbers. We shall include leading zeros so that 01 indicates addition, 02 subtraction, 03 multiplication, and 04 division.

Accumulator

In Chapter 1, we noted that within the central memory no arithmetic takes place. All computations and comparison operations are performed in the ALU (arithmetic/logic unit) and that, when such functions are required, it is one of the duties of the control unit to take numbers from central memory and place them in the ALU. In the ALU there is a special register called the *accumulator*. One purpose of this accumulator together with associated circuitry is to perform arithmetical operations.

Thus, if we wish to add two numbers together, we will need one instruction which will order the control unit to place a number in the accumulator and another instruction to identify the addition operation. Since the decimal number five has not yet been given an operation, we can use it to represent the order "place in the accumulator the number found in the given address location". Thus the order 05 32 will have the effect of placing whatever numerical value is found in address location 32, in the accumulator. Furthermore, if another location, 33 for example, has a value, we can add that

value to the number already in the accumulator. The adding of two numbers together, then, is achieved by the two instructions:

05 32   place in accumulator the value found in the address location 32.

01 33   add value of address location 33 to contents in accumulator.

Note that when the addition command (01) is used, it is assumed that some previous number has *already been placed in the accumulator*.

If we wish to place the result of the computation (which is still in the accumulator) back into central memory, say in location 34, then we shall need yet another instruction. Let us use 06 to represent that function. Thus, 06 34 will cause the contents of the accumulator to be placed in that location given in the address portion of the instruction, namely location 34.

Accumulator Used for I/O Operations

The accumulator also has another purpose. It is used with the input/output operations. Reading information into the memory of a computer from some input device is usually a complex task. The same is true for output operations. These I/O activities are normally carried out under the guidance of the operating system (Chapter 6). However, all we need to know at this stage is that, when a number is read from some input device (say a card reader), then that number is placed in the accumulator, so that it becomes necessary for the program to transfer the number from the accumulator to some location in memory. To do this, we can make use of the same instruction which was used earlier to place the result of a computation from the accumulator into a memory location, namely the function code 06.

07 may be used for the input operation and 08 for the output. Note that, since the accumulator is involved in input/output operations, there is no need to have an address part for these two instructions.

Using our eight operation codes, we can now write a simple machine code language program to read in two numbers, store them in memory,

Operation code	Function performed
01	Addition
02	Subtraction
03	Multiplication
04	Division
05	Place in accumulator number from central memory
06	Contents of accumulator placed in memory
07	Perform input from input device into acc.
08	Perform output from accumulator to output device

Fig. 2.3 Eight basic operation codes

Instrn. number	Function code	Address	Comment
1	07		Read number into acc.
2	06	33	Store acc. contents in location 33
3	07		
4	06	32	Store acc. contents in locn. 32
5	05	32	Put in acc. contents of locn. 32
6	01	33	Add number in locn. 33 to contents of acc.
7	06	34	Store contents of acc. in locn. 34
8	05	34	Put in acc. contents of locn. 34
9	08		Output acc. contents to output device

Fig. 2.4 A simple machine code program

add them together, and output the result. Figure 2.3 gives a list of operation codes and the function each one represents, whilst Figure 2.4 lists the program instructions.

The effect of instruction 3 is to read the second number into the accumulator. The effect of instructions 4 and 5 is to place that same number from the accumulator into memory (location 32) and to put a copy of that number back into the accumulator. In other words, apart from illustrating the use of instructions 4 and 5, they are really not necessary for our program. Similarly for instructions 7 and 8. Therefore, we can re-write the program using only five instructions. You are encouraged to work

through the second program (Figure 2.5) and satisfy yourself that it does exactly the same as the first example but with fewer instructions. Note that only one location, 33, is used.

1	07	
2	06	33
3	07	
4	01	33
5	08	

Fig. 2.5 Revised program with fewer instructions

Assembly Level Languages

Mnemonic Function Codes

Whilst working through the simple program, you may have already appreciated the need for a list and a commentary of the various function codes, even though there are only eight codes. Many machine languages can have up to 200 codes depending upon such factors as the size of central memory and the degree of complexity of the computer's circuitry. With 200 different function codes, such a list would be essential *if* programmers had to use the decimal number version of the machine code. But we have already noted that, since programmers use words for their everyday communication, it is only

natural that they prefer to use words when writing programs. Consequently, the decimal numbers we have chosen to represent the various functions of our computer could be written down as semi-words or mnemonics. For example, instead of using 02 to represent the subtraction function, we could use SUB. This shorter form or mnemonic is used rather than the full word itself. Figure 2.6 gives a list of our eight decimal codes and their equivalent mnemonics.

The actual mnemonics chosen are fairly standard, but some other selection of characters could quite easily have been chosen. Using these symbolic characters as our chosen mnemonics, we can re-write the simple program as shown in Figure 2.7. The binary equivalent has also been included.

Function code	Mnem-onic	Description	Function code	Mnem-onic	Description
01	ADD	addition	05	LDA	Load accumulator with value
02	SUB	subtraction	06	STO	Store contents of accumulator
03	MULT	multiplication	07	IN	Read a value into accumulator
04	DIV	division	08	OUT	Output value in acc. to output device

Fig. 2.6

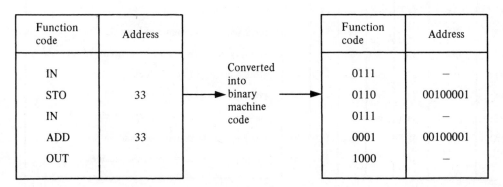

Function code	Address		Function code	Address
IN			0111	–
STO	33	Converted into binary machine code	0110	00100001
IN			0111	–
ADD	33		0001	00100001
OUT			1000	–

Fig. 2.7   Mnemonic (assembly) program

Symbolic Addressing

Not only can the function code be given mnemonics but it is also desirable for programmers to be able to give an address location a symbolic name. In the program of Figure 2.7, we have specified the actual location in memory where the first number is to be stored, namely in location 33. This is known as specifying the actual or **absolute address**. In such a simple program there is no problem in remembering the exact (absolute) address and what it was used for. But in a program using several hundred locations, this task of remembering becomes very difficult. An "absolute address list" would be required showing those locations which had been used (as well as their purpose) and a list of those locations which have yet to be used.

Let us now extend the simple program to illustrate this problem. In addition to reading in two numbers and adding them together, we shall also multiply both original numbers and then output *two* results—the addition of the two original numbers and the multiplication of the two original numbers. Figure 2.8 shows the coding for this, but note first how the number of instructions has increased and, secondly, that there is now a need to store both numbers in memory before *either* computation can take place. If this were not done, then one of the original numbers would be lost when the process of addition took place so that we could not carry out the multiplication. To help appreciate this point, Figure 2.8 includes the contents of the accumulator as each instruction is executed. Note how it is constantly changing. The contents of locations 32, 33, 34 and 35 are also shown. The dash (−) indicates that the location has not yet been given a value. The two numbers to be operated upon are 5 and 6.

One further point of interest about the above program needs to be mentioned. Look at instruction 2 (STO 32). This will store the contents of the accumulator into the absolute location 32. But after the instruction has been executed, the contents of the accumulator are not only in location 32 but also *still* in the

| Instrn. number | Functn. code | Address | Acc. | Locations for data | | | | Commentary |
				32	33	34	35	
1	IN		5	−	−	−	−	Read number into acc.
2	STO	32	5	5	−	−	−	Store acc. contents in locn. 32
3	IN		6	5	−	−	−	Read another number into acc.
4	STO	33	6	5	6	−	−	Store acc. contents in locn. 33
5	ADD	32	11	5	6	−	−	Add value of locn. 32 to contents of acc.
6	STO	34	11	5	6	11	−	Store acc. contents in locn. 34
7	LDA	32	5	5	6	11	−	Load acc. with contents of locn. 32
8	MULT	33	30	5	6	11	−	Multiply contents of acc. by contents of locn. 33
9	STO	35	30	5	6	11	30	Store contents of acc. in locn. 35
10	LDA	34	11	5	6	11	30	Load acc. with contents of locn. 34
11	OUT		11	5	6	11	30	Output acc. contents to output device
12	LDA	35	30	5	6	11	30	Load acc. with contents of locn. 35
13	OUT		30	5	6	11	30	Output acc. contents to output device

Fig. 2.8

accumulator. In other words, only a *copy* of the accumulator contents is placed in location 32.

A similar occurrence takes place with instruction 7 (LDA 32). Here the reverse of instruction 2 is taking place, namely the contents of location 32 are loaded into the accumulator. But again, because only a copy of the contents is passed over, location 32 still retains the original value. This is very useful, of course, since it means that location 32 can be used time and time again without it having to be "refilled" each time it is used.

Symbolic Names

Instead of the programmer having to keep track of each absolute address used, he can (as we shall shortly see) allocate this function to the translator program and merely refer to a location by some symbolic or mnemonic name. These names are usually restricted to three or four characters and can only contain letters of the alphabet (A–Z) and digits 0–9. We shall adopt the same policy and allow a name to have up to four characters. The first one must be alphabetic. Thus, we could give the name NUM1 (symbolic for "number one") to the location into which the first number will be read; NUM2 for the second number; RES1 and RES2 can stand for the results of the addition and the multiplication. These symbolic names are now used in place of the absolute addresses and thus, we can now re-write the program as in Figure 2.9.

It is much easier and quicker for the programmer to write programs using both mnemonic function codes and symbolic address names. Now there is no need to keep referring to lists in order to recall the decimal number function code for "loading the accumulator", or to check in which absolute address the first data number was read into. It is merely necessary to write: LDA NUM1.

If you do not fully appreciate this point, then try writing the above program in both machine code (i.e. just using decimal numbers) and then in assembly code but extending the program to subtract the second number from the first as well as adding and multiplying both numbers.

Instrn. number	Functn. code	Address	Commentary
1	IN		Read first number into acc.
2	STO	NUM1	Store acc. contents into locn. called NUM1.
3	IN		Read second number into acc.
4	STO	NUM2	Store acc. contents into locn. called NUM2
5	ADD	NUM1	Add contents of locn. called NUM1 to contents in acc.
6	STO	RES1	Store acc. contents in locn. called RES1
7	LDA	NUM1	Load into acc. contents of locn. called NUM1
8	MULT	NUM2	Multiply contents in locn. NUM2 by contents of acc.
9	STO	RES2	Store acc. contents into locn. RES2
10	LDA	RES1	Load into acc. contents of RES1
11	OUT		Output to output device acc. contents
12	LDA	RES2	Load into acc. contents of RES2
13	OUT		Output to output device acc. contents

Fig. 2.9

The Assembler

Whilst thinking about assembly languages, we must not lose sight of the fact that the machine cannot understand any of the mnemonic instructions. These will have to be converted by a translator into the binary machine code which the computer has been designed to obey. This translator is called an **assembler** or, sometimes, an **assembler program**, because it is a program in its own right.

The assembly language program written by a programmer is called the **source program** and it will become the data for the assembler program. The output from the assembler program (the translator) is the converted source program. We call this the **object code**. The source program then is what the programmer writes, the object code is that which the computer will obey. Both are the *same* program but at different stages of development. Figure 2.10 illustrates this concept using the simple program from Figure 2.7.

An assembler program has a number of duties or functions to perform. It must translate the mnemonic function code into its binary machine code counterpart and give any symbolic name found in the address portion an absolute address. Although this latter activity may sound sophisticated, in reality it is a very simple process. We can think of the central memory as being divided into three areas

Fig. 2.10 Assembler program translating an assembly source program into binary machine code

(Chapter 6 will extend this to four); the first area is used in conjunction with special registers and is normally restricted to a few locations; a second area is used to hold the program instructions; and a third area is used to hold the data upon which the program works. Figure 2.11 shows this arrangement.

Location address	Central memory
0 . . . 9	Reserved for use with special registers
10 . . . n	Program instructions
n+1 . . . 1023	Data

Fig. 2.11   Division of central memory

In our particular 1K computer memory, the memory locations are conventionally numbered from zero to 1023. It is customary in some machines to reserve the first few locations for use with the special registers. Ten locations will be sufficient for our small machine, numbered from zero to nine. Therefore, the eleventh location (i.e. absolute address 10) will always contain the first instruction of any program. If the assembler program places each instruction in

SOURCE PROGRAM

Function	Address
IN	
STO	33
IN	
ADD	33
OUT	

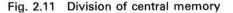

ASSEMBLER PROGRAM

OBJECT CODE

Function	Address
0111	—
0110	00100001
0111	—
0001	00100001
1000	—

a separate location and is made to count the number of instructions, it is then a simple matter for the assembler to "know" exactly where to place the first data value of the program, namely, in location $n+1$ where $n-10$ is the number of instructions.

Using the program from Figure 2.9, we can follow this procedure. However, one more instruction must be added to our program, i.e. the instruction END (decimal function code 00). This instruction is placed at the very end of the program to inform the assembler that there are no more instructions to follow and will become instruction 14 in our program.

The assembler reads in each source program instruction and translates the function code into its binary object code equivalent, and adds to a list any symbolic name found in the address portion. The first source program instruction will, of course, be placed in location 10, the next in location 11, and so on, until the END instruction is encountered. Since our program has 14 instructions, the final one, the END instruction, will be placed in absolute location 23. The symbolic name list will contain the four names: NUM1, NUM2, RES1, RES2 as used by our program. It is now very simple to allocate absolute addresses to these four names and to place them in the address portion of the relevant instructions. Thus, NUM1 will be given absolute address 24, NUM2 25, RES1 26, and RES2 27. Figure 2.12 shows the central memory locations.

As we shall see later, the assembler has several other functions to perform, but we can summarise its duties so far as being

1) Translating the source program function codes into their binary machine code equivalent.
2) Placing the program instructions into memory locations.
3) Assigning absolute addresses to symbolic names.
4) Eventually passing over to the control unit the responsibility for executing the program.

These functions will vary from assembler to assembler depending upon the type of assembly language in use and the type of computer. However, what has been presented does convey the basic concept of the assembly phase.

Logical/Comparison Operations

Of the four basic computer operations, nothing has been explained, so far, about the logical and comparison operations. In order to appreciate their role in a language, we need to discuss briefly the order in which instructions are executed. When the assembler has translated a program and it is ready for execution, the address of the location containing the first instruction (always location 10 in our computer) is passed over to the Control Unit. We saw from Chapter 1 that it is this unit which decodes and obeys the instructions. Unless otherwise told, the CU will execute each instruction one after the other, in a sequential manner. But one of the great strengths of computer programs is the ability to *repeat* a given series of instructions, and, at a particular point in a program, to *choose* not to execute the next instruction but to execute some other instruction elsewhere in the program. Obviously, some instruction is needed which will inform the CU *not* to execute the next instruction in sequence but to go elsewhere and execute some other instruction.

The simplest instruction to achieve this is the so-called **unconditional jump** instruction. We can choose 09 to be the decimal function code and the letters JUN as the mnemonic for "jump unconditionally". Other common names for this type of instruction are the *branch*, the *jump* or the *control* statement. The purpose of this instruction, then, is to order the control unit to execute an instruction which is not the next in sequence. Consequently, the address portion must supply the address of where that instruction lies in central memory. If the absolute form is used for the address, then JUN 15 will have the effect of ordering the control unit to execute the instruction in location 15.

This absolute form of address implies that the programmer has kept track of the address of

Location address	Central memory		
0 . . 9	Use with special registers		
10	0111	-------	07
11	0110	00011000	06 24
12	0111	-------	07
13	0110	00011001	06 25
14	0001	00011000	01 24
15	0110	00011010	06 26
16	0101	00011000	05 24
17	0011	00011001	03 25
18	0110	00011011	06 27
19	0101	00011010	05 26
20	1000	-------	08
21	0101	00011011	05 27
22	1000	-------	08
23	0000	-------	00
24	0000	00000011	NUM1 — read in value 3
25	0000	00000100	NUM2 — read in value 4
26	0000	00000111	RES1 — addition = 7
27	0000	00001100	RES2 — multiplication = 12
28 . . . 1023			

Program (brace spanning locations 10–23)

Data (brace spanning locations 24–27)

Unused (brace spanning locations 28–1023)

Fig. 2.12

each instruction, a rather tedious operation which, if not done accurately, can cause havoc when the program is executed. It is possible to use instead a symbolic name (or *label* in computing jargon), thus JUN LABL. But now it becomes necessary to attach the label LABL to the relevant instruction (see Figure 2.13). We now see that assembly level languages require a "label" field as well as the function code and address fields.

But note well that the object code equivalent instruction will still only have the function and address fields and not a label field. The assembler will have to replace the mnemonic label with an absolute address in the JUN instruction. Now not only will a symbolic *address* name table have to be built up by the assembler but also a table of symbolic *labels*. In the case of punched cards, a label is denoted by always starting in a particular column (e.g. column 1)

Label	Function field	Address field
LABL	IN . . . JUN	— LABL ◄──

This instruction causes the CU to return to the instruction called LABL.

Fig. 2.13

whereas other fields may begin in any column except the first (i.e. from column 2 onwards). It is then a simple matter for an assembler to distinguish between a label and a function code. When a label is identified the assembler needs to keep a note of the location into which that labelled instruction is placed so that instructions like the JUN can have their mnemonic label names (if used) eventually replaced by the absolute address.

Another type of jump instruction is one which will order the CU to jump to the instruction in the address portion provided that a certain *condition* is satisfied. A typical **conditional jump** instruction is one which "jumps to the address portion instruction *if* the contents of the accumulator are greater than zero", i.e. the contents of the accumulator are positive. We can allocate 10 to be the decimal function code and JGT as the mnemonic for "jump if greater than zero". We must note that the accumulator has to be used in this type of instruction as well as in the arithmetic and I/O statements. It should be obvious by now that, before the value in the accumulator can be tested to see whether it is greater than zero, the program should have placed a particular value in there, possibly as the result of some previous computation upon two numbers.

Another conditional jump instruction which proves to be very useful is the "jump to the address portion *if* the contents of the accumulator are NOT EQUAL to zero", i.e. they can be positive or negative. This again, as with the other four conditional instructions (contents of accumulator "equal to zero", "less than

zero", "less than or equal to zero", "greater than or equal to zero") implies that two values have been subtracted and the result in the accumulator tested for the condition imposed by the instruction. We shall allocate 11 as the decimal function code and JNE as the mnemonic for "jump if contents of accumulator not equal to zero".

We have only four more possible instructions which we can implement in our four-bit operation code, since twelve have already been accounted for out of the sixteen. Yet there are many more possible instructions which we could choose: the logical AND and OR operations; the shift operations of accumulator contents; inputting and outputting single or blocks of characters (our existing IN and OUT may only be used with numbers); the remaining four conditional instructions; and many more. If we were to increase the function code bits to five, this would give us a possible 32 instructions but at the cost of reducing the address portion to seven bits (i.e. an address range of 0 to 127). However, since we are not designing a full language we need not try to solve the problem now, thankfully, but move onto another problem, one associated with our limited addressing range.

Addressing Techniques

Our computer with its 8-bit address portion can only directly address 256 out of the 1024 central memory locations, the locations numbered 0 to 255. What then about locations 256 to 1023? There are two methods of resolving this problem, by *indirect addressing* and by *address modification*.

Indirect Addressing

This method makes use of one of the address portion bits. If this bit is set to zero, then *direct* addressing takes place (as illustrated so far in this chapter), but if the bit is set to 1, then *indirect* addressing takes place. Figure 2.14 shows this arrangement using bit 8 of the address field as the indicator.

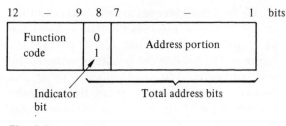

Fig. 2.14

Using the above figure, if bit 8 is set to zero direct addressing takes place and the number in bits 1–7 will give the absolute address of the location to be used with the function, but only in the range of 0–127. If a location greater than 127 is required, then indirect addressing is used by setting the 8-bit to one. The absolute address given in the address portion (still in the range 0–127) is now the address of a location in memory *in which the real address to use is to be found.*

As an example, let us suppose that it is necessary to load the accumulator with the contents of address location 330 which contains the value 16. Since the address 330 is beyond the range 0–127, we shall have to use indirect addressing by arranging to place the address 330 in one of the locations up to 127, let us say, in location 32. Thus, we use the instruction shown in Figure 2.15.

Provided location 32 has been given the value 330 before the instruction in Figure 2.15 is executed, the two-phase indirect address technique can proceed. Figure 2.16 illustrates this two-phase operation. We suppose that the instruction is held in location 15. Since the indirect address bit is set to one when this instruction is placed in the CU for execution, then the contents of address location 32 (i.e.

330) is used as the real address. The contents of location 330 will now be placed in the accumulator. The numbered arrows of Figure 2.16 show the order and direction of events. Thus, by the time the instruction has been finally executed, the accumulator will contain the value 16. Had the indirect address bit been set to zero, then the accumulator would have contained the value 330.

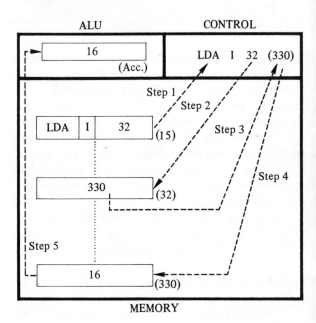

Fig. 2.16   Steps involved in indirect addressing

Address Modification

The second method involves modifying (altering) the absolute address (whether this absolute address was given by the programmer or allocated by the assembler) found in the address portion of the instruction by merely adding to it

12	9	8	7	1	
0101		1	0100000		Binary object code in memory
LDA		I	32		Assembly version with the symbol I indicating to the assembler that address 32 is to be used indirectly to obtain the real location.

Fig. 2.15

12	9	8	7	1
LDA	M	NUM3		
0101	1	0100000		

The assembler has given the symbolic name NUM3 the absolute address 32.

Fig. 2.17

a value provided in a special register called a **modification register** or **index register**. This implies that the program has to load this register with the required value (which can be either negative or positive) before address modification can take place. Figure 2.17 shows the three field instruction format similar to the indirect address format except that the symbol M is used in place of I. The presence of the M symbol in the source program will indicate to the assembler that address modification has to take place. The assembler will set the modification indicator to 1 (i.e. bit 8). If no address modification is required (i.e. bit 8 set to zero), then the address portion will be used as the direct address.

The actual address used when modification is indicated will be the address in the address portion of the instruction *plus* the contents of the modification register. If this register has previously been loaded with the value 298 (see Figure 2.18), then the instruction in location 15 will load into the accumulator the contents of address 32 + 298, in other words the contents of location 330. Thus, by the time the instruction has been executed, the accumulator will contain the value 16. Had the modification bit been set to zero, i.e. indicating a direct address mode, then the accumulator would have contained the value 126.

Final Assembly Instruction Layout

Before "labels" for use with jump instructions and other addressing techniques were introduced, the format of an assembly instruction exactly mirrored the format of a machine code instruction. The only difference was that decimal numbers were used with the latter type, mnemonics with the former. Thus, "load the accumulator with the contents of a given address" could be written 05 32 or LDA 32 (or LDA NUM1—leaving to the assembler the task of inserting the absolute address for NUM1).

However, having introduced labels and additional addressing techniques into our assembly language, we need to establish the order of the various four fields. This is left to the designer of the assembler program but a commonly adopted approach using punched cards is as follows. A label can only begin in column 1; a function code may begin in any column except column 1; an address field may begin in any column but must follow the function code and have at least one empty column as a separator between the function field and the address field; the indirect or modification symbol may be placed after the address field and separated by a comma (see Figure 2.19a), or before the address field but following the function code with at least one space acting as separators on either side of the symbol (Figure 2.19b shows this second method).

In practice, many professional programmers impose further restrictions on format layout but, of course, still remaining within the rules of

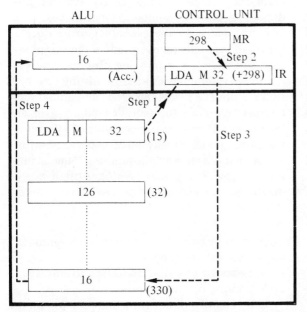

Fig. 2.18 Steps involved in modifying instruction address

Card
columns

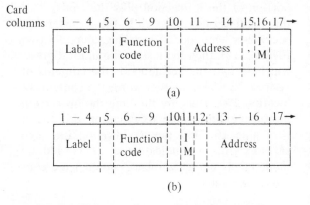

(a)

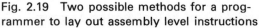

(b)

Fig. 2.19 Two possible methods for a programmer to lay out assembly level instructions

the language itself. They do so only to make their instruction listing more readable. The layout in Figure 2.19 shows this. A label field begins in column 1 (mandatory), a function field begins in column 6 whether or not the instruction has a label, columns 11–14 are used for the address portion with the comma appearing only in column 15 if the I/M symbol is placed in column 16. Figure 2.19*b* shows the alternative method with the I/M symbol appearing before the address.

The Special Registers

If address modification is used, then a modification register is required. (Indirect addressing does not need any special register.) In practice, any realistic low-level language using address modification will require more than one such register. Since registers are expensive storage locations, much more so than central memory storage locations, the actual number of registers will depend upon the market value of the computer itself. Furthermore, additional instructions will have to be included in our instruction repertoire in order to load the modification register(s) with values. They will be similar to the LDA command which loads the accumulator register with a value.

We shall not discuss these additional instructions since it is not our intention to design or learn a working low-level language. It should be

enough at this stage merely to appreciate that special storage locations of greater complexity than the central memory locations exist in the ALU and CU, such as the accumulator and the address modification register, and that they are available for use by the programmer via certain instructions.

Earlier it was stated that the first ten locations (addresses 0–9) were used for special purposes. We need not discuss this in any detail except to say that the assembler program may make use of these locations during the translating phase, and that during execution of the program some of these locations may be used to hold the number zero and perhaps the values contained in some of the registers. These locations are not normally available for storing data or program instructions.

Summary of Assembler Functions/Duties

Four of the assembler's duties have already been covered on page 45, we can now discuss the remainder. The assembler has to be able to recognise "labels" and to insert absolute addresses in place of symbolic label names. It is also customary for the assembler to produce a list of all symbolic names used by the programmer and their corresponding absolute addresses. The assembler must also distinguish between a direct address reference and an indirect address reference (or modified address) in an instruction. It must also be capable of informing the programmer of any incorrectly written instruction as well as "pin-pointing" the actual error. These "error messages" are often called **diagnostics**. Thus, our final list of assembler duties is

1) to translate the function code into its machine code equivalent;
2) to assign absolute addresses to any symbolic address or label names;
3) to identify direct from indirect (or modified) addresses and to set the appropriate bit in the address portion of the instruction;

4) to place each instruction in central memory—beginning at some "known" start address;

5) to check each instruction for correct grammatical construction (syntax) and to issue diagnostics if necessary;

6) to provide (optionally) a cross-reference table between all symbolic names used and their absolute addresses;

7) to inform the CU (if no diagnostics are issued) to execute the first instruction of the object code.

We have now completed this section on low-level languages; if you have a particular one to learn then you must not be surprised to find that your language will differ somewhat from the language we have been discussing. Also you ought to be able to appreciate that there are often several ways of doing the same thing, e.g. refer to Figure 2.19 a, b.

It is hoped that by now you can understand why low-level languages are called machine-oriented. A low-level language is designed for a particular machine; the language cannot be properly developed until the size of the central memory is known and the length of the location word. It is usual for either indirect addressing or address modification to be implemented but seldom both. The indirect method is slower because it makes use of two central memory locations. Address modification is much faster because of the use of modification registers but, in consequence, is much more expensive. Which technique is used obviously depends upon how much money is available.

An assembly language can often be the assembly version of the machine code itself. For example, COMPASS is the machine language of the CDC 6000/Cyber series, yet it is also an assembly language. The reason is quite simple. System programmers, who have to write programs or amend existing ones which control the running of the CDC computers (see Chapter 6), have to write in the machine language of the computer itself. But to do so using decimal numbers becomes a difficult and arduous task. So, an assembly version exists for use by the system programmers and which can easily be translated into the actual machine code by the appropriate assembler program.

High-level Languages

From our study of low-level languages, we can now appreciate that to add three numbers together, assuming that the three values are already stored in locations A, B and C, will require at least four low-level instructions. For example:

```
LDA   A
ADD   B
ADD   C
STO   X
```

The point to note is that these four low-level instructions can be reduced to one high-level statement in Basic:

LET $X = A + B + C$

When the assembler translates an assembly level instruction, it will generate one machine code instruction and we talk of a one-to-one correspondence between the two languages. Whereas, in the case of one high-level statement, the high-level translator will have to generate many machine code instructions for the one high-level statement. Thus we talk of a one-to-many correspondence between one high-level statement and the machine code instructions into which it will have to be translated.

The translator of a high-level language into machine code is called a *compiler program* or *compiler*, for short.

Compiler

The **compiler program** has a similar set of tasks to perform to the assembler. The source program must be converted or translated into the one and only machine language that a given computer has been designed to recognise. One compiler is capable of translating source programs written in only one high-level language.

Thus, if a given computer is capable of processing Algol and Basic programs, then two compilers are required, one to translate Basic programs and another to translate the Algol programs. Since each make of computer has a different machine language, then the Fortran compiler for an ICL machine could not be used on an IBM machine.

Like assemblers, compilers must allocate absolute addresses for any location names used by the program. Diagnostics are issued for any misuse of the high-level language (called syntax errors) and, if no syntax errors are discovered in the source program (written by the programmer), then the compiler must "inform" the CU, which can then begin to execute the object code produced by the compiler.

The main purpose of problem-oriented languages, is to enable the programmer to write programs more easily by being able to concentrate on the problem to be solved, rather than the machine level features of the computer. Although the task may be easier, the process of translating a high-level language source program into machine object code will be more lengthy and complex. Hence, compilers tend to be longer and more complex programs than

assemblers. Before the compiler program can do its work, it must be resident in the CM and, since it is a larger program than the assembler, it will occupy more space. Thus, compilers are commoner in computers with large CMs (at least 32K locations) than smaller, mini-computers. However, because of the advantages of high-level languages and the growth of certain special techniques, users of mini-computers (and micro-computers) today often have the choice of writing programs in a high-level language. The illustration (Figure 2.20) of the compilation process is applicable to a computer with a large central memory.

Character Sets

Each programming language has its own distinct character set. Our own small assembly language code had quite a restricted set. We could use letters of the alphabet A–Z but only as capital letters; the digits 0–9; and a few special symbols, such as the comma for use in the address portion to separate the index or modification symbol from the address portion (see Figure 2.19a), and the "space" to allow one field to be separated from the next. We

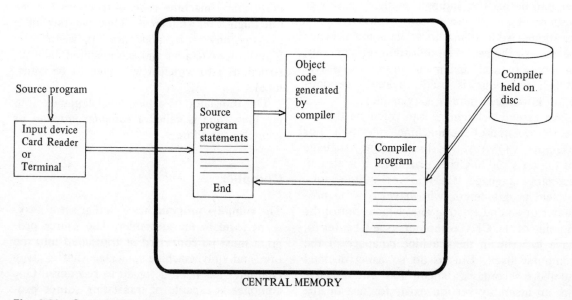

Fig. 2.20 Compilation process

could have used more symbols, had we decided to produce a full assembly code. For example, the asterisk * could be used to allow comments to be placed between program instructions. One common method is to place the asterisk in column 1 of a punch card. Everything which follows is then regarded as a comment and not a program instruction. Adopting this procedure, we now have: three special symbols, the comma, the space and the asterisk; 26 letters of the alphabet; and 10 digits, 0–9; making a total of 39 valid characters in all.

In everyday use, we have many more characters—small Roman letters as well as capital letters, many mathematical symbols and logic symbols, a range of alphabetical sets, Greek, Roman, Arabian, Hindu, Chinese, Japanese, Russian, etc. But with a programming language, it is common to have only a very restricted character set. Standard Fortran, for example, has only 47 characters—the capital Roman letters (26), the digits 0–9 (10), and eleven special symbols. The 47 Fortran characters and the 54 Basic characters are shown in Figure 2.21.

FORTRAN	BASIC
A B C D E F G H I J K L M N O P Q R S T U V W X Y Z 0 1 2 3 4 5 6 7 8 9 ( ) * + - / £ , = . "space"	A B C D E F G H I J K L M N O P Q R S T U V W X Y Z 0 1 2 3 4 5 6 7 8 9 ( ) * + - / £ , = . "space" ; > < ↑ ↓ " :

Fig. 2.21 Alphanumeric character sets for Fortran and Basic (Note that some computer systems permit additional special characters)

Reserved Words

The idea of a programming language having its own vocabulary has already been discussed. The vocabulary consists of a set of **reserved words**. Relating this to our everyday English language, we can say that a certain grouping of letters represent certain words, e.g. the group of letters H-A-L-L-O indicates the word HALLO, a reserved word used when two people meet. Programming languages have a restricted vocabulary, e.g. Basic has about 30 words (depending upon the type of Basic used). REM and DIM are two words from the Basic vocabulary to indicate a comment statement and a dimensioning statement. Others are GO TO, END, LET, etc. These words inform the compiler about a particular instruction which the programmer wishes to use—in the same way that the English words "hallo" and "goodbye" indicate the beginning and end of a meeting between two or more persons.

High-level languages have far fewer reserved words than low-level languages which can sometimes have several hundred "words" (instructions). This is because much more can be said with one high-level statement than one low-level instruction. Both types, however, have far fewer than any natural language since a programming language needs to indicate through these words only the four basic computer operations.

Operators

In addition to the reserved words, other special symbols called **operators** exist to indicate either an arithmetical operation or logical (sometimes called *relational*) operation. In many languages these operator symbols are similar to some of the symbols used in mathematics.

Arithmetic operators

$+$	addition
$-$	subtraction
$*$	multiplication
$/$	division
$\uparrow$ or $**$	exponentiation

Logical/Relational operators

$=$	equal to
$\neq$	not equal to
$>$	greater than
$<$	less than
$\geq$	greater than or equal to
$\leq$	less than or equal to

53

Please note that the arithmetical and logical operators are not used in a low-level language since mnemonics are used instead, e.g. ADD, MULT, JGT.

Again, with the logical operators, not every language will use these symbols. Figure 2.22 shows the Basic and Fortran symbols for logical operators. Fortran makes use of letters instead of symbols. The choice of operator symbols or letters is left to the designers of a particular language.

FORTRAN	BASIC	Meaning
.EQ.	=	equal to
.NE.	<> or ><	not equal to
.GT.	>	greater than
.LT.	<	less than
.GE.	>=	greater than or equal to
.LE.	<=	less than or equal to

Fig. 2.22

What is Programming?

The object of writing a program is to present to a computer a set of instructions which will achieve a desired end, i.e. to solve some problem. These instructions will have to be stored in the computer's memory and translated into the machine code of the computer concerned before they can be executed. Once the translation phase has been completed (and assuming that the program contains no grammatical/syntactical errors), then the CU will execute the instructions in turn. It has already been pointed out that computers perform only four basic operations and, therefore, it should not be surprising to find that any programming language is partly built around these four types of operations. Let us look more closely at these in relation to typical high-level languages.

(a) I/O OPERATIONS

A computer cannot do anything with an instruction or a piece of data unless it is in the central memory. Input operations are, therefore, obviously needed in order to place the information which the program works on into CM. Output operations are similarly required in order for human beings to be able to read the program results. Typical Fortran and Basic I/O statements are signified by the words READ, INPUT, PRINT, WRITE.

(b) ARITHMETIC OPERATIONS

Arithmetic operations are also necessary in a great many computer applications. Even when the application itself is not obviously involved in arithmetic, the programmer may have to perform some arithmetic within his program. For example, if it is necessary to input twenty individual pieces of data (say numbers or names of friends), then it will be necessary to count up to twenty in some fashion so that the computer "knows" when twenty data items have been input. The FOR–NEXT statement in Basic (or the DO–LOOP in Fortran) has a built-in counting process; nevertheless the fact remains that the counting process (arithmetic) has taken place.

Included as an arithmetic operation is the so-called "assignment statement", when a variable name (say N) is given some numerical value (let us say 5). Thus,

LET N = 5   in Basic
N = 5   in Fortran
N := 5;   in Algol

(c) LOGIC/COMPARISON OPERATIONS

There are two types: a decision-making instruction and a repetitive instruction.

A typical decision-making instruction in Fortran is the IF (or the IF . . . THEN in Basic). This IF statement has the condition attached to it such that, if it is true, then some other part of the program is executed next.

The repetition instruction is one of the fundamental computer instructions. Although it is a simple concept, without it computers never would have reached the stage of usefulness that they have. Let us refer to the inputting of twenty data items. Obviously the crudest approach is to write 20 input statements, each one inputting one piece of data. As well as being tedious, this approach is not necessary. All that is needed is to write *one* input statement and repeatedly execute that one statement twenty times. Some counting process up to 20 must be included, as well as a decision-making instruction in order to move to the next part of the program once the reading/inputting instruction has been executed twenty times. From your own programming experience you will already know (or will do once you begin to program in a high-level language) that there are several ways of repeating certain instructions (the FOR . . . NEXT or DO–LOOP).

This programming technique is known as *looping*.

The repetition loop must sometimes contain a decision as a means of escaping from the loop. It can take the form, for example, of a test to see that a count is complete, or that some operation has finished. Otherwise the loop could be repeated for ever (the "infinite loop").

The main point here is to underline the two distinct programming techniques of repetition and decision-making. It is easy to confuse the two on occasions because the decision-making instructions is frequently tied in with some form of repetition. But both exist, both are distinct, and both should be borne in mind when you are performing your practical programming.

(d) MOVEMENT OF DATA IN CENTRAL MEMORY

Since programs are written to work on data, a programming language possesses features which will allow the programmer to manipulate that data. By manipulation we only mean that pieces of data can be moved around in CM, and, when necessary, structured or arranged in a particular way. One example of structuring data is the *list* or *array* (by means of the DIMENSION statement in Fortran or the DIM statement in Basic). Although only one piece of data can be contained in one central memory location, it

Location	Club	Index
900		
901		
902		
903		
904		
905	Liverpool	1
906	Arsenal	2
907	Man United	3
908	Wolves	4
909	Rangers	5
910	Celtic	6
911		7
912		8
913		9
914		10
915		11
916		12
917		13
918		14
919		15
920		16
921		17
922		18
923		19
924		20
925		

Fig. 2.23 Section of CM showing the locations numbered 900 to 925. Locations 905 to 924 are grouped together, forming in effect a list (array) containing 20 football clubs

may be convenient for a programmer to arrange (structure) related items in consecutive and individual locations (see Figure 2.23). For instance, the twenty pieces of data read into CM could be the names of football clubs. If we were going to write down these names using paper and pen, it would be natural for us to arrange them one under the other to form a list. Similarly, any worthwhile high-level language will allow a programmer to arrange data in such a way. The array or list is only one way of structuring data; other methods exist but are not discussed in this book.

Computing people talk of one language being "better" or "more powerful" than another in its data structuring techniques. Pascal and PL/1 are examples of languages which allow the programmer a wider choice of how to lay out or arrange data. However, such languages are more difficult to learn than the simpler Fortran or Basic languages.

We have just completed a fairly difficult section and so it would be useful to summarise what has been said. Essentially, all that we are discussing are the tools or techniques which programmers have at their disposal. When confronted with a problem to solve, these are the only basic tools which a programmer can use. Furthermore, these few and comparatively simple techniques are related closely to the four basic operations of a computing machine. We can summarise both in Figure 2.24 and you are encouraged, when you come to write programs in a high-level language, to relate one of the four techniques to each instruction of your program.

Before leaving this section, there are two features of a high-level language which ought to be mentioned. One is an extension of arithmetic operations, the other an extension of the data arrangement operation.

Functions

Many people are already familiar with pocket calculators. Not only are they useful for adding up many numbers but they are also capable of the other arithmetical functions as well as percentages, square roots, logarithms, and so on, depending upon the sophistication (and cost) of the calculator. If we want the square root of a

	What a computer can do	What a programmer can do
1)	Input/output of data	Reading (inputting) data into or writing (outputting) from the CM.
2)	Arithmetic operations	Addition, subtraction, division, multiplication (and perhaps raising to a power) on numbers.
3)	Logical/comparison operations	Repetition statements, decision-making instructions [including jump (GO TO) type statements].
4)	Moving data or arranging data in CM	Arrange data in single or multiple locations in CM.

	Assembly-type mnemonic instructions	High-level language instructions	
1)	IN OUT	READ INPUT WRITE PRINT	
2)	ADD SUB DIV MULT	Use of arithmetic operators + . — / * **	
3)	JNE JUN JGT	IF statement (Fortran)	IF . . . THEN (Basic)
4)	Special features available	DIMENSION (Fortran)	DIM (Basic)

Fig. 2.24

particular number and we have a calculator, all we do is to enter the number and then push the button with the square root sign on it. The display panel will then show the result. We do not have to perform any calculations at all.

A similar situation has been true with high-level languages for a number of years. Instead of programmers having to write a part of their program to calculate a function, say the square root, the program can indicate very simply that the square root of a given number must be found at a certain point in the program. An additional duty of a compiler, then, is to look out for such indications and to ensure that during execution of the program, the relevant function is available to the program.

Many of these functions can be thought of as being short programs which have been previously written by other programmers. They can be stored in a special area of the computer system's backing store and retrieved from there when required. The special area of backing store is called a *library* and will contain not only function-programs but also any other useful pre-written programs for use in mathematical, engineering and computer design programs. Fortran is particularly rich in such **library programs** (often called *routines* or *library routines*) and saves individual Fortran programmers from having to re-create their own routines every time they are needed.

Preparing a Program

No-one given a problem of any complexity for computer solution begins by writing program statements one after the other without first spending some time in thinking about *how* the problem is to be tackled. One method of helping programmers to clarify their ideas is

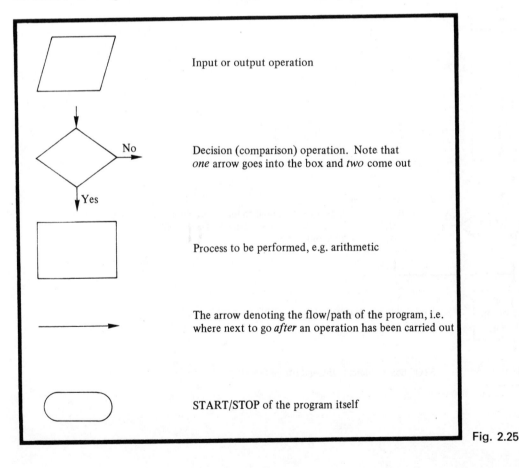

Input or output operation

Decision (comparison) operation. Note that *one* arrow goes into the box and *two* come out

Process to be performed, e.g. arithmetic

The arrow denoting the flow/path of the program, i.e. where next to go *after* an operation has been carried out

START/STOP of the program itself

Fig. 2.25

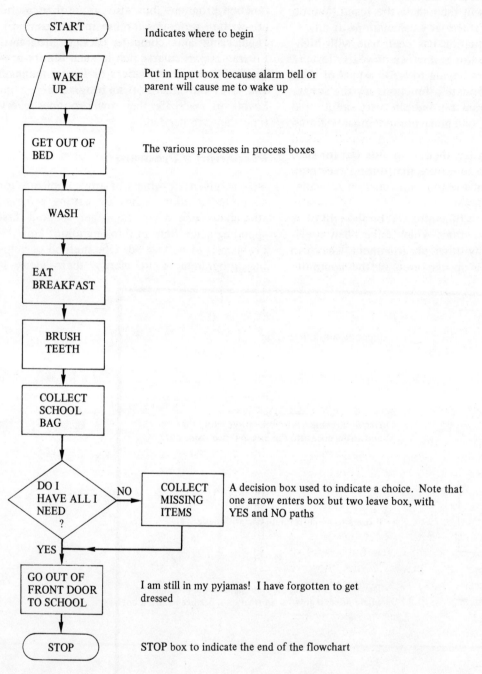

START	Indicates where to begin
WAKE UP	Put in Input box because alarm bell or parent will cause me to wake up
GET OUT OF BED	The various processes in process boxes
WASH	
EAT BREAKFAST	
BRUSH TEETH	
COLLECT SCHOOL BAG	
DO I HAVE ALL I NEED ? — NO → COLLECT MISSING ITEMS	A decision box used to indicate a choice. Note that one arrow enters box but two leave box, with YES and NO paths
YES	
GO OUT OF FRONT DOOR TO SCHOOL	I am still in my pyjamas! I have forgotten to get dressed
STOP	STOP box to indicate the end of the flowchart

Fig. 2.26

through the use of **flowcharts**. Briefly, a flow-chart is a two-dimensional or pictorial description of how the problem is to be solved, and, most important, in what order the programming instructions should occur. It is called a flowchart, then, since it charts (or plots) the flow (or path) of the program. If the flow is in the correct order (often called the *logic*) of the program, then the program instructions will be in the correct order.

(Many other pictorial methods exist, some of which are often much better at representing the program flow than flowcharts. For this reason, many practising programmers prefer to use one of the other methods.)

Flowcharts make use of several different-shaped boxes. Each box stands for a certain type of programming activity. The boxes are linked together by arrows which indicate the flow of the program itself. It is customary for each box to contain a few words to explain what event is taking place. Figure 2.25 shows the various shapes and their relation to the programming techniques already mentioned in Figure 2.24.

A Simple Non-computing Flowchart

In order to introduce flowcharting, we shall draw a chart for "going to school". Your own teacher may provide other and more computer-oriented examples for you to work on. Figure 2.26 shows, in broad outline, the events necessary from waking up in the morning to going out of the front door.

This is a simple example which can be flowcharted but which could not be given to a computer to solve. It introduces the shapes of the boxes used, and illustrates the "flow of events" via arrows, and how the decision box allows for one of two paths to be chosen depending upon the result of the question posed. Normal English words ought to be used to describe briefly the event or question for each box.

Two further points need to be mentioned. First, we can see how important it is not to forget any necessary event (e.g. getting dressed) otherwise the problem will not be able to be solved. Secondly, any one event in one flowchart symbol may have to be expanded at a later stage when a more detailed solution is required; for example, the act of getting out of bed may be expanded as in Figure 2.27.

Fig. 2.27

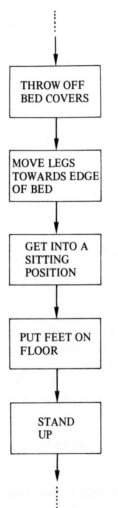

59

Let us now flowchart one problem which can be solved by computer. We have met the problem before and it is typical of a data processing activity. We shall input twenty names of current records (possibly from the pop-charts or even from some long-standing list of our own favourites) in any order, with the object of sorting them into a "top twenty", and then printing out the names of the records in that order. Note that at this point in the preparation we are not concerned with *how* to write the program instructions nor with the programming language to be used but simply with the sequence of events (via a flowchart) which will be necessary in order to begin writing program instructions. The first problem to solve is how we can indicate which of the twenty records will be the first, the second, etc. in the final list. This can be done in several ways but we shall simply include a number, from one to twenty, together with our record name to indicate that record's final placing in the list. Figure 2.28 illustrates this.

```
INPUT DATA

14    record name
 3    record name
11    record name
 .    etc. for the twenty
 .    records
 .
```

Fig. 2.28

One very sensible approach, before tackling the flowchart, is to put down on paper exactly what the final output is to be from the program. This helps to clarify the objective of the program itself. Figure 2.29 therefore shows the program output, i.e. a heading and the top-twenty list.

Obviously, this example is easy to visualise in its final output form, but demonstrates what to do for more complicated cases.

The interesting thing about this short and apparently simple problem is that it illustrates many of the topics we have been discussing in this long chapter: the four basic operations of a computer; the fundamental high-level language programming techniques; and the use of the

```
PROGRAM OUTPUT


MY LIST OF THE BEST TWENTY RECORDS

1.      record name
2.      record name
3.      record name

        etc.
```

Fig. 2.29

flowchart symbols. Although this is not an obviously arithmetical problem, its solution involves arithmetic by keeping a count so that, when the count reaches twenty, the program will "know" when to stop reading in more data and "decide" to move into another part of the program. Repetition is also involved by continually repeating the "read another piece of data" instruction. Input/output must be performed in order to place data from the outside world into the CM of the computer so that, once the data has been processed, the program results can be printed out in readable form.

The box which states simply "re-arrange into numerical order" is another example of the need to expand one English statement into many program instructions. This does not matter for the general flowchart of Figure 2.30. In order to re-arrange the list, a *sorting* procedure will be necessary, based on the number with the record name. This is not an easy task for someone new to programming and it will be necessary to draw a sub-flowchart for this activity. This is a common approach. The basic chart provides the overall series of tasks in the correct order. Then a more detailed flowchart may be required to provide details of any event which needs to be expanded.

We can conclude this section with a few observations. First, no one person will tackle a problem in exactly the same way as another person. Hence, it is usual to discover that the same problem can be represented by several different flowchart solutions. Secondly, when

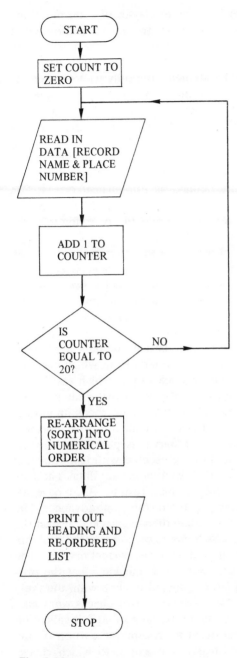

Fig. 2.30

drafting the flowchart, we often begin by drawing a rough outline first. Then that outline is amended as we add tasks overlooked the first time. The neat and final flowchart is only arrived at after the original draft has been changed and redrawn perhaps several times. Do not expect to draw a neat and accurate flowchart the first time.

Documentation

The flowchart is of *most* value to the person who drafts it, but it can also be of great value to some other person who needs to understand the program which results from the chart. Junior programmers, for example, in commercial organisations often have to show their flowchart solution (or any other method used) to a more senior programmer to verify that the events are in the correct order and that nothing has been omitted. It is only after this stage that the junior programmer is allowed to begin to write program instructions.

The flowchart then can be used as part of the description of the program itself. This description is often termed **documentation** and forms as important a part of the total solution as the program itself. Other additions to the total documentation may include the list of program instructions (the *listing*) with comment statements to give meaning to groups of program instructions; a written description of the purpose and aim of the program; details and examples of the input data (how it is arranged, on what medium it is, e.g. punched cards or paper tape, magnetic tape or disc, etc.) as well as the *test data* used to check whether the program works correctly; details and examples of the output produced; and instructions on how to operate the program for anyone not familiar with the computer system. Naturally, not all of these are required for short and simple programs, but when large and therefore complex programs are written, good documentation forms an essential part of the solution.

We can list the minimum set of requirements for documentation for complex programs.

1) Contents
2) Program description
3) Description of the hardware system used
4) I/O details and examples
5) Test data
6) Flowchart or other pictorial form
7) Program listing with comments.

Errors

As any professional programmer knows, it is not usual for a complex program to execute correctly the first time it is run on a computer. There are many reasons for this: some are due to the human element, others are due to the use of certain programming features (e.g. too many GO TO statements) which can lead a programmer into various traps. Research is being undertaken into this problem and several languages have been designed (e.g. Pascal) which attempt to minimise the use of those features. However, further discussion about this problem is unfortunately out of place in this book. We must take it for granted that, in practice, errors do occur when writing programs and may be caused by one or more of the following reasons:

a) A simple misprint when writing a program statement may result in a mis-punch on a punch-card machine or a wrong pencil mark on a mark-sense card or the use of the wrong key on a terminal keyboard or paper-tape punch. For example, instead of writing LET in Basic we might write LAT.

b) Mistakes in the use of the programming language can lead to grammatical and syntactical errors. For example, in Basic,

$$LET \ A + B + C = X$$

This is a syntax error—wrong construction of a Basic statement.

$$LET \ X = B.$$

This is a grammatical error—full stop is not used to end a statement.

It will be part of the function of the compiler to detect the above types of error when it checks for the correct spelling of reserved words and syntax during the translation stage. Error messages, called **compiler diagnostics**, will be given to help the programmer trace the mistakes.

c) There are various classes of "run-time" errors. We shall discuss two in this section and a third in section (*d*). If the program has faulty logic, such as *going to* the wrong instruction via a GO TO statement, the only way a programmer can know this is when the time comes to look at the program results. Neither the compiler nor the computer can be expected to recognise such a mistake.

However, a second type of run-time error can be spotted by the computer and these can be broadly defined as *arithmetical* errors. For example, attempting to read in a 91st piece of data when there are only 90; or trying to put a piece of information into the 91st location of a 90-element list. Since the compiler is no longer functioning once a program is being executed, it can only be the *operating system* (see Chapter 6) which can detect such errors and issue error messages called **system diagnostics**.

d) Errors can also exist in the data itself upon which the program operates, in which case the program will produce results which will be incorrect. Consequently, any worthwhile program should attempt to make some check upon data as soon as it has been read into CM. Furthermore, before a program is passed as satisfactory, it should be presented with test data that contains valid as well as invalid data. The correct data will produce results which have already been "worked out" in advance. The program results can then be checked against the known results to make certain that the program is operating on data in the correct manner. The deliberate errors are of the kind that the program has been designed to cope with, thus verifying that the program error checks work successfully. It should be noted that full validation checks can often form a major portion of any program. Clearly, the extent to which checks are made will depend on the importance of the program itself.

e) A final category of errors comes not from the programmer, the program or data, but from the computer itself, either from the computer hardware or from some faulty computer operating system program. Although computer hardware is one of the most reliable pieces of machinery ever created by man, it can develop faults. As an example, if the read/write mechanism (see Chapter 3) of a disc unit should suddenly fail and drop onto the disc surface, information on the surface will become "corrupted". However, if such accidents occur, a respectable operating system will inform the computer operator and the program using the disc at that time that some accident has taken place and therefore to re-run the program.

As we shall see in more detail in Chapter 6 on operating systems, programs called *computer system software*, written, of course, by human programmers, actually drive the hardware units. These programs themselves are therefore prone to all the errors listed so far. Usually, these software programs are very thoroughly tested before being allowed to control the computer hardware.

We can summarise errors as follows:

If the programmer has carefully thought out the solution and represented this by means of some graphical description, and only begins to write program instructions (*coding*) when he or she is satisfied that the pictorial representation is correct, the chances are that the program will work correctly. Well-prepared test data, system and compiler diagnostics are all additional aids for the programmer to use. But there is one final method which can be used before the program is presented to the computer. Once the program has been coded, the programmer should act as the "computer" by going through the instructions and making use of the test data. This procedure is commonly known as a *desk check* or a *dry run* because the program is checked at the programmer's desk and not on the computer. It is often in this way that mistakes in the program logic ("bugs") can be spotted and corrected before the program is run on a computer. If all these methods are carefully put into practice, then the program should be able to work the first time correctly.

Mis-punching and syntax errors	detected by the compiler—compiler diagnostics.
Execution time (run-time) errors	detected by the operating system software—system diagnostics.
Hardware faults causing errors	detected by operating system—system diagnostics.
Operating system program errors	detected by user "complaints"

Important Words and Terms in Chapter 2

low-level languages
   machine-oriented languages
machine code
high-level languages
   problem-oriented languages
assembly level languages
mnemonics
operation/function code
address in central memory
accumulator
absolute address
assembler program

compiler program
source program
object code
branch/jump instruction
loop instruction
conditional/unconditional jump instruction
address field
label field
indirect addressing
address modification
modification/index register
compiler and operating system
   diagnostics
character set
reserved words

arithmetic operators
logical/relational operators
library routines
flowcharts
documentation
program listing

desk check/dry run
test data
syntactical errors
arithmetic errors
execution errors

Exercises 2

1 Which of the following high level languages is mainly used for commercial programming: Basic, Fortran, Cobol, Algol? (*EAEB* 1977)

2 Complete the following statement by writing in appropriate words chosen from the list below:
"Diagnostics are the ... available to help a programmer ... a program. Error messages are produced if there are faults at ... time. Run-time errors may occur if the program ... is faulty."
   name, logic, debug, aids, compile, interpret, deletions
(*EAEB* 1976)

3 Which word best completes this sentence? "The working out, by the computer, of any problem is known as ..."
a) processing *b*) programming *c*) files *d*) addressing *e*) registering

4 Explain why a low-level language is so called.

5 What is the input to a compiler? What is the output from a compiler? (*AEB* spec)

6 Explain briefly the meaning of the terms *object program* and *source program*. (*AEB* spec.)

7 Explain what is meant by the phrase "a one-to-many" correspondence between a high-level language statement and the machine code into which it is translated by the compiler.

8 Why do we say that there is a "one-to-one" correspondence between an assembly instruction and the machine code of a given computer?

9 What is the purpose of assemblers and compilers?

10 List the functions of a compiler.

11 List the functions of an assembler.

12 What are the fundamental operations of any computer?

13 The following diagram shows a program instruction for a simple computer that is designed with a fixed word length of 14 bits.
a) Of how many different functions is the machine capable?
b) How many directly addressable locations are available? (*AEB* spec.)

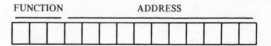

FUNCTION   ADDRESS

14 Describe briefly the difference between low-level languages and high-level languages. (*WJEC* 1977)

15 Complete the following sentence by writing in appropriate words chosen from the list below:

"A high-level language program will take longer to ... and to ... than a low-level program to do the same job but it is easier to ..."

run, compile, write

(*SWEB* 1977)

16 A flowchart is (chose from below the best answer to complete the sentence)

a) a method of programming

b) usually difficult to understand

c) only used by CSE students

d) seldom used in industry

e) a method of displaying a problem in simple steps. (*EMREB* 1977)

17 Draw a flowchart to read one hundred numbers and output their sum. (*EAEB* 1977)

18 Mention with reasons two kinds of program error that would be found by a compiler, and describe one that would not, explaining how this might be found. (*OLE* 1976)

19 The following information represents a machine code program in a certain computer.

The computer has the following instruction code:

01 n load contents of address n to accumulator
02 n add contents of address n to accumulator
03 n subtract contents of address n from accumulator
04 n copy contents of accumulator to store n
05 n jump to address n for next instruction

If the locations 100, 101 and 103 contain the numbers +7, +29 and +149 respectively, describe what the program does. (*AEB* spec.)

Location	Function	Address
50	01	100
51	02	101
52	04	102
53	03	103
54	04	104
55	05	55

20 *a*) Complete the following statement by writing in appropriate words chosen from the list below. (*EAEB* 1977)

"A high-level ... can be used on any computer which has an appropriate .... The compiler is a ... which translates each ... of the source program into ... code. The program, when it has been translated, is called the ... program and may then be ... provided no ... were found.

Fortran, machine, compiler, value, executed, language, person, variables, errors, object, statement, program, interpreted.

b) Give one example of a run-time error and suggest a possible cause.

21 A certain computer's machine language contains the following instructions:

FETCH n   copy the contents of the location whose absolute address is n into the accumulator,

SUB n   subtract the number contained in the location whose absolute address is n from the accumulator,

STORE n   copy the contents of the accumulator into the location whose absolute address is n,

BNEG n   branch (jump) to location n if the number in the accumulator is negative,

STOP   end of program.

The following instructions are stored in locations 17 to 21 inclusive:

location 17   FETCH 66
        18   BNEG 21
        19   SUB 69
        20   STORE 69
        21   STOP

Before these instructions are executed, the accumulator contains +75.

What will be the contents of the accumulator and locations 66 and 69 after execution if, before execution,

(i) location 66 contains +21, location 69 contains −78;

(ii) location 66 contains −21, location 69 contains +78?

(*OLE* 1978)

22 *a*) Of what is the computing term BIT an abbreviation?

b) In a certain computer instructions are stored in 12-bit words. The four left-hand bits are the operation code. The remaining 8 bits give the address of the data word whose contents are used in the operation.

The first four operation codes are as follows:

0001 LOAD a copy of the contents of the addressed word into the accumulator.

0010 STORE a copy of the contents of the accumulator in the addressed word.

0011 ADD a copy of the contents of the addressed word to the contents of the accumulator and leave the answer in the accumulator.

0100 SUBTRACT a copy of the contents of the addressed word from the contents of the accumulator and leave the answer in the accumulator.

i) The next operation in the list is MULTIPLY followed by DIVIDE. Their codes follow the logical sequence. Give their codes.

ii) Complete the table by coding the instructions in binary. Enter the values which will appear in the accumulator and data words as the instructions are executed. The first line has been done for you. (*EAEB* 1976).

23 If a mistake occurs in a computer system, it is usually for one of the reasons listed below:

a) Mechanical or electrical failure

b) Operating errors

c) Programming errors

d) Basic design fault of the system that is being run on the computer

e) Errors when data is copied on to the input medium.

For each of these FIVE things:

i) Explain how the errors occur.

ii) Say what precautions should be taken to lessen the chances that such errors can occur. (*MREB* 1976)

24 In a certain computer instructions are stored in 12-bit words. The four left-hand bits are the operation code. The next six bits give an address. The last two bits give the address of one of four special words called registers. The registers have addresses 0, 1, 2, and 3. The contents of register 0 are always zero.

Three operation codes are as follows.

0001 LOAD a copy of the contents of the addressed word into the accumulator.

Binary Instruction		Instruction		Accumulator and Data Word Contents				
Op. Code	Address	Op. Code	Address	Accumulator	Word 13	Word 14	Word 15	Word 16
0001	00001110	LOAD	14	0	+4	+2	−1	+10
		ADD	15	+2	+4	+2	−1	+10
		SUBTRACT	13					
		STORE	15					
		LOAD	16					
		ADD	15					

0010 STORE a copy of the contents of the accumulator in the addressed word.

0011 ADD a copy of the contents of the addressed word to the contents of the accumulator and leave the result in the accumulator.

After each instruction is executed the CONTENTS of the specified register are added to the ADDRESS to give the ACTUAL ADDRESS to be operated on.

Example

Suppose register 3 holds +6,

INSTRUCTION	ACTION
then <u>0001</u> <u>000101</u> <u>11</u> LOAD 5 3	will cause the contents of word 11 to be loaded into the accumulator because the actual address is 5+6 = 11.

a) Given that registers 1, 2 and 3 hold +4, +8 and −2 respectively, decode the instructions
0001 000111 10
0010 010000 00
0011 010100 11
in the way shown in the example above.

b) Complete the table below. Write the decoded version of each instruction in the table and enter the values which will appear in the accumulator and each word as the instructions are executed.

The first line has been done for you to show the decoded instructions and the contents of the words. (*EAEB* 1977)

Binary Instruction
0 0 0 1 0 0 0 0 1 0 1 1
0 0 1 1 0 0 0 0 1 1 0 0
0 0 1 0 0 0 0 0 0 0 1 1
0 0 1 0 0 0 0 0 1 1 0 1
0 0 1 1 0 0 0 0 0 1 0 0
0 0 1 0 0 0 0 0 0 1 1 1
0 0 1 1 0 0 0 0 0 1 1 0
0 0 1 0 0 0 0 0 1 0 0 1

Instruction		
LOAD	2	3

Accumulator and Word Contents

Accumulator	Registers					
	Word 0	Word 1	Word 2	Word 3	Word 4	Word 5
0	0	0	0	+1	0	0
+1	0	0	0	+1	0	0

67

3 Input/Output and Secondary Storage Devices

In this chapter, we shall discuss input, output and secondary (auxiliary) storage devices, that is all the devices which are peripheral (external) to the CPU—hence the term *peripheral device*. Input devices are necessary to convert our everyday information into a form which can be understood by computers. Most computing depends on the *daily* collection, preparation and input of large amounts of data. Once collected, it is either converted to a machine-readable form and as a second operation input to the computer, or it is input to the computer system in one step using a **direct entry** method. A great deal of manpower is tied up in this aspect of the computing process, known as **data preparation**, and in many an organisation it represents a significant proportion of the overall computing costs. Table 3.1 describes some common input devices.

Once information has been processed, we need to see the results. Output devices convert computer information into a form readily understood by human beings. Table 3.2 describes the more common output devices.

Secondary storage devices exist to supplement the limited main memory of the CPU, either for storing programs and data for future use in a machine-readable form, or during processing to hold data on a temporary basis. See Table 3.3 for a brief description of these auxiliary storage devices.

Punched Cards

Since the early 1950s, one of the principal methods of placing information into the computer memory has been to punch the data on cards and to input the cards via a *card reader*. Today the punched card is not so widely used since more direct methods of entering data are favoured, e.g. key-to-tape and key-to-disc.

The traditional punched card is known as the Hollerith card. It is named after Herman Hollerith who in the 1880s pioneered the development of punched card equipment and the use of punched cards in data processing (see historical section). The standard card is 7·375 inches by 3·25 inches (187 mm × 82·5 mm) and is divided into 80 columns and 12 rows (Figure 3.1). A character is represented by a single rectangular hole, or a combination of two or three holes punched in a single column. Since only one character can be represented per column, a single card can hold a maximum of eighty characters.

The machine used to punch out the holes is called a **keypunch**. The device has a keyboard similar to an ordinary typewriter. To punch out the code for a required character simply involves depressing the corresponding key, known as "keying" or "keying-in". On most keypunches, the character is printed at the top of the column at the same time as the holes are cut out, so that the characters on the card can be checked visually. Some punches do not provide this interpretation and a separate device called an **interpreter** may be brought in to do the job.

It is important to ensure that the computer is not asked to process wrong information which has been punched on cards. The established method of checking the accuracy of punching involves the use of a **verifier**, a device in outward appearance similar to a keypunch. An operator enters each punched card in the verifier and attempts to key-in the same data again. But, instead of punching out the code, the verifier checks against the code already punched on the card. The device indicates any mismatch between the two.

Table 3.1 Input devices

Device	Medium	Purpose
Punch card reader	Punched card	Input of information (data) punched in coded machine-readable form on cards (typically 80 characters per card).
Paper tape reader	Paper tape	Input of information punched in coded machine-readable form on continuous roll of paper tape.
Mark reader	Cards or special forms	Input of information marked by pencil or pen on specially pre-printed cards or forms.
Optical character reader	Documents	Input of information printed on documents using special type faces.
Magnetic ink character reader	Documents (e.g. cheque)	Input of information inscribed in documents using ink containing magnetized particles.
Terminal (teletype or VDU)		Direct keyboard entry of data particularly for on-line enquiries and for updating existing files.
Point-of-sale terminal		Direct entry of sales information at the point-of-sale.
Magnetic tape	Magnetic tape	High speed input of data pre-stored on tape in machine-readable form (the data may have been input in the first place from another device, e.g. magnetic ink character reader or directly using a key-to-tape system).
Key-to-tape	Magnetic tape or cassette/cartridge	Keyboard entry of data directly to magnetic tape without preparing it first on some other medium
Key-to-disc	Magnetic disc or floppy disc (diskette)	Keyboard entry of data directly to magnetic disc.
Light pen on cathode ray tube device		Direct entry via visual display.
Audible signal receiver		Direct entry via spoken word.

Table 3.2 Output devices

Device	Medium	Purpose
Line printer (or character printer, e.g. teletype)	Paper (continuous fan-fold, or pre-printed forms)	Listing out information in human readable form.
Visual display unit (VDU)	(CRT screen)	Display of information (results, messages) for visual consideration (the information is not lasting—lines are lost to allow fresh information to be displayed). Some visual display units are designed to display graphical symbols as well as ordinary alphanumeric characters.
Computer output microfilm reader	Microfilm roll/ microfiche	Display of information recorded on film, particularly suited to information which only needs to be referenced from time to time.
Graph plotters	Paper (and other materials such as plastic)	Tracing out graphs, maps, designs, etc. to a high degree of accuracy.
Magnetic tape unit	Magnetic tape	Output of information in machine-readable form in readiness for future input.
Magnetic disc unit	Magnetic disc	Although disc is considered primarily as a secondary storage, the medium is used for output of information in machine-readable form in readiness for future input (i.e. in the meantime the disc acts as a store).
Card punch	Card	Output of information in machine-readable form ready for future use.
Paper tape punch	Paper tape	Output of information in machine-readable form ready for use again; useful for transferring information from one computer system to another.
Audible signal generator		Produces sound patterns to simulate speech.

Table 3.3 Secondary storage devices

Device	Medium	Purpose
Magnetic tape unit	Magnetic tape	Retaining files of information which can be accessed in strict sequence.
Magnetic disc unit/floppy disc drive	Magnetic disc/ floppy disc	Retaining files of information which can be accessed at random (in any order).
Magnetic drum unit	Magnetic drum	Retaining files of information which can be accessed at random, and for holding information to which very high speed access is important.

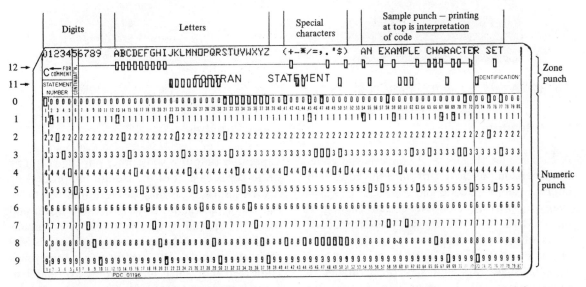

Each digit is represented by a single numeric punch.

Each letter is represented by a single zone punch and a single numeric punch.

Each symbol is represented by a combination of one, two or three punches (zone and/or numeric).

Fig. 3.1 80-column punched card; representation of digits, letters and special characters using the Hollerith code

Note that 0 (zero) is used as a zone punch as well as a numeric punch

71

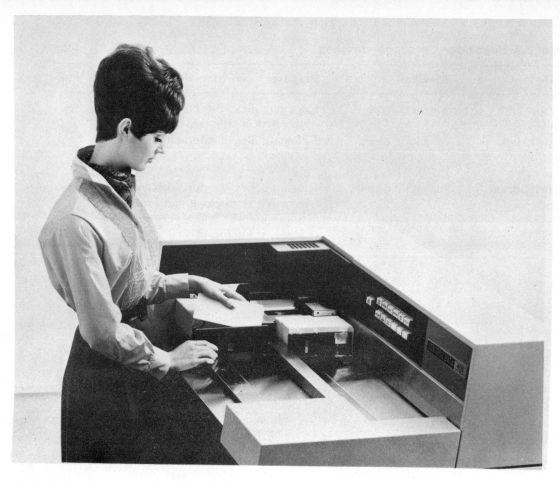

Fig. 3.2   A card reader (Courtesy *CDC*)

Card Readers

A card reader (Figure 3.2) converts the coded characters on punched cards into the equivalent internal computer code and transfers it in electronic form to the computer for processing. In the modern card reader, the presence or absence of holes in each column is detected by means of photoelectric cells. Each card passes between light rays and sets of photoelectric cells (Figure 3.3). Light passing through the punched holes activates the cells which in turn register the code. Each card is sensed twice. If the two readings match, the character is passed to the computer. Card readers operate at varying speeds up to 2000 cards per minute depending on the type and the model but 1000 cards per minute is a typical rate.

Card Punches

Computer output is sometimes punched directly on to cards as part of the computing process by a **card punch**. This may be desirable when the computer results are to be processed again and are not required in the meantime in a human-readable form. A typical punching speed is 300 cards per minute. The card punch is sometimes combined in a single unit with a card reader to form a card reader/punch.

Advantages and Disadvantages

One distinct advantage of the punched card is that the characters are visually understandable (when interpreted) as well as being in a machine-readable form. The cards therefore

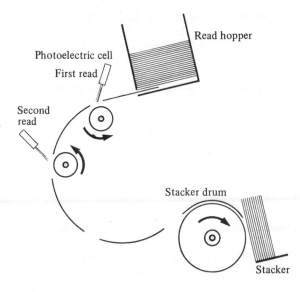

Fig. 3.3 Principle of operation of a card reader

comparatively cheap form of storage but it is bulky for a large volume of data. A big disadvantage is the slow rate of the transfer of information from cards to the computer, compared with the transfer of data stored on magnetic devices.

Paper Tape

Paper tape is another traditional medium for input to computers and, like the punched card, it can also be used directly as an output medium. Historically, the use of paper tape is associated more with input and output on smaller computers, and like the punched card its significance is declining. Paper tape permits a continuous recording of information, and in this way the medium differs fundamentally from the punched card which is of a fixed length (80 characters maximum).

A character is represented by one or more punches *across* the width of the tape (Figure 3.4). The code used is determined by the number of punched **channels** or **tracks** running in parallel the length of the tape. Eight-channel tapes are common. Character density is 10 characters to the inch, the tape is an inch wide (25.5 mm), and a reel may be several hundred feet (or over a hundred metres) long. Five-channel tapes, first used for transmitting telegraph

provide a meaningful record and they can be processed by the computer as often as is necessary, or until the cards need replacing through wear and tear. Punched cards are easy to correct and change, in that one card contains only a small amount of data that can readily be repunched. Retaining information on cards is a

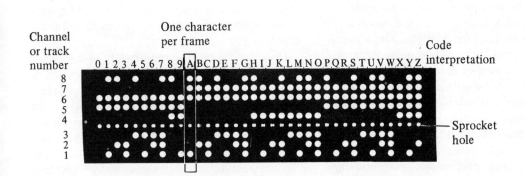

Fig. 3.4 Eight-channel paper tape

messages over wires as early as 1870, are also in use.

Punching Tape

Tape can be punched using a special keyboard device but often paper attachments are built into other machines to enable the automatic recording of information as a by-product of some other typing or keying process, e.g. in the use of some cash registers, accounting machines and typewriters. Some teletypewriter terminals can record simultaneously on paper tape, and paper tape output can be obtained directly from the computer at speeds around 300 characters per second.

Paper Tape Readers

The presence or absence of holes is sensed using similar principles to those in card reading. Reader speeds vary considerably from as low as 100 characters per second to as high as 2000 characters per second. The higher speeds are obtained using photoelectric techniques. Data on punched tape may be copied to magnetic tape via a special converter to provide a faster rate of input to the computer.

Advantages and Disadvantages

Compared with cards, paper tape is compact, easier to store, and more easily transported. It is cheaper and the data does not have to be arranged in blocks of fixed length. The automatic recording of data as a part of another process reduces the cost of data preparation. A big disadvantage of the continuous nature of tape is that corrections and insertions of data are tedious to arrange. Transfer rates are typically slower than those associated with cards, and of course considerably slower than input and output involving magnetic media (magnetic tape and disc). Paper tape is also difficult to read visually.

Mark and Character Recognition

Equipment has been developed that enables information to be read directly from marked or printed documents and cards. Three types of recognition are distinguishable:

1) Mark reading
2) Optical character recognition
3) Magnetic ink character recognition.

Mark Reading

Mark reading concerns the detection of ordinary pencil or pen marks made on specially pre-printed cards or documents. To be detected, the marks have to be made precisely and in specified positions, otherwise reading errors occur. The positions on a card, for example, may correspond to those of the holes made by a keypunch in which case the same character code is being used. The documents or cards may be so designed that the presence of a single mark in a particular position signifies an item of information, e.g. a *yes* answer to a survey question or that the person asked the question is *female.*

Mark reading is performed in two different ways. One method relies on the conductivity of graphite to determine the presence of a pencil mark. This reading process is sometimes referred to as *mark sensing.* The marks must be made *only* in pencil and a soft pencil is recommended since the graphite deposit is more pronounced. The second method of reading is based on the reflectance of light. The presence of a mark is indicated by a drop in light reflectance. Marks other than by pencil may be acceptable.

Data can be transferred directly to a computer but, because of the slow operating speeds of mark readers, typically 200 documents per minute or less, the information is more likely to be transferred to magnetic tape first. Some mark readers are designed to handle both punched cards and marked cards.

Mark reading is not a significantly important method of input. Use is very much restricted to certain applications in which the information to be recorded can be expressed meaningfully and easily by a mark or series of marks, and when it is sensible to record the information in this way at source. The medium is suitable for handling questionnaires for market research and multiple choice testing, and for recording the simple numeric data as presented by gas and electricity meters in our homes.

Optical Character Recognition (OCR)

An OCR device not only detects the presence of a printed character but distinguishes one character from another by its *shape*. Information can therefore be typed in a normal way straight on to documents, and converted directly into coded form without the need for an intermediate step. The information is in a human-readable form as well as a machine-readable form and this is an advantage for all who are involved in the particular data processing operation.

The importance of OCR has gradually increased over the last fifteen years. The first readers were designed only to recognise characters printed in a specific type face, for example the American National Standard OCR-A (Figure 3.5) or the European counterpart OCR-B. These readers are still the most common, but more versatile readers have since been developed capable of recognising characters printed in any of a number of different type faces, including characters generated by standard typewriter fonts or even by hand-printing.

OCR readers scan each character photoelectrically and convert the shape into a pattern of electronic signals. The pattern discovered is then matched against the stored patterns for all the possible characters until an exact match is found, thus identifying the character. When a match is not found, because a character has not been properly formed, it is normal for the document concerned to be rejected by the reader. Reading speeds vary considerably from 100 to 1600 documents per minute (i.e. up to 2500 characters a second), depending on the size of the documents and the number of character fonts the device is designed to detect. The single-font readers are the fastest. The information may be read directly into the computer or transferred to magnetic tape for subsequent input.

The readers are expensive compared with other reading devices. However, many firms and organisations with a large and regular daily volume of data for processing by computer make use of OCR. The advantages gained from preparing documents, designed for specific tasks, using conventional typing methods, and from not having to key the information a second time to get it into a machine-acceptable form, are considerable. Banks, insurance companies, airlines, and numerous commercial and business concerns make use of OCR. Some retail outlets also use optical scanners connected to modified cash registers or terminal devices to record the sale of goods. Each item on sale is marked with a product code which can be read by the device.

Research into producing readers capable of reading handwriting as well as hand-printing continues. However the many different styles of handwriting make it a difficult task.

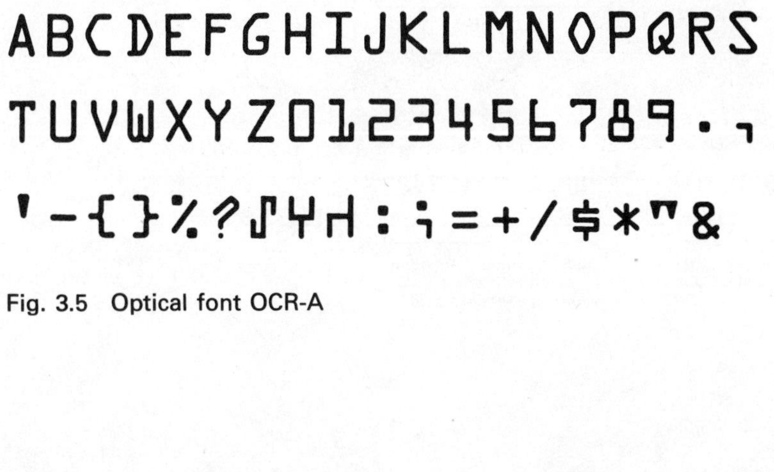

ABCDEFGHIJKLMNOPQRS
TUVWXYZ0123456789·,
'-{}%?∫≠⊢:;=+/$*"&

Fig. 3.5 Optical font OCR-A

Magnetic Ink Character Recognition (MICR)

MICR, as the name suggests, concerns the recognition of characters inscribed on documents with ink containing magnetized particles. As a method it is invaluable to the world of banking for the processing of cheques. The cheque number, the number identifying the bank, and the customer's account number are pre-printed along the bottom of the cheque in magnetic ink (Figure 3.6). After the cheque is presented to a bank for encashment, the amount of the transaction is added using a special key-operated machine. The four items can then be read from the cheque, the characters converted into the internal computer code, and transmitted to a computer for processing. Since one cheque may eventually be handled by a number of banks, it is essential for the characters to be printed in a common style.

As early as 1966, two standard MICR fonts were agreed, one for use in the USA and the UK, known as E13B (Figure 3.7a), and one for use in France and the rest of Europe, known as CMC7 (Figure 3.7b). There are only fourteen characters in the E13B set, the digits 0 to 9 and four special characters, each with a particular meaning, but this is sufficient for the banking application. The CMC7 set includes the letters

Fig. 3.7a MICR font E13B

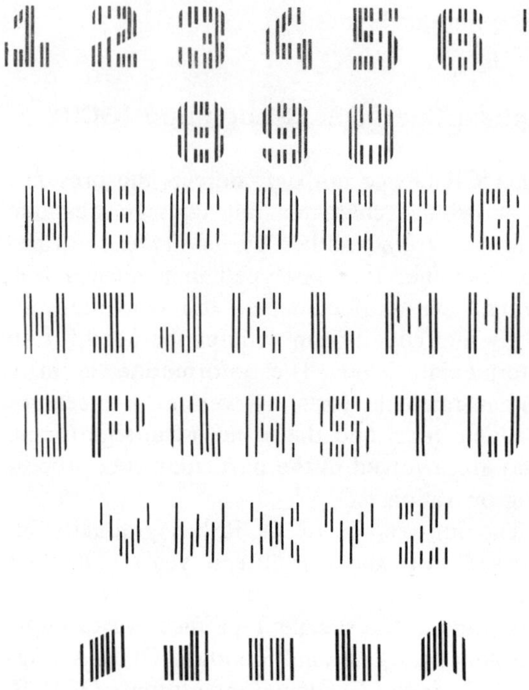

Fig. 3.7b MICR font CMC7

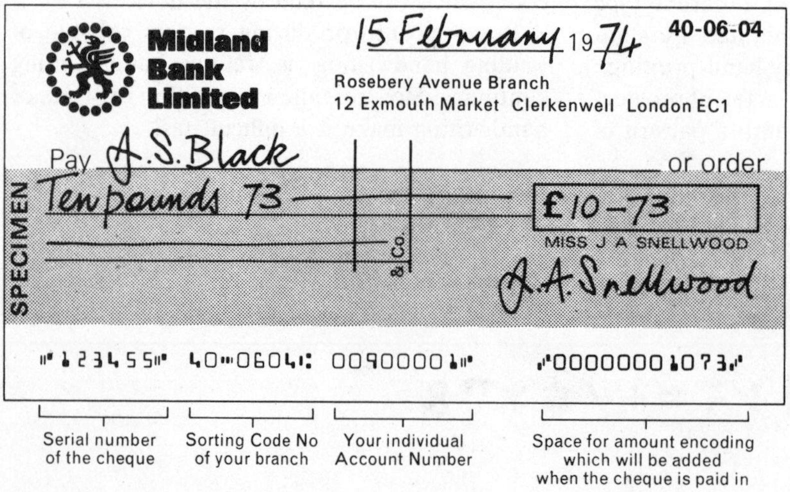

Fig. 3.6

Serial number of the cheque	Sorting Code No of your branch	Your individual Account Number	Space for amount encoding which will be added when the cheque is paid in

of the alphabet and five special characters as well as the digits. With both fonts the character shapes must be distinctively styled, and for successful MICR reading a high level of printing accuracy is required.

An MICR reader detects the magnetic patterns formed by the characters and matches them, as in OCR, against the stored patterns of all the possible characters. Documents are rejected when a pattern cannot be matched. Reading speeds compare favourably with card readers with some devices capable of handling up to 2500 documents a minute. Typically information is read direct to the computer or to magnetic tape for processing later.

Printing with magnetic ink and to the level of accuracy required is comparatively expensive. Use of MICR is therefore restricted to special applications. Significantly for banking, creasing a cheque does not normally affect the readability of the special print. Cheques sent through the post may be handled many times before they eventually arrive at the computer centre, where they can be submitted directly as input to the computer without the need for any further data preparation.

Light Pen

The light pen was originally developed in the late 1950s and came into common use in the early 1960s. It is a small rod-shaped device, rather like a felt-tip pen in shape and size, which is connected to the graphics terminal by a wire. It appears to behave like a pen since it can be used as an input device for drawing or moving items on the graphics screen. Inside the barrel of the pen there is a photosensitive device or cell. An aperture at the tip of the pen allows light emitted from the screen to pass to this cell which, in turn, passes a signal back to the computer. Thus, it works in reverse to a normal pen.

In order for the photosensitive cell to become energized, the spot at which the pen is pointing must be of the right colour and intensity. Since it is the computer system in the first place which is generating the light detected by the light pen, the controlling computer graphics program "knows" the point at which the pen is pointing. Once the computer has detected the spot at which the pen is pointing, it usually generates a small pattern on to the screen, such as a cross or circle, to inform the human operator that the pointing activity of the pen has been detected.

In order to draw images on to the screen or to move images around, additional commands must be supplied such as: DRAW or MOVE and may refer to drawing/moving spots or vectors or lines onto or around the screen. To support the activity of light pens and similar input devices to a graphics terminal, a considerable amount of software must be available. Thus, this branch of computing tends to become a specialised area for computer personnel.

A type of light pen is also used in conjunction with point-of-sale terminals and for reading bar codes (see p. 82).

Audible Signal Receivers and Generators

Input to and output from the computer in the form of spoken words is no longer the preserve of science fiction fantasy. Some 300 voice data entry (VDE) systems are currently in use. Such a system can analyse and identify words or phrases spoken into the system. Each word spoken should be followed by a short break (of about 0·1 seconds), i.e. speaking should be "clipped". A vocabulary word may be a digit, a word in any language or a short phrase, or several digits lasting no more than four seconds. The entire vocabulary of such systems may range from 64 to 192 words.

Initially, each user has to "train" the system to recognise his or her particular pronunciation by repeating each word ten times. The system can be retrained easily by repeating this process and thus eliminating problems arising from temporary illnesses which may affect the user's pronunciation. When in use, the system reduces the user's entered word to a string of binary bits. This string or pattern is matched against the stored words generated during the training process. The best match is then selected and

Fig. 3.8　Light pen in use
(Courtesy *IBM United Kingdom Ltd*)

usually displayed on to a screen for visual identification by the user.

In these early days of VDE systems, there are only a few satisfactory application areas associated with vocal data entry, machine control and quality control. Apart from voice entry, computer systems can also generate spoken words. The words are delivered more slowly than those in normal speech. Again, only a limited vocabulary is possible which reduces the number of application areas to those in which this limitation is not unduly restrictive.

Terminals

A **computer terminal** is essentially two devices, an input and an output device. It consists of a keyboard for inputting information direct to the computer, and either a printer or a TV screen for displaying information from the computer. A terminal may be situated at the computer site or situated at a place where the data to be input is more readily available.

Terminals within 500 feet (150 m) or so of the computer are frequently linked to the computer system by a direct cable and are known as **hard-wired** terminals. But for more remote terminals, communication to the system is established via **telecommunication** lines. An ordinary telephone line can be used but a **modem** at both ends of the line is required. Modem is an acronym for *mod*ulator/*dem*odulator. It takes binary pulses received from a computer or a terminal and converts those signals into a continuous analogue signal which is used on telephone lines, and vice versa.

Telegraph lines and microwave channels are also used for data transmission, and space satel-

78

lites can act as microwave relay stations for long-distance transmission between continents.

Although computer terminals are normally able to receive messages from the computer and to display them in some form, certain terminals are designed to transmit data only. A terminal situated at the point-of-sale to record goods sold, or one on the factory floor to record items drawn from stock, are such examples. The advantage of placing terminals where such activities occur is that information is collected in machine-readable form with no further preparation required.

Two principal types of keyboard terminals are identifiable, teletypewriters and visual display units (VDUs).

Teletypewriter Terminal

The **teletypewriter**, or **teletype** for short, is the most common terminal device (Figure 3.9). It consists of a keyboard, for sending information to the computer, and a printer, for receiving information from the computer. Because the printer prints a character at a time, as does an ordinary typewriter, it is called a **character printer**. The output is typed on to a continuous roll of paper at speeds typically between ten and thirty characters a second. The speed of input depends upon the typing speed of the operator.

A paper tape reader/punch is sometimes incorporated in the design of a terminal to enable

Fig. 3.9 A teletype being used in a computer room (Courtesy *CDC*)

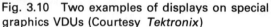

Fig. 3.10 Two examples of displays on special graphics VDUs (Courtesy *Tektronix*)

information to be keyed-in and punched on to paper tape for subsequent input to the computer. Information from the computer, for example a complete program, may also be copied on to paper tape. In place of the paper tape reader/punch, some later machines have magnetic tape cassettes incorporated for the same purpose.

Visual Display Units (VDU)

The distinctive feature of a **VDU** is its cathode ray tube (CRT) similar to a television tube. Results and messages are output on a screen rather than printed on paper. A keyboard is normally fitted below the screen for input of data. There are two types of VDU, those which display only ordinary alphanumeric characters (alphabet, digits 0–9, and a few special symbols), and those which can display special graphical symbols as well.

The screens vary in size from 8 inches (203 mm) up to 20 inches (508 mm) and can display up to 30 lines. The number of characters per line also varies from machine to machine, from 32 characters to 80, so that a full screen can display up to 2400 characters in a matter of a few seconds. It is this rapid display which makes the VDU an attractive terminal device for enquiry applications, e.g. airline reservations and other applications for which a printed copy of information is not necessary.

The special graphics VDU (Figure 3.10) enables information to be displayed rapidly and meaningfully in pie chart, histogram and graphic form. Objects can also be represented graphically in two or three dimensional form as well as in colour. The device is a valuable aid to design. Shapes and plans can be viewed and modified until a suitable design is discovered. Applications include engineering, building design, as well as mapping and plotting seismic recordings.

Copies of selected displays may be taken using a "hard copy" device, linked directly to the VDU (Figure 3.11), and which uses special sensitized paper. Copies may also be made on computer output microfilm (for viewing at a later date), using a device which provides the option of printing any required plot from the microfilm.

Fig. 3.11 Graphics terminal linked to hard copy unit (shown right) (Courtesy *Tektronix*)

Point-of-Sale Terminals

The retail trade is making increasing use of computers to help process sales of goods at the point-of-sale. Typically a terminal is situated on the shop floor with a communication link to a central computer. A large store may have the computer on site whilst a branch store is more likely to be linked to head office or a district office. The terminal acts as a cash register but also transmits sales data to the central database, thereby maintaining automatic stock control and providing valuable information about buying trends.

Numerous methods of capturing data are employed and this is reflected in the way the articles for sale are marked with such information as stock number and price. Some point-of-sale systems are designed to read coded information from perforated (or punched) tags or cards (sometimes referred to as KIMBALL tags). Another method involves the use of a hand-held *wand* or pen reader. An operator waves the wand over the sales information to be recorded and through this action the information is read, using optical character or magnetic character recognition techniques. Sometimes, the marking of goods is done using bar codes rather than normal characters for ease of recognition.

This bar code (see Figure 5.3 on page 131) consists of binary combinations of thick and thin vertical black bars. The code is read typically by means of a light pen used in conjunction with a portable data-capture terminal. Bar codes are used in libraries, at points of sale in retail/wholesale stores, for stock control in industry, etc.

In all these methods the accuracy of the collection of the data is the responsibility of the machine. There are also many types of advanced cash register in use which are linked to computers and which rely on human operators to key in sales data (Figure 3.12).

Printers

Results from computer processing are fre-

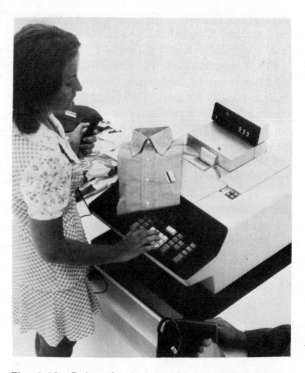

Fig. 3.12 Point-of-sales terminal showing an assistant keying in the sales data; the magnetic wand reader in her left hand can be used with those goods which are magnetically encoded (Courtesy *IBM United Kingdom Ltd*)

quently required in printed form. The printer, therefore, is an output device of considerable significance. Printing may be on continuous fan-fold paper, or multi-leaved stationery to provide multiple copies, or it may be on pre-printed forms designed for gas or telephone bills, bank statements, or salary slips.

There are two types of printer, character and line. A **character printer** prints one character at a time at speeds ranging from 10 to 120 characters per second, with speeds generally at the lower end of the scale. Printers on teletype-writers are of this type.

A **line printer**, on the other hand, is a more complex and expensive device that operates at higher speeds, ranging from 200 to 2000 lines or more per minute with up to 136 characters per line. At such speeds it is able to give the appearance of printing an entire line in one action, hence the term line printer (Figure 3.13).

Fig. 3.13 A line printer in a working situation (Courtesy *CDC*)

All the letter As required in one line are printed out, then any letter Bs, etc., until the entire alphabet has been completed. Digits and special symbols are dealt with in the same way. Once all the required characters for a complete line have been printed, the printer will move on to the next line and the process is repeated.

Two different printing techniques are used, impact and non-impact. An **impact printer** presses or hammers each character against an ink ribbon and on to paper. The **non-impact printer** forms characters by chemical or electronic means and is more expensive since the process requires special sensitized paper. The printing operation is almost silent and speeds are high, even above 2000 lines per minute, but with this technique no multiple copies can be printed using carbon paper.

There are two main types of line printer, chain and drum, but they both operate upon the impact principle. The **chain printer** is the more common device. A chain, normally comprising six complete sets of characters, rotates in a horizontal plane over a set of print hammers, each corresponding to a print position (Figure 3.14). As the selected character passes the required position, the character is pressed against the paper with the ink ribbon between. The speed of rotation is so great that a complete line appears to be printed all at once.

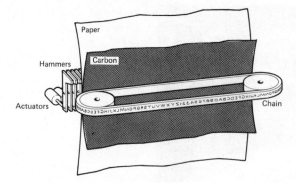

Fig. 3.14   Chain printer

Computer Output Microfilm (COM)

Much of the information obtained from computer processing is only required for reference. In printed form, it can be very bulky and it can take time to find individual items. **Computer output microfilm (COM)** provides a speedy and efficient method of handling this category of information. Large amounts of information can be recorded and retained in a small space.

A COM device displays computer output, obtained on-line from the computer memory or, more likely, from magnetic tape, on to a CRT screen, and records the display on film, normally 16 mm or 35 mm, and then moves on to the next display. Each display is equivalent to about a page of line printer output. The microfilm copy is in roll or microfiche form, and additional copies can easily be made. Microfiche (pronounced micro-fee-sh) is a rectangle of film consisting of a number of frames arranged in rows. Common fiche sizes on which 60 and 30 frames can be recorded respectively are 105 mm × 148 mm and 75 mm × 125 mm. The speed of recording is on average 25 to 50 times faster than printing and costs are less.

A special COM reader is required to view the film (Figure 3.15). It displays a frame at a time on a translucent screen about the size of A4 paper (210 mm × 298 mm). A printing unit is often combined with a reader so that good-quality printed copies can be obtained as required. Computer indexing of the film enables the reader to trace the requested frame in a matter of seconds.

Special COM devices are able to display

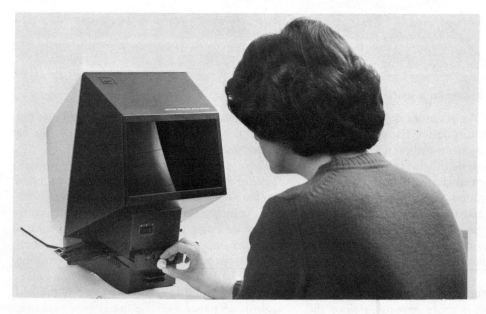

Fig. 3.15   A COM reader, showing the feed-in point of the microfiche (Courtesy *Kodak*)

graphical symbols as well as the alphanumeric characters. This enables the recording of graphs, designs and plans on to microfilm. An accurate plot can be obtained over one hundred times faster than achieved by a conventional plotting device. The processing of microfilm is in itself inexpensive but the capital cost of the equipment is comparatively high.

Graph Plotters

Special plotting devices are capable of tracing out graphs, designs and maps on to paper, and even on to plastic or metal plates. A high degree of accuracy can be achieved, even to within one thousandth of an inch (2 to 3 hundredths of a millimetre). Plotters may be driven *on-line* or *off-line*. Computer systems dedicated to design work are more likely to operate their plotter on-line. Systems used for other applications, as well as graphic applications, are more likely to be driven off-line by specialised equip-

ment. This equipment obtains its instructions from magnetic or paper tape produced by the user's graph-program. It may often take many minutes to complete a design, hence the need for the graph plotter to be off-line.

There are essentially two types of plotter, drum and flat-bed. A **drum plotter** plots on paper affixed to a drum. The drum revolves back and forth, and a pen suspended from a bar above moves from side to side taking up new plot positions or plotting as it moves. The device is suitable for routine graph plotting and for tracing out such things as fashion designs.

On the **flat-bed plotter** the paper lies flat. The bar on which the pen is suspended itself moves on a gantry to provide the necessary two-way movement. Colour plotting is usually possible. Some plotting beds are very large. Those used to assist aero design may be as large

Fig. 3.16 A small flat-bed plotter designed for on-line use, providing A2 size copies, with felt-tip, ballpoint or ink pens (Courtesy *Tektronix*)

as $6\,\text{m} \times 15\,\text{m}$. In some cases designs can be etched on materials such as plastic to form master plates for creating manufactured goods.

Keying to Magnetic Media

Data can be keyed direct to magnetic storage media for subsequent input to a computer. The following methods are identifiable:

1) Key-to-tape (i.e. magnetic tape)
2) Key-to-cassette/cartridge
3) Key-to-disc

Key-to-Tape

This method of recording data directly on to magnetic tape, without first preparing the data on some other media and inputting to the computer for subsequent transfer to tape, was first introduced in 1965. Essentially, the device, variously called a **magnetic tape encoder** or a **data recorder**, consists of a keyboard, a small memory, and a tape-reading mechanism. A small amount of information, equivalent, for example, to one punched card, is keyed in, held briefly in the memory, edited if necessary, and transferred as a block on to $\frac{1}{2}$ inch standard magnetic tape. As a method it saves data preparation time and the cost of the materials previously used in data preparation, e.g. punched cards. Once the data is on magnetic tape it can speedily be input to the computer for processing and the same tape re-used to retain fresh data.

Key-to-Cassette/Cartridge

The principle of operation is the same as key-to-tape format but in this case the information is represented on cassette tape or cartridge similar to that used in home recording systems. The tape is normally $\frac{1}{4}$ inch wide and the number of storage tracks varies from 2 to 8. A cassette typically holds up to $250\,000$ charac-

ters and a cartridge a similar amount. Data from one or more cassettes or cartridges is normally converted with the aid of a special tape/cartridge reader and combined on a standard $\frac{1}{2}$ inch magnetic tape for subsequent input to the computer.

Keying to cassette or cartridge is a simple operation and as a method of data input is growing in importance. The loading of the tape is virtually automatic and the compactness of the device encourages the capture of data at source, that is at the place where the information is generated. The recording of the data may be a by-product of a more conventional operation, e.g. registering the sale of goods.

Key-to-Disc/Key-to-Diskette

Key-to-disc systems, first introduced ten years ago, provide a more versatile and fully automated method of collecting and inputting data. A full system consists of a number of keying-in stations (between 8 and 64), a magnetic disc, a mini-computer, a tape unit, and an operating package to make the whole system functional.

On many modern systems each keyboard station is equipped with a visual display to allow verification by sight before data is transmitted. The mini-computer and the operating package program control the input from the various stations, permit editing and the arrangement of the data onto disc as required.

As a method of data input, key-to-disc/diskette is growing in significance. Many business organisations with large data processing requirements once based on punched cards now operate key-to-disc systems. The process is more efficient and cost effective. Data is easier to verify and the quiet operation of the key stations compared with the noisy clatter of keypunch machines provides a more congenial working environment. Hardware requirements are less and therefore fewer operational staff are needed. Remember that when punching cards there is a second operation using a different device to verify the punching. It is estimated that 9 key-to-disc stations can handle the same volume of work once undertaken from 16 keypunch machines.

Fig. 3.17   A key-to-diskette station (Courtesy *IBM United Kingdom Ltd*)

Figure 3.17 shows a key station for data entry, consisting of a visual display, a keyboard, and diskette drive.

Magnetic Tape

Magnetic tape is extensively used as a medium for secondary storage because it permits the sequential storage of large amounts of data. It is also important as a medium enabling fast input and output of computer data.

A standard tape is $\frac{1}{2}$ inch wide and 2 400 ft (732 m) in length, though smaller as well as larger sizes are sometimes used. The tape is made of plastic and covered on one side with a thin coating of metal oxide on which coded information is recorded in the form of magnetized and non-magnetized spots representing binary 1s and 0s. The tape width is divided into tracks or channels for the recording of data. Standard tape is either 7 or 9 track. The more modern tape drives are designed to read and write with 9 tracks. Figure 3.18 shows both 7-track and 9-track codes.

The code used for 7 tracks is known as **BCD (Binary Coded Decimal)**. The arrangement for 9 track is an extension of the 7 track and is called **EBCDIC (Extended Binary Coded Decimal Interchange Code)**. A character is recorded across the tape in a "frame". An extra track in the frame, called the **parity track**, is set aside for checking purposes. A so-called *even parity* tape is one on which all the frames contain an even number of 1 bits. If a frame contains a character represented by an odd number of 1 bits, the parity bit will be set to 1 in order to make the number of 1 bits across the frame even. If the character already has an even number of 1 bits, then the parity bit is set to 0 to retain the even number of 1 bits across the frame.

When information is transferred from one device to another, the number of 1 bits is checked to ensure that they are even. If they are not, then the computer system suspects that

87

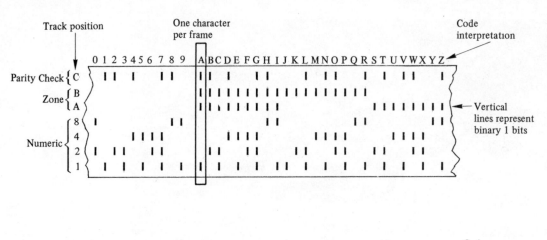

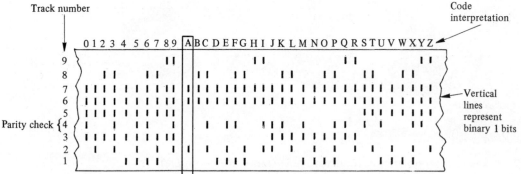

Fig. 3.18 7-track and 9-track magnetic tape codes

an error occurred when transferring the data and it will re-read or re-transmit the data. If the number of 1 bits is even, however, then the data is regarded as having been transmitted correctly. Note that this is not a foolproof method. Other methods also exist which are built into the computer system to ensure accuracy when transferring or manipulating data. Some tapes operate with an *odd parity* check.

A **tape drive** or tape unit performs the operation of writing (that is, recording) on to tape, and of reading information from tape. Normally this is carried out under direct computer control, i.e. the computer outputs information to tape or inputs data from tape. As we have seen, key-to-tape systems enable data to be transferred directly to tape without involving computer processing.

Figure 3.19 shows a magnetic tape unit installation and Figure 3.20 shows the principle of operation.

Tape is fed from a supply reel past a set of read and write heads onto a take-up reel. The tape loops down on either side of the read/write heads in two vacuum chambers. This play on the tape is needed to prevent it from snapping when the tape speed varies, as for example when starting or stopping. There is a read and write head for each track of the tape. The action of reading causes a *copy* of the information to be transferred to the computer, thus allowing the original information to remain on the tape. This means that data can be stored on tape and accessed again and again, as often as required without the data being changed or lost. The action of writing causes information to be copied onto the tape, **over-writing** anything that might have been there before. This means that tape can be re-used for the storage of different data on each occasion.

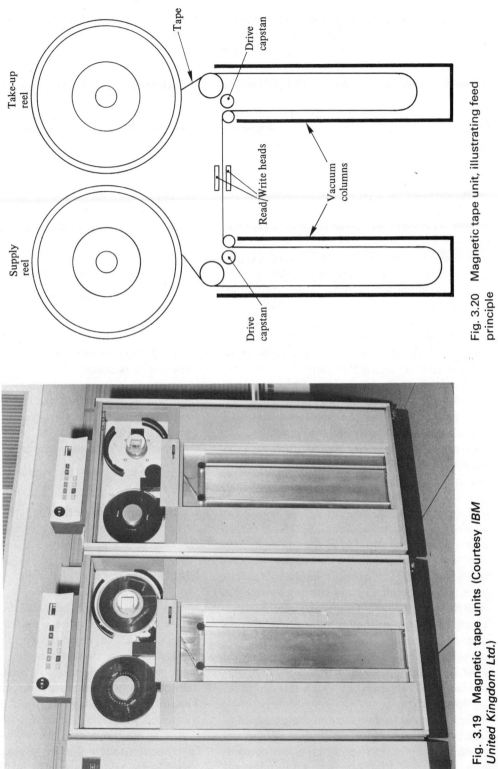

Fig. 3.20 Magnetic tape unit, illustrating feed principle

Tape

Take-up reel

Drive capstan

Read/Write heads

Vacuum columns

Supply reel

Drive capstan

Fig. 3.19 Magnetic tape units (Courtesy *IBM United Kingdom Ltd.*)

Data is normally stored on the tape in **blocks**. On some tapes the block is of a fixed length, on others it is variable in length. The blocks are separated by an interrecord gap, typically $\frac{3}{4}$ inch (19 mm) in length. A read action transfers all the data in one block. A block corresponds typically to one or more data records (see Chapter 4) of a practical size, e.g. a customer's name and address and/or current account statement, or the amount of information previously recorded on one punched card.

The capacity of a tape is determined by the density at which characters are recorded. The density is measured in characters per inch. Rates of 556, 800 and 1600 characters per inch are standard, though some devices support even higher rates. The **character transfer rate**, i.e. the speed of reading and writing, is determined by the density and the speed of the tape movement past the read/write heads. Typical transfer rates range between 30 000 and 320 000 characters per second. A standard tape holds between 10 and 40 million characters depending on the number of records permitted in a block of data as well as the density per inch. To punch the same amount of data on cards would require a minimum of 125 000 to 500 000 cards.

Magnetic tape is a convenient form for data storage. It is compact, easy to handle, low cost, and can be repeatedly used. The medium is ideal for data which needs referencing in sequence, e.g. a mailing list, but not so useful for accessing records at random. The 150th record is only found after looking at the previous 149. The 100th might then be found by working backwards from 150 or more likely by rewinding the tape completely and starting again. It is ideal for storing data temporarily, or for collecting raw data, prior to inputting to the computer for processing, since the fast rate of transfer, some 100 to 1 000 times faster than card input, is nearer to, though by no means comparable with, the speed at which the computer can handle data.

Tape is prone to damage and the presence of dust can lead to a distortion of data. When not in use it is important to store tape in a controlled environment to ensure a suitable temperature, correct humidity and a dust-free atmosphere.

Magnetic Tape Cassettes and Cartridges

Cassette tape and cartridge are often used as storage media to support mini-computer and microprocessor systems, as used in small business systems and word processing systems. As we have seen, data can be keyed directly to cassette and cartridge tapes. The data may then be converted and stored on standard sized magnetic tape for subsequent input to a computer.

A tape cassette typically measures

$$2\tfrac{1}{2}\,\text{in.} \times 4\,\text{in.} \times \tfrac{1}{4}\,\text{in.}\ (63.5\,\text{mm} \times 101.5\ \text{mm} \times 5.5\ \text{mm}).$$

The $\frac{1}{4}$ in. tape, housed in a cassette, resembles that used on home recording systems and one reel stores approximately 200 000 characters. The information is stored and accessed in much the same way as on standard sized tape. The cassette provides protection for the tape and makes it very easy to load the drive.

A cartridge typically measures

$$4\,\text{in.} \times 6\,\text{in.} \times \tfrac{1}{2}\,\text{in.}\ (101.5\,\text{mm} \times 152.5\ \text{mm} \times 12.5\ \text{mm}).$$

It differs from the cassette tape in that it is sprocket driven but the capacity is about the same.

Magnetic Discs

Magnetic discs have become the most commonly used form of storage media for retaining large volumes of data and for the temporary storage of data that is awaiting entry to the main memory of the computer. Each individual item of data stored on disc is directly accessible. This distinct advantage means that data is retrievable at random, i.e. in any order.

A disc is about the size of a long-playing LP record though thicker. Both surfaces are coated with oxide material, just like tape, and this allows the recording of data in the form of magnetized spots. The presence of a spot signifies a 1 bit and the absence a 0 bit. The data is stored as a string of bits along a track. There are typically 800 tracks on a surface laid out in the form of concentric circles. Each track can hold the same amount of information. Thus the characters on the inner tracks are simply packed more tightly together. To enable data to be stored in addressable locations, the surface is further divided up into sectors.

Typically six or more discs are mounted together on a spindle to form a **stack** (Figure 3.21). Storage capacity varies from several million characters to 200 million or even more, depending on the number of discs in the stack.

A disc unit is the device responsible for both the recording and the retrieval of information. The disc stack may be permanently fixed to the drive or it may be removable as a complete pack (Figure 3.22). The removable disc pack feature is very useful as it allows a pack to be set aside for the storage of data files for a particular application. The pack is only mounted on the drive when required. By purchasing a number of packs the capacity of the disc unit is increased.

The drive rotates the discs pack constantly. Typical speeds are between 2400 and 3600 revolutions per minute. As the discs rotate, read/write heads can either pick up or record data. The speed of rotation causes the heads to "float" approximately 1/400th of an inch (0·064 mm) from the surface. Dust particles can therefore be a problem. As with magnetic tape, data can be repeatedly retrieved (copied) without being actually removed and new data can be placed on the disc by overwriting data no longer required. Disc space can therefore be re-used repeatedly.

There are two classifications of drives relating to the operation of the read/write mechanism, these are fixed-head and moving-head. On a **fixed-head drive**, for every usable surface (not the very top one or very bottom one of the stack) there is a set of read/write heads equal in number to the number of tracks. The time taken to find an item of data is of the order of 10–50 milliseconds. On a **moving-head drive**

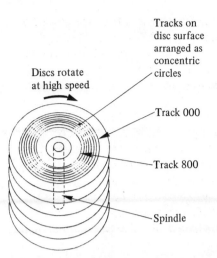

Fig. 3.21 A stack of magnetic discs mounted on a spindle

there is only one read/write head per disc surface. The heads are fixed to arms that move in and out in unison between the discs. Access time is slightly slower, 25–100 milliseconds, since the arm has to move to the right position to seek out the specified track. Transfer rates to and from disc and main memory are in the order of 100 000 to 2 000 000 characters per second.

Many computer systems are dependent on discs for their auxiliary or back-up storage. There are a number of factors in their favour: large storage capacity, direct access to data items selected at random, very fast character transfer rate, and the fact that they can be re-used again and again. Disc drives are expensive pieces of equipment but the replaceable pack feature allows storage capacity to be built up relatively cheaply. Disc packs though are more expensive than magnetic tape reels.

Fig. 3.22   A disc storage unit with four drives,
showing one disc stack being loaded (Courtesy
IBM United Kingdom Ltd)

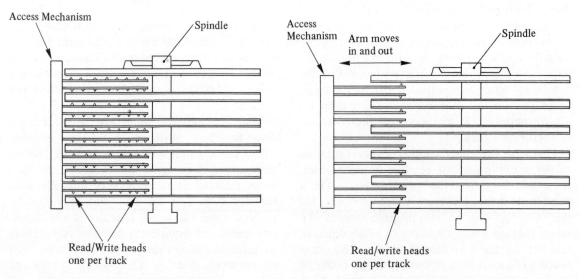

Fig. 3.23   Fixed-head magnetic disc drive   Fig. 3.24   Moving-head magnetic disc drive

Floppy Disc/Diskette

The **floppy disc**, or diskette as it is sometimes called, is a small-sized and low-cost method of storage associated with the use of mini-computers, microprocessors, word processing systems and, in conjunction with some keyboard device, for the capture (recording) of data at source, i.e. in places where the information is generated.

It is a single flexible disc, hence its name, only $7\frac{1}{2}$ in. (190·5 mm) in diameter and about 1/40 in. (0·64 mm) thick, and for protection the disc is enclosed in a plastic jacket or cartridge. The entire cartridge slots into the floppy disc drive and it is very easy to load and unload. (see Figure 3.25).

The way in which the information is stored and the method of retrieving and recording data is similar to standard disc, but the capacity is substantially smaller. A floppy disc can retain only 250 000 characters or more. However, they are very cheap and with the growth in the use of mini-computers and microprocessors they are becoming more popular.

Fig. 3.25 A diskette being removed from its plastic envelope (Courtesy *IBM United Kingdom Ltd*)

Magnetic Drum

Magnetic drum is another medium used for auxiliary storage. It is similar in concept to magnetic disc except that the information is stored on the outer surface of the drum, rotating at a high speed, as opposed to the surface of a disc. A drum, as the name suggests, is cylindrical in shape, typically about 3 ft (914 mm) in length (Figure 3.26). The outer surface of the drum is coated in ferro-oxide, enabling the storage of information in coded form as magnetized or non-magnetized spots. Data is stored in tracks and the tracks are arranged in parallel with several hundred on the surface of a drum. The drum can store between 100 000 characters and as many as 10 000 000 characters of information. There is a read/write head for each track. This provides fast access to informa-

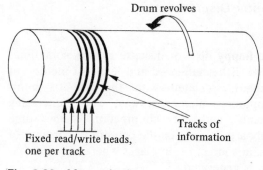

Fixed read/write heads, one per track

Tracks of information

Fig. 3.26 Magnetic drum

tion. Drum storage is more expensive than disc and it is used only in applications where the slightly higher speed of access to the information is important. The drum is not used as much as it was ten years ago.

Important Words and Terms used in Chapter 3

access speed
addressable locations
audio signal receiver and generator

binary coded decimal (BCD)

card punch
cathode ray tube (CRT)
chain printer
channels
character density
character printer
character transfer rate
CMC7 font
computer output microfilm (COM)

data preparation
data transmission
direct entry
disc pack
disc stack
drum plotter
drum printer

even parity
extended binary coded decimal
    interchange code (EBCDIC)
E13B font

fan-fold paper
fixed-head disc drive
flat bed plotter
floppy disc or diskette

graph plotter
graphics visual display unit

hard copy
hard-wired terminals
Hollerith card
Hollerith code

impact and non-impact printing
interpreter
interrecord gap

keyboard
keypunch
key-to-cartridge
key-to-cassette
key-to-disc
key-to-tape

light pen
line printer

magnetic disc
magnetic drum
magnetic ink character recognition (MICR)
magnetic tape
magnetic tape encoder
mark reader
mark reading
mark sensing
microfiche
microfilm
microwave channels

microwave relay stations
modem
moving-head disc drive
multi-leaved stationery

odd parity
off-line
on-line
optical character recognition (OCR)
optical character reader
optical scanner
over-writing

paper tape
paper tape punch
paper tape reader
peripheral device
point-of-sale terminal
printer
punched card
punch card reader

random access
read/write heads

serial access

teletype or teletypewriter
tracks

verifier
(verification)
visual display unit (VDU)
voice data entry

Exercises 3

1 A common output device is
a) a punched card b) a line printer c) an arithmetic unit d) a coding sheet e) paper tape (*EMREB*)

2 A graph plotter is
a) an input device b) an output device c) a backing store d) a storage device e) a sequential access device (*EMREB*)

3 MICR is used in
a) reading magnetic tape b) reading punched cards c) reading bank cheques d) graph plotting e) reading paper tape (*EMREB*)

4 What do the following stand for: VDU, OCR, COM.

5 Which of the following can be used for *both* input and output?
a) a graph plotter b) OCR c) a terminal d) a telephone e) a line printer

6 How many columns does the standard punch card contain?
a) 12 *b*) 21 *c*) 100 *d*) 80 *e*) 8 (*EMREB*)

7 A magnetic disc can transfer data at a rate of about
a) 2000 characters per second *b*) 20 000 ch/sec *c*) 200 million ch/sec *d*) 1 million ch/sec *e*) 20 million ch/sec (*SWEB*)

8 How many punching positions are there for each column of a standard 80-column punched card?
a) 12 *b*) 10 *c*) 14 *d*) 800 *e*) 960 (*EAEB*)

9 Computer peripherals are
a) staff in a computer installation *b*) input and output devices *c*) logic units *d*) programs *e*) punched cards (*EAEB*)

10 A verifier would normally be located in
a) the disc unit *b*) the tape library *c*) the data preparation area *d*) a multiplexer *e*) the control unit (*EAEB*)

11 What device provides hard copy output at high speed?

12 What is a peripheral device? Name *four* peripheral devices. (*WJEC*)

13 Explain the reason for the loops of tape between the reels and read/write heads of a magnetic tape unit. (*SWEB*)

14 Give one advantage and one disadvantage of a teletype when compared with a VDU with a keyboard. (*AEB*)

15 What is the purpose of a parity bit?

16 What are the advantages and disadvantages of optical character recognition?

17 Explain the following two terms and give an example of a medium suitable for each:
a) random access storage *b*) serial access storage (*JMB*)

18 What advantages are there in retaining information on microfilm?

19 Name *three* types of input device. In each case briefly describe the purpose of the device and how it operates.

20 Name *three* types of output device. In each case briefly describe the purpose of the device and how it operates.

21 Describe briefly how data is arranged on *either* punched cards *or* paper tape.

4 Data Processing and Files

Introduction

Man has been recording information for as long as history can determine; in the earliest times as scratches upon rocks and trees or marks on the mud walls of houses. The oldest surviving records were made on clay tablets by the ancient Sumerians as long ago as 3700 BC. The wet clay was marked with the cut end of a reed. To preserve the tablets of clay they were dried in the sun or baked in an oven.

The information contains details of the history of ancient civilisations, accounts of wars and, very important, accounts of the trading activities or transactions between tribes or nations. The first records of actual business transactions date back to 2600 BC in Babylon, a large and civilised commercial centre even before that date.

Papyrus was another common medium for recording information. Thin sheets of bark were taken from the tall water plants abundant on the banks of the Nile. When these were soaked, pressed together and dried, they formed a reasonable surface upon which to make marks with sharp-pointed reeds. Papyrus was gradually replaced during the 3rd century AD by parchment, the dried skins of animals. Although paper first originated in China in the 2nd century AD, it was not until the 8th century that paper was introduced more generally to the rest of the world through the Arabs. Paper was introduced into Europe by the Moors when they conquered Spain in the 12th century. By the second half of the 14th century the use of paper had become well established in Western Europe. With the introduction of paper, advances were made in the design of writing implements as shown in Figure 4.1.

Over the past twenty years or so, a new term

```
Lead pencils c 1590

Metal pens, in common use 1828

First practical typewriter in 1868

Fountain pens in 1880
```

Fig. 4.1

data processing has replaced the older terms *paperwork* and *record keeping*. The activity is the same, only the implements used have changed. Today, "data processing" refers to the process of recording information by the use of computers. Although computers were first used as a means of calculating numbers very quickly and accurately, it soon became evident that they could also perform many of the routine clerical tasks of everyday commerce. Over 80% of computer applications are now of a commercial nature so that one no longer talks about computers being electronic calculating machines but of their being **processors of information**. By the term "information processing" we simply mean the recording, the manipulation and the retrieval of information by computers.

In order to process information a computer requires two things, a complete set of instructions telling it exactly what to do (i.e. a *program*) and *data* upon which the program works. Data can include many everyday facts and figures, letters, words, symbols, etc. In scientific applications data tends to be restricted to numbers and involves the use of programming languages especially designed to facilitate the writing of mathematical formulae. Commercial applications have no such restrictions on the type of data but normally the arithmetic performed is of a minor nature and forms a very small part of the total activity. The term "data processing" has come to be more generally equated with commercial applications rather than with scientific ones. Consequently, in this chapter where we concentrate on the subject of data processing, we shall refer to commercial applications and discuss some of the terms and techniques employed in this large and important area of computer activity.

Information and Data

It is necessary in this chapter to make a distinction between two terms which so far have been used interchangeably, namely *information* and *data*. **Data** is the material which computer programs work upon. It can be numbers, letters of the alphabet, words, special symbols. But by themselves they have no meaning. For example, the following sequence of digits 181240 is meaningless by itself since it could refer to a date of birth, a part number for a washing machine, the number of dollars spent on a Government or university project, the number of people employed in a large organisation, etc. Once we know what the sequence refers to then it becomes meaningful and can be called **information**.

What transforms data for computers into information? Simply the program which has been written for a particular set of data. The program will inform the computer how to interpret the data which has been organised by the programmer in a particular manner. This will become clearer once we look at a specific data processing application and at the same time many of the associated problems can be discussed.

A Data Processing Application

The application chosen is the one related to a school environment. Let us suppose that a class of twenty-five students is getting ready to select their subjects for CSE and O-level examinations. The teacher in charge of the class has decided to "computerise" the student records. What will this entail?

The first and most important step is for the teacher to be absolutely clear as to what *output* is required from the computer. Once this has been clarified the teacher can then and only then decide *how* to do it. This point is often overlooked by beginners. They are too anxious to begin writing programs and to make use of the computer. But this step of writing programs is really the last part of the whole operation and cannot be attempted properly until one knows exactly and in great detail what is required.

Output Required

There are twenty-five students and let us suppose twelve possible subjects which they can each take for State examinations. Not every student will take all twelve and so the teacher wishes primarily to create a list of how many are entering for each examination. Figure 4.2 illustrates the eventual output. Furthermore, since Examination Boards require to know the names, dates of birth and sex of each student, this information will have to be provided and can be output as a second list by the computer. Again, the first decision to make is how the list will be designed. Figure 4.3 shows one possible solution.

Finally, the teacher will need a third list which will provide information about the subjects each student will take (Figure 4.4). This third list combines information from both previous lists but it shows the teacher exactly which subjects each student will take, together with the students name, date of birth, whether male or female, and finally, the total number of subjects each student is taking at both O-level and CSE.

Files and Records

Before proceeding any further with the student examination application, we shall need to take

	Subject	No. of pupils at O-level	No. of pupils at CSE level
1	English grammar	25	–
2	English literature	25	–
3	History	20	–
4	Geography	20	–
5	French	8	–
6	German	3	–
7	Chemistry	–	18
8	Biology	–	14
9	Physics	–	18
10	Mathematics	10	15
11	Computer studies	8	8
12	Home economics	–	10

Fig. 4.2 List 1: number of students per subject
NB. Some subjects are taken only at O-level,
some only at CSE level, and 2 at both O and
CSE levels

Name of student	Date of birth	Male/Female
ALLEN, J. T.	21.12.64	m
ARCHER, D.	3. 6.65	m
BROWN, P. J.	24. 5.65	f
BUTLER, R. R.	14. 4.65	m
CARR, M. B.	12.12.65	f
CARTER, P. T.	5. 7.65	m
CLARK, R. V.	10.10.65	m
CRIPPS, M.	28.12.64	m
DAVIDSON, T. K.	26. 8.65	f
DAVIES, R. L.	15. 9.65	f
EVANS, D. T.	6. 6.65	m
EWINS, D. F.	19. 9.65	m
FARMER, J. F.	23. 8.65	f
FARREL, G. K.	30.10.65	f
FREEMAN, T. H.	24. 9.65	m
FULLER, L. J.	27. 7.65	m
GALE, D. J.	16. 5.65	m
GEORGE, M. H.	20. 7.65	f
GREEN, M. T.	4. 1.66	f
GRIFFITH, R. K.	9.10.65	m
HAGEN, G. H.	16. 8.65	m
JACKSON, B. D.	13.10.65	f
KENNEDY, J. L.	4. 4.65	m
LUCAS, J. J.	19. 5.65	m
MARTIN, F. J.	12. 9.65	f

Fig. 4.3 List 2: alphabetical list of names,
dates of birth, and sex

note of a few terms used in data processing. If we go back to Figure 4.4 the entire information contained in the output (list three) is more commonly referred to as a **file**. The whole file consists of information about 25 students and we refer to each of the 25 students individual information as being a **record**. Thus a file consists of a number of records. In each record there are seventeen pieces of information, each one being called an *item of information* or **item** for short (Figure 4.5).

A file then consists of a number of records and each record consists of a number of items as shown in Figure 4.6. List 2, the output file described in Figure 4.3, again contains twenty-five records but, in this case, each record consists of only three items of information.

Name of pupil	Date of birth	Sex	Eng. gr.	Eng. lit.	Hist.	Geog.	Fren.	Germ.	Chem.	Biol.	Phys.	Math.	C/std.	H.Econ.	Total O-level	Total CSE
Allen, J. T.	21.12.64	m	O	O	O	O	O	N	C	N	C	O	O	N	7	2
Archer. D.	3. 6.65	m	O	O	O	O	N	N	C	C	C	O	O	N	6	3
Brown, P. J.	24. 5.65	f	O	O	O	O	N	N	C	N	N	C	C	C	4	4
Butler, R. R.	14. 4.65	m	O	O	O	O	N	N	C	N	C	C	C	N	4	4
Carr, M. B.	12.12.65	f	O	O	N	O	O	N	C	C	C	O	N	C	5	4
Carter, P. T.	5. 7.65	m	O	O	O	O	N	N	C	N	C	C	N	N	4	3
Clark, R. V.	10.10.65	m	O	O	O	O	N	N	C	N	C	C	N	N	4	3
Cripps, M.	28.12.64	m	O	O	O	N	O	O	C	C	N	O	N	N	6	2
Davidson, T. K	26. 8.65	f	O	O	O	O	N	N	C	C	C	O	N	C	4	4
Davies, R. L.	15. 9.65	f	O	O	O	N	O	O	C	C	N	O	O	C	7	3
Evans, D. T.	6. 6.65	m	O	O	O	N	N	N	N	C	C	C	N	N	3	3
Ewins, D. F.	19. 9.65	m	O	O	O	O	N	N	C	C	C	O	O	N	6	3
Farmer, J. F.	23. 8.65	f	O	O	O	N	N	N	C	C	C	C	N	C	3	5
Farrel, G. K.	30.10.65	f	O	O	O	O	N	N	C	C	C	O	O	C	6	3
Freeman, T. H.	24. 9.65	m	O	O	O	O	N	N	C	C	N	C	C	N	4	3
Fuller, L. J	27. 7.65	m	O	O	N	O	O	N	N	C	N	C	C	N	3	3
Gale, D. J.	16. 5.65	m	O	O	N	O	O	O	O	N	C	O	O	N	7	2
George. M. H.	20. 7.65	f	O	O	N	O	N	N	N	C	N	C	C	C	3	4
Green, M. T.	4. 1.66	f	O	O	N	O	N	N	N	N	N	O	C	C	3	4
Griffith, R. K.	9.10.65	m	O	O	O	O	O	N	C	N	C	C	C	N	4	3
Hagen, G. H.	16. 8.65	m	O	O	O	O	O	N	N	N	C	O	O	N	7	2
Jackson, B. D.	13.10.65	f	O	O	O	O	N	N	C	C	C	O	N	C	5	4
Kennedy, J. L.	4. 4.65	m	O	O	O	O	O	N	C	N	C	C	N	N	5	3
Lucas, J. J.	19. 5.65	m	O	O	O	O	N	N	C	C	C	C	O	N	5	4
Martin. F. J.	12. 9.65	f	O	O	O	N	O	N	C	N	C	C	C	C	4	5

Fig. 4.4 List 3: individual student records showing the examinations taken by each student

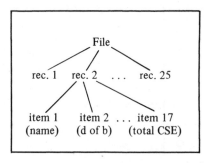

```
Item 1:   name of child

    2:    date of birth

    3:    sex of child

4 – 15:   a C indicates the subject is
          taken at CSE, an O at O-level,
          N means not taken.

   16:    total number of examinations
          to be taken at O-level

   17:    total number of examinations
          to be taken at CSE level
```

Fig. 4.5

```
                File
          /      |      \
     rec. 1   rec. 2  ...  rec. 25
          \      |      \
     item 1   item 2 ...  item 17
     (name)  (d of b)    (total CSE)
```

Fig. 4.6

Computer Hardware

Another important consideration for anyone responsible for computerising a data processing application is the actual equipment to be used. At the heart of the computer hardware there will be the central processing unit, but the actual input and output devices will influence the way in which the information is prepared and the way in which the results are eventually presented. Sometimes one has no choice. If you have access to a computer, you will have to use whatever I/O and secondary storage devices are available. Usually, the larger the computer installation, the more choice the user will have.

Let us imagine in our case that the school has its own micro-computer with a teletypewriter, a VDU screen and keyboard as I/O devices, and a floppy-disc drive for secondary storage. This would be quite a luxurious hardware *system* (that is the collection of hardware units) for most schools today but one which could be within the grasp of most schools in a few years time. The VDU can be used for both input and output of information in situations where no permanent copy is required. The teletypewriter can be used for both input and output of information when it is necessary to retain a printed (**hardcopy**) record of whatever has been entered into or output from the micro-computer. The floppy-disc will provide external storage for all programs and files of data. The hardware is illustrated in Figure 4.7.

Now that the teacher has decided what is required from the computer and knows the equipment available, the next phase of the work, namely how to achieve the objectives, can begin. In this step, an important consideration is the data itself and in particular how it is to be organised. Note that so far we have not yet considered the program. Programs are written to work upon data. If we do not know how the data is to be organised then it is quite pointless to try to write the program. Thus, the next section is devoted to the data itself and how it is going to be arranged. This phase is sometimes called the **data creation phase.**

Data Creation

Since three lists are going to be produced by

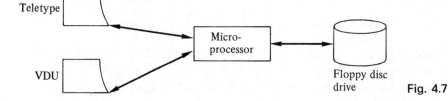

Teletype

VDU

Micro-processor

Floppy disc drive

Fig. 4.7

the computer program, a simple approach would be for the teacher to prepare three sets of data, each one corresponding to Figures 4.2, 4.3 and 4.4. But if this is done, the teacher duplicates the names, dates of birth and the sex of the students in lists 2 and 3, thus wasting time and effort as well as wasting storage space in the floppy-disc by having repeated information. Furthermore, the teacher may just as well have used an ordinary typewriter to type the output lists. Computers are meant to save time and effort and so this very simple approach does not make much sense.

A better approach is to give the computer one set of information from which it can generate all the required information. If we look more closely at the information in the three lists, we see that the only information the computer program needs is

1) The names of the 25 students
2) The dates of birth
3) The sex of each student
4) Whether a student is taking or not taking a given examination
5) The names of the twelve subjects and whether each one can be taken at O-level only, CSE level only, or at both levels.

From this information alone, the computer via the program is able to produce the three lists and to perform all the necessary totalling. It would be pointless for the teacher to add up all the totals when the computer can be made to do this much more quickly and accurately.

The problem which faces all designers of any data processing application is how to arrange or organise the necessary input data in some meaningful manner. In our case, the teacher will have to create an input data file consisting of a series of twenty-five records, one for each student, with each record containing the fifteen items of information as required in 1–4 above. Figure 4.8 shows one possible arrangement.

Organising data into meaningful information, i.e. creating items within a record, is not as straightforward as one might think. For example, let us consider how to enter one of the items of data, the date of birth. Dates may be

Item 1	2	3	4	5	6	7	8	9	10	11	12	13	14	15
Name of pupil	Date of birth	Sex	Eng. gr.	Eng. lit.	Hist.	Geog.	Fren.	Germ.	Chem.	Biol.	Phys.	Math.	C/std.	H/Econ
Allen, J. T.	21.12.64	m	O	O	O	O	O	N	C	N	C	C	O	N
...														
Martin, F. J.	12. 9.65	f	O	O	O	N	O	N	C	N	F	C	C	C

File

Fig. 4.8 Input data per student O ≡ O-level; C ≡ CSE; N ≡ exam not taken

12.10.24
12/10/24
12th Oct 1924
12th October 1924
12-10-24
12 10 24

24-10-12[†]

[†] The USA manner in which the year is given first, then the month, then the day, i.e. the reverse of the British method.

Fig. 4.9

A field is the place which will contain one item of data. Since our record has fifteen items, it will have fifteen fields. It is easy to confuse the two terms item and field, but if we think about a similar situation brought up in Chapter 1, where we discussed an *address* and the *contents* of an address, we ought not to get the two confused. The term "field" can be likened to the address of a location in central memory; the term "item" to the contents of an address location.

It is common to turn one of the fields into what is called a **key-field** or *key*. The purpose of the key is to enable one particular record in a file to be found. In our file, for example, there are twenty-five records. How can we find one of the records, say the record belonging to Carr, M.B. (that is the 5th record)? In a manual system, we simply pick up the first record and look at the name. If it is Carr, M. B., then we know that we have found the record. If it is not the name we require, then we go to the second record and again look at the name field to see if it corresponds to the name we are looking for. This procedure is repeated until we find a *match* between the name we are looking for and the name in the name field of a record. What we are doing is to use the name field as a key in order to find a particular record.

In a computerised system, a similar procedure is adopted. One of the fields is used as a means of identifying a record. This field then is used as the key or identification of the entire record. Often one of several fields can be used for the key, but in most cases one field presents itself as being more suitable than any other. Thus, for our records, the most obvious field is the name field. The date of birth field could have been used but in practice would be less appropriate. Figure 4.10 illustrates the key–field.

written in many ways, a few are given in Figure 4.9. Whatever method is chosen for one record will have to be adopted for *all* the records in a file. Remember that a program works on the data of every record and therefore it expects the data to be consistent. If a program expects the date to be in "day–month–year" format, then it would be pointless to have this data entered in the American fashion for some records since these, being the wrong way round, would produce an incorrect data. Thus, 12–10–24 is the 12th October, 1924 in the British fashion, but 24th October, 1912 in the American. Furthermore, if the month is given as a number, 1 to 12, then the program is written in such a way as to expect a number. If a word version of the month suddenly appears in one of the records, then the program would not be able to recognise the month.

Let us now work out in detail how we shall arrange each item in our record. The basic structure of the input data record has already been designed in Figure 4.8. Each record has fifteen items. We now meet another term, **field**.

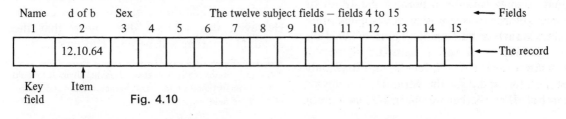

Fig. 4.10

Subject Field

The length of any record depends upon the total number of characters used to describe each item. In the case of our record each of the subject fields has to indicate whether the subject is to be taken at CSE or O–level or whether the subject is not to be taken at all. If we simply insert the character C for CSE, this will reduce the number of spaces required from three to one; the character O can stand for O–level; and the character N, in place of the word NO, to show that the subject is not to be taken. Thus, only one space is needed for each of the subject fields instead of sometimes three (CSE) or sometimes two (NO). Not only does this save space on the secondary storage device but it also reduces the time spent in preparing the records. The C, O or N forms the data but the information which this data supplies is whether an individual subject is to be taken or not, and at which level.

A similar approach can be adopted for the sex field (field 3). We could go to the trouble of writing out "male" or "female" and of having to reserve six spaces in each sex field for the six characters of "female". But if we use the characters M for male and F for female, then only one space need be reserved.

Date Field

Space can be saved in this field too if we write the date in numerals rather than with letters. Furthermore, let us agree that we shall adopt the British method of putting the day first followed by the month and finally the year. Thus 20.12.24 means the 20th December, 1924. One nice point here is that we can ignore the digits 19 in the year since no student in the class could possibly have been born in the 1800s or in the 2000s. Thus, for the date we use only eight characters and employ periods or full-stops between each set of digits, i.e. there will be 2 digits for the day, 2 for the month, 2 only for the year, and 2 for the periods†. If a day or month is below 10, then we shall use a blank (i.e. a space) character for the leftmost digit or a leading zero. Thus 19th June, 1978 becomes 19. 6.78 or 19.06.78.

Name Field

Like dates, names can be written in one of many ways (a few are shown in Figure 4.11). We shall have to decide on one method. Initials rather than full Christian names will be adopted and the surname will precede the initials, thus, Evans, D. T. However, unlike the data held in other fields, we cannot tell exactly how many characters each name will contain. The name above has ten characters but Macmillan, J. P. has fifteen.

David Thomas Evans
Evans, David, Thomas
Evans, D.T
D.T.Evans
Evans   D.T.

Fig. 4.11

This raises a problem frequently faced by data preparation designers. In some cases, the data in a field is of *variable* length (as with names and addresses). Designers have two main methods of solving this problem. First, they can allocate a sufficient number of spaces to accommodate the longest name (or address) possible; in our case, we could allow a maximum of twenty spaces for the name. This is the simplest solution whereby the entire field is of a **fixed length**, but it can be wasteful in space because, even if a name does not require twenty spaces, the field will have been allocated twenty. A name which uses only nine characters will have to leave the additional eleven spaces unused. However, this solution does mean that the eventual program will be easier to write.

---

† Are the periods really necessary? Leaving them out would reduce even further the number of characters input and the size of the date field.

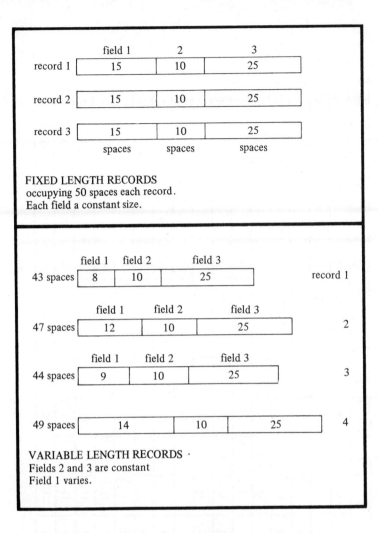

FIXED LENGTH RECORDS
occupying 50 spaces each record.
Each field a constant size.

VARIABLE LENGTH RECORDS ·
Fields 2 and 3 are constant
Field 1 varies.

Fig. 4.12

The alternative solution is to use as many characters per name as required. This will result in each name field in each record having a different or **variable length** (see Figure 4.12). This certainly avoids wasting space in storage but at the expense of having to make the program more complicated.

Whichever solution is chosen depends upon whether it is more important to save space or to write less-complicated programs. The latter should always be favoured wherever possible. In our design we shall have fixed-length records and less-complicated programs. Each record will occupy forty-one spaces.

Item 1	Name field	20 spaces
Item 2	Date of birth field	8 spaces
Item 3	Sex field	1 space
Items 4–15	Subject field	12×1 space
	Total	41 spaces

Our input file will look like the illustration in Figure 4.13. Many other arrangements are possible. This one was chosen more for its simplicity than for any other quality and contains twenty-five records, one for each student. However, as yet we have not supplied the names of

15 fields holding items of information

Name of pupil	Date of birth	Sex	Eng. gr.	Eng. lit.	Hist.	Geog.	Fren.	Germ.	Chem.	Biol.	Phys.	Math.	C/std.	H.Econ.
Allen, J. T.	21.12.64	m	O	O	O	O	O	N	C	N	C	O	O	N
Archer, D.	3. 6.65	m	O	O	O	O	N	N	C	C	C	O	O	N
Brown, P. J.	24. 5.65	f	O	O	O	O	N	N	C	N	N	C	C	C
Butler, R. R.	14. 4.65	m	O	O	O	O	N	N	C	N	C	C	C	N
Carr, M. B.	12.12.65	f	O	O	N	O	O	N	C	C	C	O	C	C
Carter, P. T.	5. 7.65	m	O	O	O	O	N	N	C	N	C	C	N	N
Clark, R. V.	10.10.65	m	O	O	O	O	N	N	C	N	N	C	N	N
Cripps, M.	28.12.64	m	O	O	O	N	O	O	C	C	N	O	N	N
Davidson, T. K.	26. 8.65	f	O	O	O	O	N	N	C	N	C	C	N	C
Davies, R. L.	15. 9.65	f	O	O	O	O	O	O	C	C	C	O	O	C
Evans, D. T.	6. 6.65	m	O	O	O	N	N	N	N	C	C	C	N	N
Ewins, D. F.	19. 9.65	m	O	O	O	N	N	N	C	C	C	O	O	N
Farmer, J. F.	23. 8.65	f	O	O	O	N	N	N	C	C	C	C	N	C
Farrel, G. K.	30.10.65	f	O	O	O	O	N	N	C	C	C	O	O	C
Freeman, T. H.	24. 9.65	m	O	O	O	O	N	N	N	C	C	O	C	N
Fuller, L. J.	27. 7.65	m	O	O	N	O	N	N	N	N	N	C	C	N
Gale, D. J.	16. 5.65	m	O	O	N	O	O	O	N	C	C	O	O	C
George, M. H.	20. 7.65	f	O	O	Ń	O	N	N	N	C	C	O	C	C
Green, M. T.	4. 1.66	f	O	O	N	O	N	N	N	N	C	C	C	C
Griffith, R. K.	9.10.65	m	O	O	O	O	O	N	C	C	C	O	O	N
Hagen, G. H.	16. 8.65	m	O	O	O	O	N	N	C	N	C	O	O	C
Jackson, B. D.	13.10.65	f	O	O	O	O	O	N	C	C	C	O	C	C
Kennedy, J. L.	4. 4.65	m	O	O	O	O	O	N	C	N	C	O	N	N
Lucas, J. J.	19. 5.65	m	O	O	O	O	N	N	C	N	C	C	N	N
Martin, F. J.	12. 9.65	f	O	O	O	N	O	N	C	N	C	C	C	C

25 records forming the actual input file

Fig. 4.13 Input data file 1

Subject number	Subject name	Level
4	English grammar	1
5	English literature	1
6	History	1
7	Geography	1
8	French	1
9	German	1
10	Chemistry	2
11	Biology	2
12	Physics	2
13	Mathematics	3
14	Computer studies	3
15	Home economics	2

Fig. 4.14   Subject names; input data file 2
1≡O-level; 2≡CSE; 3≡both O and CSE

the twelve subjects or whether that subject is taken at O or CSE level.

There are various ways of presenting this information. One way is to enlarge the original input data file by supplying the information there. But this means repeating the names of the twelve subjects for each record. Another method is to create a second input file (see Figure 4.14). This file will consist of 12 records, one for each subject; each record contains three items and therefore three fields.

Field 1 contains a number between 4 and 15, field 2 the name of the subject, the third field indicates whether the subject is O–level or CSE level or both. Notice that in this third field the character 1 stands for O–level, 2 for CSE, and 3 is used to indicate that the subject can be taken at either level. We could have used three separate fields to represent this last bit of information, one for each situation, resulting in a record with five fields. However by adopting our simple technique we need only three fields for our record, making use of one field to indicate one of three possibilities. This is quite a common technique amongst data preparation designers.

What is the purpose of the subject number field? Somehow we need to link the fields 4 to 15 of the input data file 1 to the names of the subjects supplied in the input data file 2 since the names of the subjects are not included in the first data input file. The item in field 1 of the second data input file can do this. The program will have to be written in such a way that it can cross-reference information between the two input files. Thus, item 4 of the *first* input file relates to the subject name in the *second* input data file with the number 4 in the subject number field. Item 5 of the first file relates to the subject numbered 5 in the second input file, and so on. Figure 4.15 shows how this cross-referencing takes place.

From these two files, the program can select all the information it needs to produce the final output lists. The number of spaces shown below are reserved for each item of data in input file 2. Thus each record will require twenty-one spaces. Note that again we have used a fixed length record by reserving a maximum of eighteen spaces for item 2, since the longest subject name is "English Literature".

Input date file 2—Subject Information
Item 1—Subject number field—maximum of two characters   2 spaces
Item 2—Subject name field—maximum of 18 characters   18 spaces
Item 3—Subject level field—one character   1 space
Total   21 spaces

INPUT FILE

Item 1	2	3	4	5	6	7	8	9	10	11	12	13	14	15
Name of pupil	Date of birth	Sex	Eng. gr.	Eng. lit.	Hist.	Geog.	Fren.	Germ.	Chem.	Biol.	Phys.	Math.	C/std.	H/Econ
Allen, J. T.	21.12.64	m	O	O	O	O	O	N	C	N	C	O	O	N
Martin, F. J.	12. 9.65	f	O	O	O	N	O	N	C	N	C	C	C	C

SUBJECT NUMBER FILE (INPUT FILE 2)

Item 1	Item 2	Item 3
Subject number	Subject name	Level
4	English grammar	1
5	English literature	1
6	History	1
7	Geography	1
8	French	1
9	German	1
10	Chemistry	2
11	Biology	2
12	Physics	2
13	Mathematics	3
14	Computer studies	3
15	Home economics	2

Fig. 4.15 Cross-reference between subject fields of input file 1 and the subject number and subject name fields of input file 2

Input Device for Data Preparation

The teacher is now in a position to move on to another phase, that of collecting and preparing the data for computer entry. If our input device had been a card reader, then the input would be punched onto cards. But our micro-system does not have a card reader, only a teletype-writer and a VDU. If the teletype has a paper-tape attachment, then the teacher has a choice of preparing data onto paper-tape or of directly inputting data via the keyboard of the teletype or the VDU. The former would be an example of *indirect data preparation* since, having punched off-line all the data onto paper-tape (i.e. step one), the tape itself would then have to be fed through the teletype paper-tape attachment for entry into the storage device, i.e. resulting in a second step. But if the keyboard is used, only one step is involved. As each item of a record is typed in (called **keying in**), it will be stored immediately or *directly* onto the storage device, namely a track on the floppy disc. The choice will depend on the individual preference.

The Systems Analyst

Having designed the output list required from the computer, designed the input files and prepared the data, the teacher can now set about writing the actual program itself. This stage does not concern us in this chapter since it requires a detailed knowledge of programming. We are interested only in the application itself and have been considering the actual design of the input files and the method of preparing data. In fact what we have done so far has a technical name. It is called **systems analysis** and we can discuss this in a little more depth later on. The *systems analyst*, the name given to the designer who has prepared all this work, would at this stage pass on the details of the files (both output and input) to a programmer who would study the details and then write the program or programs which will achieve the objectives. In other words, the systems analyst in normal circumstances does not become involved in writing the actual programs.

Let us assume that the programmer has now completed his program. His next step is to find out whether the program works correctly. He will use a set of input data very similar to the real input data files, except that this set of data is usually much smaller and will have been provided by the systems analyst. The systems analyst will have worked out the expected results in advance by hand from this smaller set of data. The computer will process this so-called **test data** and produce results. The output from the computer is then compared with the known results. If both sets of results are the same, then the programmer knows that the program must be working correctly and the program can be released to process the real data. If the two sets do not match, then the program will have to be corrected.

This may seem to be a lengthy procedure but it should be remembered that a program is written to be used time and time again, especially a data processing program. A *payroll program* for example is used every week to prepare the weekly salaries of the employees of a company. Even our own application can be used each year by the teacher and therefore it is most important to make certain that it works correctly. If it does, the same program can be used again to work on a different set of similar data.

Figure 4.16 shows the various stages we have discussed. In practice, professional data processing personnel may follow a slightly different order, but nevertheless the six steps shown illustrate the various stages in the design of any computer application.

Figure 4.17 shows the input files to the program and the output files (or lists) expected in our student examination application. This is a typical example of the diagrams which a systems analyst will have to produce and eventually show to the programmer responsible for writing the program and is called a *systems chart*.

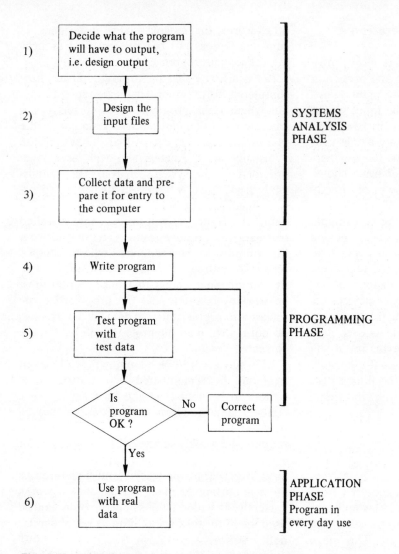

Fig. 4.16   Design stages of a computer application

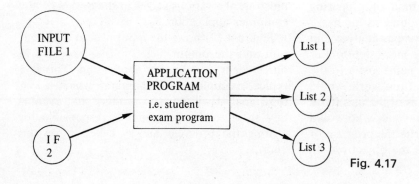

Fig. 4.17

Updating

This is by no means the end of our study. All we have really discussed so far is the *creation* stage of the application. There is another stage which we have yet to discuss which will have to take into account any possible changes to the original input data. For example, suppose that another pupil joins the class. His record will have to be prepared and added to the original input file 1. Again, it is possible that some pupils may decide to alter their original choice of examination subjects. In both situations, the original input file will have to be amended or, to use the data processing term, **updated**. Input files can be updated (really meaning "brought up–to-date") in several ways.

In the case of our application the simplest and easiest method would be for the teacher to make the alterations by hand. To do this means having to retrieve the input file from the storage diskette and then having to select the record which needs changing. The new information can then be added and the application program re-run to produce a new set of output lists. This procedure is quite simple since the teacher can select and make changes to any record by a special program called an **edit program**. These are supplied by the manufacturers of computers for this type of activity.

In the case of a new pupil, the records will now number twenty-six. If the teacher had written the program to accept only twenty-five records, then the program will have to be amended. This of course would be inconvenient to say the least. But if the teacher anticipated the possibility of new pupils arriving, then the program would have been written in such a way that it could cope with more than twenty-five student records. Any good systems analyst will always be able to anticipate such possible events and will provide the programmer with these details so that the program will be made as flexible as possible. This is one of the secrets of writing successful programs.

However, in most data processing applications, where many records need changing frequently, it is not convenient to update input records in such a manner via an editing program. Instead, a special program will be written which will perform all updating tasks. First, all the amendments are collected together into one file. This file together with the original input file become the two input files for the "updating program". This procedure is shown in Figure 4.18. Note that the update program can be made to output reports on to the line printer so that up-to-date information can be inspected by the management. In addition, any incorrect data from the amendment file could be reported at this time and corrected later by the data preparation staff.

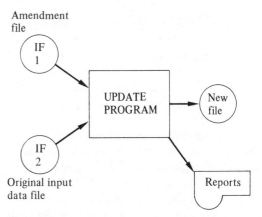

Amendment file

Original input data file

Fig. 4.18

The update program will amend the original input file according to the data in the amendment file and produce as its output a new updated input file. It will be this new file which becomes the input file for the main application program to work on. This process is quite sophisticated, and professional data processing personnel spend several years learning the art. We can do little here except to appreciate some of the basic ideas.

A More Realistic Data Processing Application

The example of student examination records was a simple one and has been useful in introducing many of the basic ideas and terms used

Item										
1	2	3	4	5	6	7	8	9	10	11
Name	Address	d of b	Sex	Relgn.	Illness	Doctor's name	Ward	Date of entry	Date of leaving	Outpatient clinic

Fig. 4.19

in data processing. Now we shall take a more realistic application in order to introduce some other features. Consider a hospital which has computerised its records on patients. Each patient will need a record as outlined in Figure 4.19, where eleven fields containing relevant items of information are shown. In practice much more information will be recorded but for our purposes this would become difficult to consider in detail. Clearly, the hospital will need to record the name and address of each patient, the sex, age and religion; the nature of the patient's illness, the name of the ward, and the name of the attending doctor; the date when the patient entered hospital as well as the date of leaving (this latter field will of course be left blank if the patient is still in hospital); and, finally, whether the patient has to return to the hospital for follow-up treatment as an outpatient. For simplicity, we shall choose a small hospital with 200 beds. The patients' file will however contain more than 200 records since hospitals keep records of those patients who have left the hospital.

Furthermore, the file will have to be updated each week since new patients will enter the hospital frequently. The files will be held on secondary storage so that whenever lists are required they can be found or retrieved at once. The main patient file shown in Figure 4.19 is often called the **master file** since it contains all the relevant information. From this one input file many different lists can be produced. For example,

A list of all patients in the hospital—for the administration staff.

A list of all patients under a particular doctor—for the doctors concerned.

A list of all patients in a given ward—for the ward sisters.

A list of all the patients attending outpatients—for the sister in charge of the outpatients clinic.

A list of all patients with a particular illness and whether they are currently in hospital—for statistics.

A list of all patients in the hospital of a given religion—for the religious ministers; and so on.

The program will be written so that whichever list is required can be produced from the master file. For example, to get a list of patients currently in a given ward, the program will have to look at item 8. If the ward name is the same as the one required, the other relevant information can be extracted such as the name and possibly the address of the patient, the illness, the name of the attending doctor, religion, etc. However, before printing out such details, the date of the patient's leaving hospital will have to be looked at, item 10. If this is blank then the patient is still in hospital and therefore the details can be printed. But if it is not blank, then the patient has left hospital and the details will not be required by the ward sister.

A list of all patients with a given illness can be printed out by the program by comparing item 6. Such a list would need the patient's name and address, the doctor's name, the ward name, whether the patient is still in hospital or has left, and if so whether he/she has to attend the outpatient's clinic.

Clearly, this master file contains details not only of the patients in hospital at any given date but also of those who have previously been in hospital. This list could become very large over a number of years and eventually contain more past patients than current patients, thus making the search for current patients a rather long process. If it is necessary to keep details of past

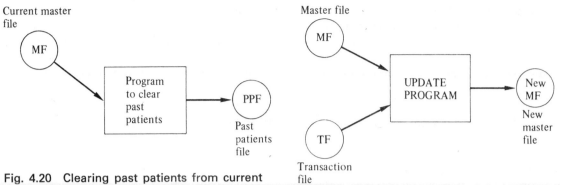

Fig. 4.20   Clearing past patients from current master file

Fig. 4.21   Creating a new master file

patients on this master file for only one year, then periodically another program will have to look at item 10 and remove those patient records whose date of leaving hospital exceeds one year. Since all hospitals have to keep records of past patients for much longer than one year, these records will have to be kept on another file which we can call the "past patients file". This process is illustrated in Figure 4.20 and would probably take place at monthly intervals. Thus, if the record of a patient who was in hospital over a year ago was required, then the past patients file would have to be searched.

Now let us turn to the problem of updating the master file. Each week, as new patients arrive and existing patients leave, new records will have to be made out and old ones amended. These will be collected together into what is called officially a **transaction file** but is the same as the amendment file of Figure 4.18. The updating program will now update the master file with the information in the *transaction* file to produce a new master file (see Figure 4.21). It will be from this new master file that current and up-to-date information is produced for any of the lists.

From this example of patients' records, we are now in a position to understand the term **information retrieval** used frequently in data processing. All this term means is that information can be retrieved from one or more data files held in the computer's storage system. Usually, the term refers to specialised applications

which require an immediate answer to a given enquiry. For example, in the hospital patients system, a doctor may require details concerning a particular patient. The doctor will type in the patient's name, and the computer program(s) will search for and output all information concerning that patient. Air-line reservation and library and banking systems are other examples.

Note that not every commercial application is an information retrieval system. A payroll system which generates weekly payslips, gas and electricity billing systems, stock-taking, etc. could not be called information retrieval systems.

The subject of information retrieval then is concerned with the methods and procedures for extracting information from files. Two important considerations are: first the way in which the data is arranged or structured in the file(s); and secondly, the speed at which the programs can produce the required information. Further discussion on this aspect of data processing is beyond the scope of this text and is more applicable to data processing professionals.

Data and Files

Preparation of Data

Without data, programs would have nothing to work on and it should be obvious by now that the process of collecting and preparing data

113

forms an important phase of any data processing application. In many organisations where there is much data to prepare, a team of people known as data preparation staff are employed. Either they will transcribe data onto punch cards or paper tape, or, as is becoming increasingly popular, enter data directly from a keyboard onto some secondary storage device such as magnetic disc (or the smaller floppy disc) or magnetic tape via key–to–disc or key–to–tape devices.

In order to reduce mistakes when entering data in this fashion, most of the key–to–disc or key–to–tape devices have a screen similar to a television screen. Every item of data typed at the keyboard is shown on the screen. If any mistakes are noticed they can be corrected by re-typing the data. Another method is to have a program which can *prompt* or *cue* the operator for the required data. This special cuing program knows exactly what data items have to be entered. It will produce a short statement or prompt, and wait for the operator to enter the data. Figure 4.22 illustrates this in relation to the patients' records application. Usually, the prompt will be in capital letters, whilst the data supplied by the operator will be in small letters.

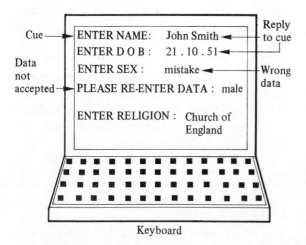

Fig. 4.22   Prompt example

However, mistakes can still be made even when checking by sight or in response to cues because the human operator may become dis-

tracted or begin to lose concentration, especially when large volumes of data have to be entered. The prompt program can therefore be made to perform another task, namely to check the validity of the data entered. For example, in reply to the prompt ENTER SEX the only two answers possible are "male" or "female" (or m and f). If any other character(s) is given then the program can reject the data and issue another cue such as PLEASE RE-ENTER DATA.

Some items cannot be checked by the program in this way as in the case of names and addresses. Any errors that do arise in these instances will only be discovered at some later stage (if at all!). But most items can be verified in some way. Dates of birth can be checked to make sure that no ridiculous age is given, such as a person being born well over a hundred years ago, or born *after* the present date. The computer could have a list of all the doctors' names, ward names, illnesses, etc. If an answer is given to any of these which is not contained in the computer's lists, then a reply can be given by the validating program to that effect and issue a request for the data to be re-entered. With both the human operator and the computer program checking the data, many mistakes can be eradicated, thereby reducing the danger of incorrect data entering the computer storage.

In the case of the student examination application, the teacher did not have a cuing program which would also check data, but it is possible to write a program which would "look at" every data item in either the transaction file or the original input file or both and perform some validation on it. As we have said, names are difficult to verify, but if the computer produced a record for every student, the teacher could pass these onto each student and let them verify the information. Any mistakes would be reported and the records updated in the manner already described. Dates of birth can easily be checked by the validation program to see that they lie within a certain range. Since each student will be about fifteen years old, the year of birth must be approximately fifteen less than the current year. Thus if the current year is 1980, then the year of birth is approximately 1965. The program can check, therefore, that the year of birth is not less than 1964 and not greater than 1966. Such a check, and a simple one at that, which does not demand any great programming skill, can reduce errors in dates of birth.

Even results produced by the application program can be checked by the program itself. For example, the final total of examinations taken by any one student cannot be greater than 12 since there are only twelve subjects. Here again by making sure that every total lies within the range of 1 and 12, any silly errors produced by the program can be detected and reported. Many of us know the story of the electricity bill for £1 million being sent out to a householder and other stories of bills for £0.0 being repeatedly sent out and payment demanded within seven days. Now if the program which produced these bills had a simple check to see that all bills lay within a given range of possible amounts, then these silly errors could not have occurred.

We have discussed two stages at which errors can be discovered. Errors in data are discovered by a **data validation run** before the application program processes any data. The second stage at which errors can be detected is during the processing of data by the application program, perhaps as a result of invalid data not being detected during the validation run. The point to make here is that any self-respecting data processing application should always involve *both* stages, one on the data itself, the other on the results produced. This will mean, of course, an increase in the time taken to run the application as well as in programming effort.

It is perhaps convenient at this time to point out that it is the comparison-type operations of a programming language which allow programmers to check data and results. In Basic the IF...THEN or IF...GOTO type statements are examples which make use of the "greater than", "not equal to" comparisons mentioned in Chapter 1 and Chapter 2.

Security of Files

Having gone to the trouble of writing programs and creating data files it would be disastrous if they were to be lost. This can happen! Computers are machines and like other pieces of equipment can develop faults. Also they can break down as a result of external forces such as a sudden outbreak of fire, loss of electricity due to power cuts, or even floods or bomb attacks. For this reason precautions have to be taken to ensure that, in the event of a failure, data files and programs are not totally lost or destroyed. One of the commonest methods is the **ancestral file system** which applies to data files rather than to programs.

Let us return to Figure 4.21 where we saw that the new master file was generated by both the old master file and the current transaction file which contained all the updating information. Let us call the old master file, file X and the new master file, file Y. In ancestral terminology the old master file (X) is called the *father* file and the new file (Y) the *son*. If the father file is kept together with the transaction file after the son has been created, then should the son be destroyed or lost in any way, it can be re-generated by simply repeating the process which created it in the first place. At a later stage when another transaction file is created to update the son (file Y), the new master file generated will now be called the son (file Z), the previous son (file Y) will now become the father, and the old father (file X) will now become the grandfather. Hence the term ancestral files. Figure 4.23, illustrates this process with files X, Y and Z.

In this way should both the son and the father be destroyed or corrupted, the grandfather file X together with the transaction file can re-generate the father file; and the father file together with its transaction file can re-generate the son, file Z. It is seldom necessary to go back more than two generations, and consequently in due course the present grandfather file can be taken out of service. If it is on a magnetic tape, the tape can be re-cycled.

In addition to ancestral files, it is sensible and

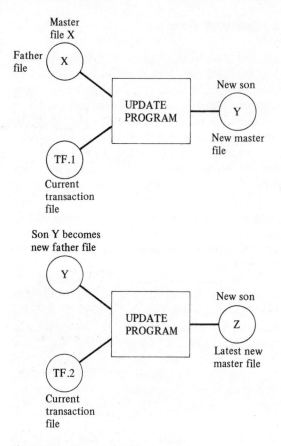

Fig. 4.23   Ancestral files

again a common method to have more than one copy of a file or program. If we have a particular cassette tape containing our favourite music which we would not want to lose, we sometimes go to the trouble of copying the contents onto another cassette. If we ever lose the first then we have another copy. This precaution can be taken into the data processing field and is especially useful with long and complicated programs. For example there should always be several copies of the compiler program (the translator of high-level languages, see Chapter 2), each held on different storage devices preferably, since it would cause untold chaos if the one and only copy was ever lost. In some cases where the program or even data is especially important, different copies are actually held in different buildings so that in the event of fire,

flood or bombing, the other copies can still be accessed. Air-line reservation systems often go to such lengths to preserve their highly expensive files.

Certain sensitive information held in a computer's storage area which can be accessed by more than one person may have to be protected from unauthorised people. For example, if our teacher wished to keep records of his students' progress, he would probably not wish any of the students to be able to see the information. How can this be kept secret? For those who have used a computer terminal system, they know how easy it is to call up a data file from storage and ask for the information in the file to be shown on the VDU screen or printed out by the teletype. Each data file has a unique name to distinguish it from other files held on the same storage medium. By typing in the name of the file, together with a special command such as GET, "filename", that file can be selected from all the others. Another command such as LIST, "filename" will then list the contents of the file. But by attaching a password to the name of the file, only those who know the password and type it out will be allowed to have access to that file of information. Thus, instead of merely typing, GET, "filename", one now has to type in GET, "filename, password" where "password" is a set of characters known only to the creator of the file. Of course, if the password becomes generally known, then anyone can read the information in that file. So it is up to the creator of a file of sensitive data to keep the password secret and in this way be sure that only he can have access to the information in the file.

Searching, Sorting and Merging Files

So far we have said little about the programmer's involvement in typical data processing applications. One reason for this is that it is an area which rightly belongs to specialists who have to spend several years learning their skill. Consequently, we can only discuss briefly some of the techniques used. To help us do this let us think back to the two examples illustrated in this chapter. Essentially, both application programs are simply "looking at" the data files and compiling information from them in various ways. The student examination application produces three lists. But the program could quite easily be extended to produce other information (other lists) without the original input data files having to be increased. A list of all the girls in the class or a list of all the boys could be output rather than the combined list of Figure 4.4. All that would be involved in programming terms is to organise a **search** through the input file to "look at" item 3 (the sex field) in each record. If this field contained an f for female then the required details held in the other fields could be printed out. This ability to search files forms an essential activity of most commercial application programs. Some arithmetic may be performed, such as the total number of students taking each examination, or the classical payroll program which computes employees' salaries.

In the main it is simply this ability of the computer to compile many and varied lists from a basic set of input data that makes it so useful. The patients' records application is a good case. Six different lists can be produced very quickly and efficiently from the input file. Were these lists to be done by clerical staff the time and effort involved would be far greater.

However, because input data files have to be updated every so often, other data processing programs have to perform two other tasks. In the student examination example it was noted that the teacher had to add another record to the existing input file. But where should the new record be put? Suppose the new student's name is Jones, F. E. To retain the alphabetical order of the input file, this record should be placed between record 22 (Jackson) and record 23 (Kennedy). It is not possible to insert it without re-arranging the existing order of the file. This is a common situation in most commercial applications and is solved by having a special program called a **sort/merge program**. As shown in Figure 4.24, the sort/merge program produces a re-arranged or sorted master file from the data given in the transaction file.

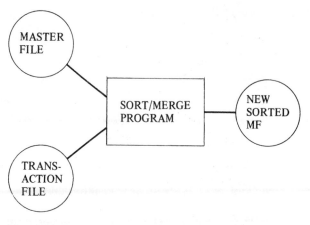

Fig. 4.24

The original data in the master file can be re-arranged in whatever way the application demands. In the student examination application, the sort will be based on an alphabetical arrangement so that Jones's record will become number 23, following on from Jackson's record, Kennedy will now become number 24, Lucas 25 and Martin 26.

The sort procedure in our simple example will be based upon the characters or letters of each student's name. This involves comparing the starting letter of each name to see if it equals the J of Jones. When the procedure comes to Jackson, both starting letters are the same and, so, the second letters will have to be compared to determine which is the lower (i.e. nearer to the beginning of the alphabet). Alphabetical comparisons are time consuming, and in practice most records make use of numbers for their key field since they are quicker and easier to compare. Thus, a more realistic patients' record system would give each hospital patient a number and any sorting would be based on this number instead of the patient's name as we have implied (see Figure 4.25). A payroll file would similarly have an employee's number as the key field to individual records.

Sorting becomes quite a complex procedure when files are too large to be held at one time in the computer's main memory. Usually, the sort program will read in as many records as the main storage permits. These are sorted internally and written out to a temporary storage

Field 1	2	3	4	5	6	7	8	9	10	11	12
Patient hosp. no.	Name	Address	d of b	Sex	Relgn.	Illness	Dr.'s name	Ward	Date of entry	Date of leaving	Outpatient clinic

↑
Key field

Fig. 4.25 Patient's records with numerical key field

area on disc or to a magnetic tape. The next block of records are then read into main memory, sorted and written out to another part of secondary storage. The process continues until the entire file has been partially sorted in this manner and will require the use of two or more temporary or intermediate work tapes or disc areas containing many series of partially sequenced records. It now remains for these series to be **merged** together, probably involving several partial merges before the final re-sorted file is formed. The more tape drives or discs available, the faster the sort and merge phases. So we can conclude this section by noting that commercial programs perform three main types of activity on files of data: searching files to provide required information; and sorting and merging data files to produce updated files for the main application program to work on.

Random and Serial Access to Records

Certain commercial applications process all the records of a file at one run. Thus, a payroll program has to process each record since each employee wishes to receive his/her salary. Other applications may wish to select only one or two records from a data file. Thus if details of only one patient are required from the patients' input file, all the others are ignored. If the file is held on a disc storage medium, then it is possible to locate that one record straight away. But if the storage medium is magnetic tape then it will be necessary to look at each record in turn until the required one is found. The first method is called **direct access** or **random access**, since the arrangement of records on a disc

allows individual records to be located directly or at random. The second method is called **sequential access** or **serial access**, since the only way to get to record 21 is by first going through all the previous 20 records. Chapter 3 discussed this in more detail but it should be pointed out here that the designer of a computerised system needs to consider the type of storage medium required by the application. Magnetic tapes are cheap, but slower for applications which only need to access a few records in an entire input file. Discs are much faster for direct accessing of individual records but are much more expensive devices than magnetic tapes. Cost and performance have to be weighed by any designer of a commercial system, i.e. the systems analyst.

Systems Analysis

We have already used the term *systems analysis* earlier in this chapter to refer to the process of designing a computerised application. When a company decides that it might like to computerise some part of its commercial activity (the payroll system, the invoicing procedures, the control of stock, etc.) computing specialists called *systems analysts* are consulted. These people may actually be employed by the company if it is a large organisation or they may come from consultancy firms who specialise in such work. There are two stages in the work of a systems analyst. First, the analyst performs a detailed analysis of the existing system in operation and, secondly, designs a computerised system based upon the analysis. Thus the term itself is a little misleading since there is much more than merely analysing the system.

Today it is accepted that there are two types of systems analyst. The **business analyst** who understands the business side of the commercial world and specifies the design of the system; and the **technical analyst** who takes the design specification and assumes responsibility for the design problems associated with the computer system.

One of the first duties of the business analyst is to study the existing system in use and to decide whether it is feasible for this system to be computerised. If the existing system is working successfully it may be inadvisable to spend money converting it. Honesty is an important attribute of analysts at this stage because if they do not consider it worthwhile to convert the manual system they are in effect stopping their own work. This phase then, not surprisingly, is called the **feasibility study**. It should include the likely problem areas which will need special attention if the decision is to go ahead with the computerisation: the most suitable computer equipment required, and the probable cost in terms of money, staff and time. It is from the feasibility study that the management of the company decide whether to go ahead with the plan or not, or whether to review the situation again at some future date. But if they do decide to go ahead, then a full and much more detailed analysis is undertaken, resulting in a full system specification. Finally, the technical analyst will take this design and become involved in the actual implementation of it as well as the testing of the system once it has been programmed.

Any errors in the design can have devastating effects once the computerised system goes into everyday use, and become very difficult and costly to correct. Consequently, another important characteristic of the systems analyst is thoroughness not only during the design stage but also during the testing stage. It takes several years of practical experience to become versed in all the arts and crafts of systems analysis and we can only afford a few paragraphs on this major area of data processing. The following list indicates a little more about the work and duties, although they will not be carried out necessarily in the order given.

The feasibility study.

Detailed examination of the existing manual system.

Gather all relevant information by questionnaires, personal contact with staff members.

Communicate with company personnel who may fear that their jobs will be taken over by the computer—possible involvement with trade unions.

Choose a suitable programming language for the application.

Prepare test data.

Keep within the time schedule and budget originally estimated in the feasibility study.

Prepare documentation on the new system via the written word and system charts for those staff members generally involved, the programming department, the management, the systems analysis department, etc.

Re-train company personnel in the use of "new" practices as a result of the computer equipment.

Implement the system.

Test the system, i.e. ensure that it does what it is supposed to do.

Review the performance of the system periodically once it is in everyday use.

Reliable Computer Results

If the original data input for the computer program is incorrect, then the results produced must also be incorrect. This raises the interesting problem of how far to trust output generated by a computer. This really depends upon several factors:

1) The extent to which data has been checked by both the human being and the number of validation checks incorporated into a data validation program.

2) The thoroughness with which the original design of the application has been undertaken.

3) The thoroughness of the test data used to check the application program itself. The preparation of test data can sometimes take longer

than the actual writing of the program and should cover every conceivable condition which could occur during the actual execution of the program.

4) The number of checks built into the program so that results produced can be validated before being output.

Databases

In many current commercial data processing applications, data is often repeated by being stored in several different data files. An employee's name, for instance, will appear in the payroll application data file as well as in the personnel application data file simply because each application has its own set of data file(s). If an employee decides to leave an organisation or is promoted, not only will the payroll application data have to be updated but also the data file of the personnel application system. Periodically, checks or controls have to be carried out to ensure that data common to several applications is the same and that it has been updated correctly.

In a **database system**, data is stored only once. The different application programs can access the same database via a set of controlling programs known as the **database management system** (DBMS). The main benefit of a DBMS is that data is stored only once (i.e. apart from any additional copies held for security purposes), thus reducing the amount of space used in secondary storage. Updating records can be performed much more quickly and easily and the need for control checks on several data files with common data is eliminated. Although it is *possible* for many existing computer systems to have databases, the design of practical DBMSs is a complex matter. As a result such systems currently are limited.

Important Words and Terms in Chapter 4

data processing
processors of information
information and data
file, record, item, field, key-field
hardcopy
data creation phase
data preparation
test data
data validation run
variable and fixed length records
keying in
input data file
transaction file
master file
updating
information retrieval
edit program
cuing program
application program
updating program

ancestral file system
    grandfather, father, son files
random (direct) and serial (sequential)
    access to records
database
DBMS—database management system

systems analysis
systems analyst
feasibility study
business analyst
technical analyst
systems chart
searching, sorting, merging files

Exercises 4

1 What is meant by data preparation? (*EMREB* 1977)

2 Describe the importance of 1) validation and 2) verification in relation to the input of data. (*UCLES* 1976).

3 List the stages in producing a computer program from the first idea to the production of useful results. (*OLE* 1976)

4 Explain the terms: file, record, field, key, item.

5 *a*) Data records on punched cards may be *interpreted* and *verified*. Explain the terms in italics.

b) Explain what is meant by the term *file* as used in data processing.

c) What is a record key?

d) Explain why *sorting* is a necessary operation in processing magnetic tape files. (*EAEB* 1976)

6 In everyday life, information is often recorded or conveyed in coded form. Give at least three examples.

7 A company previously without a computer is to make a study of the cost of installing a computer system. List four cost factors other than computer hardware which might be included in the study.

8 After your initial training period as a programmer, you are asked to complete a program which has been started by another programmer.

a) What documentation would you expect to be given to enable you to complete the job?

b) Why is program documentation so necessary? (*YREB* 1976)

9 The examination marks of Peter Jones are as follows:

English 58   Geography 61   Science 45
Maths 52   History   48   Art   37
Craft 72   Woodwork 83

Draw a flowchart to show the grades obtained by Peter in each subject (i.e. credit, pass or fail). Assume marks are in the order as shown on the form and that the form is pre-printed so that only the result column needs to be filled in.

Subject	Result
English	
Mathematics	
Geography	
History	
Science	
Art	
Craft	
Woodwork	

To pass an examination, Peter must obtain at least 45 marks. A credit is given for any subject with a mark above 70.

10 Imagine that you are the chief systems analyst for a lending library that is about to get a computer system to store and process its records. Explain what your job would entail. Describe some of the information which you think would be stored and analysed by the computer, how you think this information could be organised, and what processing would be required. What kinds of peripheral equipment would the computer need? (*OLE* 1977. This question carried 20 marks awarded as 7,3,3,3,4.)

11 An algorithm is a set of rules or instructions for carrying out a process. The diagram will, when completed, give an algorithm for making a call from a coin box telephone.

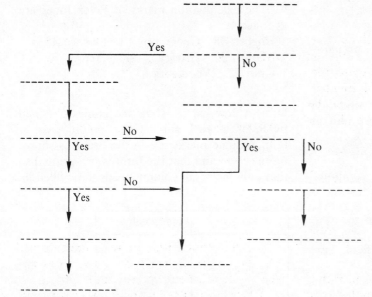

Complete the diagram by writing in appropriate phrases chosen from the list.

Lift receiver.   Ringing tone?
Try again later.   Pay tone?
Dialling tone?   Number is unobtainable.
Engaged tone?   Dial number.
Phone out of order.
Call enquiries.
Speak when pips stop.
Put coins in.

12 Distinguish between the roles of a programmer and a systems analyst. (*AEB* spec.)

13 The best boiled eggs are cooked by placing them in boiling water and cooking them for exactly $3\frac{1}{2}$ minutes. Below are the parts of a flow diagram for doing this. Re-draw them and link them together to make a working flow diagram. (*SREB* spec.)

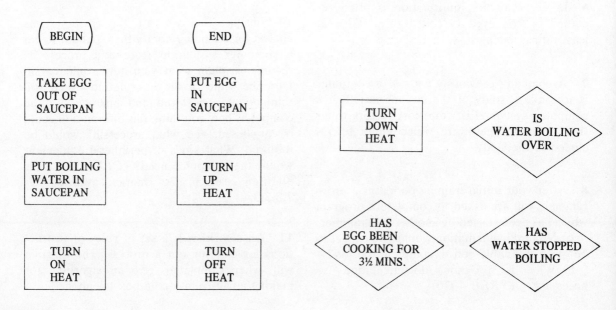

14 The diagram shows input and output files for a payroll program.

a) Apart from name and payroll number, give one other item of data which would be included on the master file for each employee.

b) Apart from name and payroll number, give one other item of data which would be included on the work file (transaction file) for each employee.

c) Give one reason why the information on the two input files would appear in payroll number order rather than employee name order.

d) Give one reason why pre-printed line-printer paper would be used in this application. (*WMEB* 1977)

15 A hire purchase company keeps records of all its customers' accounts on computer files. The master file contains details of customers' names, addresses, amount owed, and monthly payments due. Each week all the details of that week's payments arrive at the computer centre on a magnetic tape called the transaction file. This tape is processed against the master file. Below are two possible ways of doing this, system A and system B.

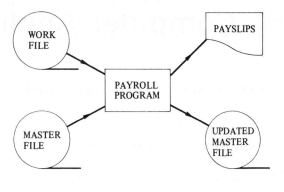

a) Which system uses a direct access device?

b) Why *must* system A have a sort program when system B does not use one?

c) What is meant by grand-father-son files? Which system uses these?

d) If master files were accidentally corrupted during processing, which system would be better at recovering correct files? How could the other system be improved to overcome this difficulty?

e) Which system could be adapted for real time processing? Explain why. (*MREB* 1977)

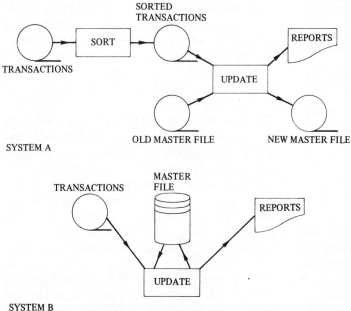

5 Computer Applications

Introduction

Before we consider the many and varied uses to which computers are put, it is as well to remember that the machine is only capable of carrying out the following four basic operations:

1) Input/output operations
2) Internal movement of information from one part of the CPU to another
3) Arithmetic operations
4) Comparison and logical type operations.

The apparent versatility of the computer stems from the fact that so many tasks can be expressed as a series of simple, logical steps involving only the four operations mentioned above. Any cleverness is in the human action of breaking the problems down to these simple steps.

Why has the computer been so successfully applied to so many tasks? The characteristics or attributes listed below provide the key.

1) *Speed* of computation and retrieval of information.
2) *Accuracy* of computation and movement of information.
3) *Storage* capability, including secondary storage for the retention of information on a permanent basis.
4) *Automatic* nature of processing.

Speed

The speed of the electronic computer is such that millions of operations and calculations can take place in a single second. What does this mean? Calculations can be carried out which the human mind could not begin to manage, e.g. in areas of scientific research. Data can be

processed fast enough to influence the next, possibly corrective, action, e.g. in space flight control and in the operation of intensive care units in hospitals. On request, items of information can be speedily traced and retrieved from a mass of information, e.g. obtaining an up-to-date statement of a customers account in a bank, searching police records to check a suspect.

Accuracy

The accuracy of the machine is consistently good, no matter how many times operations are carried out. Methods of error detection are built into the design of computers to guard against mistakes occurring as information is manipulated and moved from one part of the computer system to another. Errors do sometimes happen in computing but they are almost entirely due to human mistakes during the program development stage or in the introduction of invalid (nonsense) data.

Storage

The memory of the machine enables a complete program of instructions to be held in store, and this in turn makes the running of a program fully automatic, i.e. once loaded, the computer can work without human intervention. It also allows the program to modify (change) its own instructions as it is being processed and in this way clever things are seen to be done.

Secondary storage can be added to a computer system to enable information to be retained on a permanent basis. This information can very quickly be retrieved and brought into the main memory when required. Information stored in this way is never forgotten and it can be so arranged that any one item is just as easy to get at as any other (just as if the dictionary always opened at the correct page and the eye always focussed immediately on the right word).

Automatic

Once loaded with a program, the computer continues to operate without the need for human intervention until all the instructions in the program have been carried out. The program may also be designed to operate continuously in order to control an industrial process, e.g. refining oil, or to control the movement and behaviour of individual machines or tools, e.g. assembly line production.

Human intervention may of course be necessary to supply data to a computer program whilst it is in operation, e.g. making an enquiry about a seat reservation at the airline check-in desk or requesting information about a book in a library.

The early computers were built at universities and scientific establishments to carry out specific tasks, e.g. ENIAC, to undertake in-

numerable calculations in the field of ballistics (science of projectiles moving under the force of gravity after initial guided thrust, e.g. trajectory of shells). Later it was demonstrated that computers could be designed for use as aids to general business and office administration, e.g. in accounting and payroll. Once this was appreciated the future of the computer industry and of computers was guaranteed.

Most computer applications today fit into one or other of these two broad classifications. On a much smaller scale the computer is used in the humanities and this now provides a third classification, as illustrated in Figure 5.1.

Examples of scientific and engineering applications:
Satellites and space flight control
Patient monitoring and medical research
Earthquake calculations
Processing in the chemical industry
Testing designs for stress, e.g. bridges, buildings, airplanes
Weather forecasting
Research in high energy nuclear physics
Solution of mathematical equations.

Examples of business and administrative applications:
Payroll
Billing and invoicing
Stock control
Sales forecasting
Hospital bed allocation
Insurance premiums
Bank accounting and handling cheques
Finger-print identification
Railway timetables
Telephone directory updating and collating
Word processing
Census and questionnaire analysis

Examples of applications in the humanities:
Archaeological research
Concordance [1]
Music analysis and composition
Computer art
Linguistics [2]

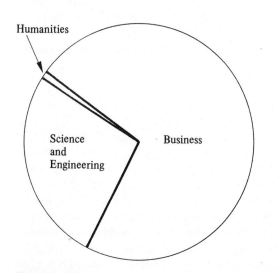

Fig. 5.1 The three broad areas of computer application

[1] Text analysis, particularly counting the frequency of words and phrases within a text, may also be included in this category. A concordance may be undertaken to test the origin of a piece of literature written many years ago. Much work has been done in finding the relationship between books in the bible, e.g. checking for a common style in those epistles which have for long been attributed to St. Paul.

[2] Science of languages, concerned particularly with the structure of languages. Development is going on into the use of computers for language translation. The task is more difficult than first envisaged because of the idiomatic use of many words and phrases within a language. Successful translation is not a matter of translating one word at a time because the correct meaning often depends on the context in which a word is used.

Commercial Data Processing

In commercial data processing, data is the name given to the various details related to the activities of a business or organization, e.g. customers' orders, different goods in stock, market cost of raw materials, number of hours worked by employees and other details required for payroll. There is a need to process this data into meaningful information so that the business can be organized and run efficiently. It is the function of the data processing (DP) department to collect all the data together and convert it into a useful form. Computers are widely used to help in this task. Indeed, today, the use of the term data processing is generally taken to imply that a computer *is* used.*

Computers are used in data processing to carry out tasks in two main areas:

1) Routine administration
2) Provision of information for management

---

* The term electronic data processing (EDP) is sometimes used to distinguish it from a manual or mechanical system.

Routine Adminstration

Many routine office jobs involve following set procedures and are repetitive in nature. These traditional clerical tasks are ideal for computers to handle. Typical examples are payroll, sales recording, invoicing and other aspects of company accounting, as well as the maintenance of staff (personnel) records.

Management Information

Much of the data assembled together for routine administration can, when analysed, provide information useful to the planning and control of an organization. The computer is able to process the data fast enough for management to use the information and take decisions before the information is out of date. Examples are the maintenance of more realistic levels of stock from inventory or stock control, sales forecasting and production planning, and estimating labour requirements from job costing exercises. The computer may also be used in the overall planning of new enterprises to find the best solution from a number of different options. This may involve simulating the problem (i.e. building a model of the real situation) and testing it out in various ways.

Systems which are designed essentially to provide management with information are sometimes called *management information systems*.

Payroll

The most common application of the computer in business is processing the payroll, involving the preparation of payslips for weekly wage earners and monthly salaried staff.

Fresh data for each run of a payroll program includes such items as number of hours worked per employee (obtained from clockcards), hours overtime, and days sickness. Records for each employee are also stored on the system as permanent files (using magnetic tape or disc). These files are accessed and updated during

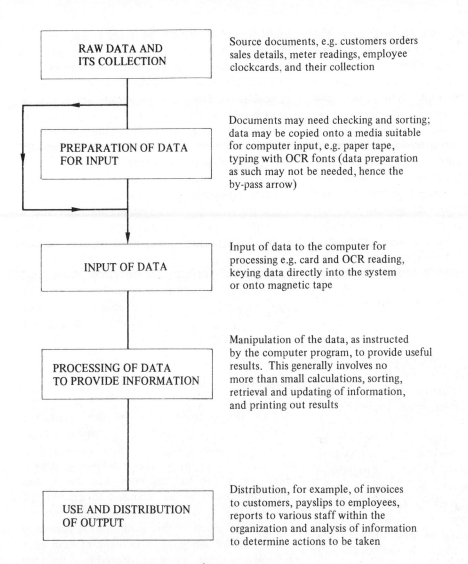

RAW DATA AND ITS COLLECTION	Source documents, e.g. customers orders sales details, meter readings, employee clockcards, and their collection
PREPARATION OF DATA FOR INPUT	Documents may need checking and sorting; data may be copied onto a media suitable for computer input, e.g. paper tape, typing with OCR fonts (data preparation as such may not be needed, hence the by-pass arrow)
INPUT OF DATA	Input of data to the computer for processing e.g. card and OCR reading, keying data directly into the system or onto magnetic tape
PROCESSING OF DATA TO PROVIDE INFORMATION	Manipulation of the data, as instructed by the computer program, to provide useful results. This generally involves no more than small calculations, sorting, retrieval and updating of information, and printing out results
USE AND DISTRIBUTION OF OUTPUT	Distribution, for example, of invoices to customers, payslips to employees, reports to various staff within the organization and analysis of information to determine actions to be taken

Fig. 5.2 Stages in data processing

each program run. They contain information of a permanent nature such as grade of employee and personal tax code, and also information that will be required on the next payroll run in updated form, e.g. total pay to date for the current financial year, total tax deducted, and national insurance and pension contributions to date. Also retained by the system for common reference are general data such as hourly rates for different grades and salary structures, and tax and national insurance tables.

The payroll processing involves only simple calculations like hours worked times rate of pay for the job per hour, but most of the time is spent in retrieving information, updating and sorting files, and printing out individual payslips using forms already preprinted with headings and subdivided into sections.

A complete payroll solution may be provided by a number of closely related programs or routines, each responsible for a particular part of the solution, rather than one large program.

Typically the payroll suite of programs will include a coin analysis program to determine the exact numbers of the different notes and coins required.

Complete *computer business systems* are now marketed. These comprise a small computer and the necessary peripheral equipment, plus standard *packages* of programs (see below) to carry out general business applications. They are ideal for a small or even medium size business. Advances in micro-technology mean that a complete operational system can be made available for as low a cost as £8000. Typical packages available for such systems include general book-keeping, sales order processing, stock control, payroll, and word processing (see below).

Packages

A package consists of a set of closely related programs which collectively carry out a particular task by using procedures accepted as typical to the application. For example, there are established procedures for sales accounting. Therefore a general program can be written that is suitable for use by firm B as well as firm A. It may be necessary to adapt procedures within a firm to fit the specifications of a package, or to amend the package to suit the local needs. An essential part of a package is clear and detailed documentation providing all the information necessary to enable the package of programs to be successfully run on the system and maintained. Who writes the packages? The so-called software division of the computer manufacturer or a special programming firm (a bureau) whose business it is to do just this.

Word Processing

Increasing use is being made of computers to assist with the production of text material. Typically, text is typed in at a keyboard, displayed on a CRT screen to allow a visual check, and stored on magnetic media such as floppy disc for future use. A word processing package al-lows the material to be edited, i.e. permits errors to be corrected, words changed, and even the insertion or deletion of whole passages of text. Material stored by a word processing system is therefore easy to update and it can be reproduced without typing it again in full. The program also automatically formats (lays out) the text without the typist having to consider layout other than to specify how it should be done.

Some computer systems are used totally for word processing. Such systems may include a high quality printer so that copies can be taken from the printout. Other systems may be designed to typeset automatically the text in a variety of fonts ready for conventional printing. In a business situation, word processing may be used to generate reports, prepare and update the firm's telephone directory, and prepare standard letters and circulars.

Systems Analysis

Before the computer can be used within a business or an organization, to carry out tasks previously undertaken by other means, it is necessary to examine the established procedures by which the business operates to see how they need to be changed to enable the efficient use of the computer. Systems analysis is the term given to this study and it generally results in the design and implementation of a completely new system, probably involving wide changes within the organization. A systems analyst is the person who carries out the so called "analysis" and produces the redesigned system.

Computers are only able to perform the tasks for which they have been exactly programmed. The analyst must therefore pay considerable attention to detail when drawing up the systems specification. It is from this specification that the programs are eventually written. If any eventuality remains unconsidered or any step is left out at the design stage, the computerized system will inevitably malfunction before it has been in operation very long.

The following stages are involved in systems analysis:

1) Investigation
2) Analysis
3) Design
4) Implementation

Investigation

Before investigation commences it is very important for the analyst to be absolutely clear about the objectives of the suggested computer application as defined by management. Only when the so-called terms of reference are understood in all their detail, including any restrictions that may have been imposed, does the investigation begin.

The main part of the investigation consists of a fact-finding exercise aimed at finding out how the work is currently performed, by whom, and in what circumstances. The analyst, or team of analysts depending on the extent of the problem to be solved and the size of the organization under investigation, carries out the fact finding by a variety of methods. These may include: a study of the formal work procedures as laid out in instruction manuals; a study of the forms and documents completed by staff as they carry out their duties; the interviewing of personnel and/or the use of questionnaires; an inspection of statistics and work records; and observation.

Crucial to the fact-finding exercise is the recording of the facts so that they can easily be referenced and used in the subsequent analysis and in the design of a new system. To retain the information in a useful form the analyst makes use of such aids as organization charts, flowcharts, decision tables, and systems charts.

Analysis

The analysis stage is used to examine critically all the facts obtained from the investigation and thereby to make an assessment of the existing system, and to look at all possible options. The analyst considers such things as whether the purposes of the procedures are being fully met, whether they are reliable, whether information is being presented in the best possible way and in time for corrective or productive action to be taken, whether the procedures can be simplified sufficiently for a computer to carry them out, and also whether it is economic to do so. As a result of the analysis, the strengths and weaknesses of the existing system should be apparent and management should be able to decide whether it is feasible and sensible to proceed with computerization.

Design

The analyst now creates the design of the new system to carry out the specified function using a computer, and the plans and procedures to be followed are detailed in the form of a systems specification. This part is normally performed by the technical analyst (Chapter 4, page 119).

OUTPUTS In creating the new system, the analyst has to consider and define the types of output to be produced, how often they are required, and what media to use. Are pre-printed forms needed such as those used for pay slips? Is it sensible to run the program to prepare invoices every morning of the week or should it be carried out on the night shift on Tuesdays and Thursdays? Who needs the output and in what form? Is a visual display of information needed to allow the user to interrogate the system more easily? Are multiple copies of documents required from the line printer to post to customers and to distribute internally within the organization? Would it be useful to be able to recall information from time to time by viewing microfilm?

INPUTS The forms of input have to be defined. It is necessary to consider how the data is collected and to what extent it is checked for accuracy. Also to be thought about is the structure of the data records, the design of the source documents, and the types of input media and devices needed. Could the data be recorded as a part of some other process, e.g. at the point-of-sale? Can the details of one transaction be conveniently fitted into a file of a certain size, made up of so many records? How much of the input data is going to be re-used or used in updated form each time the program is re-run, e.g. accumulating totals of salary and tax paid to date in a payroll program? Is there sufficient volume of data to justify the use of optical character recognition equipment? Does the application depend on enquiries made on-line, therefore necessitating the use of some type of computer terminal?

FILES   In the design stage the analyst is concerned with file structure and organization. The handling of the files depends on both input and output requirements, and the volume of data to be retained within the system for subsequent reference or for bringing up to date. How best can the files be arranged for ease of access? What is a sensible size for an output file? Are disc packs desirable or would magnetic tapes be more appropriate?

Another problem to be considered at this stage is the security of the information on the files. This concerns guarding against the contamination or loss of information through the action of the system and also guaranteeing that the information is not misused or the privacy broken by unauthorized persons gaining access to the information.

PROCEDURES   Incorporated with the computer programs in the complete design are all the various procedures which link the entire system and which have to be followed to make it operational, e.g. all the steps to be taken in the collection of the data and in the handling and distribution of the output from the computer.

SYSTEMS SPECIFICATION   The analyst provides detailed documentation of the entire system in the form of a systems specification. This not only serves as a complete record of the system but also as a passing on of information to all personnel who are going to be concerned with its use, e.g. the clerks who collect the data, the programmers who write the programs, and the operations staff who run the computer.

The specification also provides management with a complete picture of what is involved and all the possible choices that have been considered. A final decision can then be taken on whether to implement the new system.

The detail of the specification includes examples of source documents, outputs, flowcharts for each program, test data together with expected results, and a time–scale for getting the system working (implementation), and plans to enable a smooth changeover from the old to the new system.

Implementation

The analyst's tasks are not completed until the system is fully operational and sufficient time has passed for it to be thoroughly reviewed under working conditions. Implementation involves co-ordinating a number of activities and will normally include the testing of the programs using specifically prepared test data, the training of all the staff who will be contributing to the use of the new system, and the creation and updating of files in their new form without destroying master copies in the old form.

It may be practicable to run the new system side by side with the old until the new has been thoroughly proven. On the other hand it may be necessary to make a complete break and discontinue the old system at the time when the new system becomes operational. The second method puts more reliance on the quality of the design since any errors can only be corrected whilst the system is live.

Systems Personnel

A systems analyst needs to have technical expertise in computing as well as knowledge of the business organization under consideration. Ability to communicate easily with people drawn from all levels of the organization is another quality required.

An organization may employ its own systems analyst or team of analysts. The analyst may work within the computing or data processing department or function from outside the computer centre reporting directly to senior management. Alternatively, consultant analysts may be hired from outside the company to carry out a specified analysis and system design, working for several months, or however long it takes to see the job through to its conclusion.

Computers in Stores and Supermarkets

The retail trade is making increasing use of computers to help to process sales of goods. Typically a terminal is situated on the shop floor at the point of sale (POS terminal) with a communication link to a central computer. A large store may have the computer on site whilst a branch store is more likely to be linked to head office or a district office. The terminal acts as a cash register but also transmits sales data to the central database, thereby maintaining automatic stock control and providing valuable information about buying trends.

Numerous methods of capturing data are employed and this is reflected in the way the articles for sale are marked with such information as stock number and price. Some point-of-sale systems are designed to read coded information from perforated (or punched) tags or cards (sometimes referred to as KIMBALL tags). Another method involves the use of a

HEINZ TOMATO SOUP   15¼OZ
10053-7
YOU PAY
16P
UNIT PRICE   **16.5p**   PER LB

CROSSE & BLACKWELL BAKED BEANS 15½OZ
15120-9
YOU PAY
15P
UNIT PRICE   **15.5p**   PER LB

LOCKWOODS GARDEN PEAS   10OZ
21054-2
YOU PAY
11P
UNIT PRICE   **17.6p**   PER LB

Fig. 5.3 Examples of bar codes (see also p. 82)
(*Courtesy Harland Data Systems*)

hand-held *wand* or pen reader. An operator waves the wand over the sales information which is read using optical character or magnetic character recognition techniques. Sometimes, the marking of goods is done using bar codes rather than normal characters for ease of recognition by the reading device (Figure 5.3).

In all these methods, the accuracy of the collection of the data is the responsibility of the machine. There are also many types of advanced cash register in use which are linked to computers and which rely on human operators to key in sales data.

Computers in Industry

Computers are used in industry in an administrative role, e.g. payroll, personnel records, etc. Stock control is another important application, particularly in those industries in which products are assembled using pre-manufactured parts. It is not unusual for computer terminals to be found on the factory floor, in much the same way that POS terminals are used in stores and supermarkets, to record data at source and to obtain information from the system.

In some industries machine tools are driven by computer programs which control their every action, and there are also examples of complete assembly line production under computer direction, e.g. car assembly in some factories on the continent of Europe.

Computers and Process Control

In some industries computers are used to control processes without human intervention. The application is classified as process control when the controlling action partly depends on monitoring the progress of the process and taking action according to the observed conditions. Production of various chemical products and oil refining, paper manufacture, rolling and cutting steel to customer requirements, and load control of electricity power stations are examples. In general terms, process control is

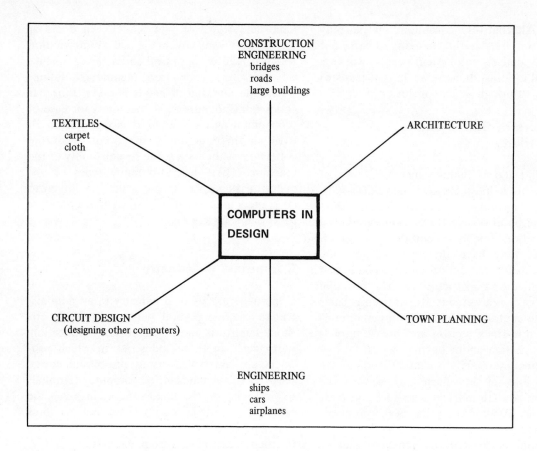

likely to lead to greater efficiency and, in such applications as chemical processing, to improved safety standards.

Computers in Design

The computer is an invaluable aid in design Using programs, or rather packages, stored in the system, the designer can create images of a design and display them for visual appreciation, typically at a graphics VDU. The images may be line or shaded drawings, two-dimensional or three-dimensional, in either black and white or full colour. The drawings may also be animated.

A design package normally permits a design, or a section of a design, to be enlarged and to be viewed from different angles. Thus every detail can be studied and the perspective and visual correctness checked.

By keying commands, entering fresh data or using a light pen or similar device, the designer can quickly modify a drawing and can do so again and again until satisfied. The computer can then draw out detailed and accurate plans via a graph plotter, or prepare microfilm copies of the various interactive displays. The number of plans that are needed to complete a large-scale engineering project may run into many thousands. Computers are useful in reducing

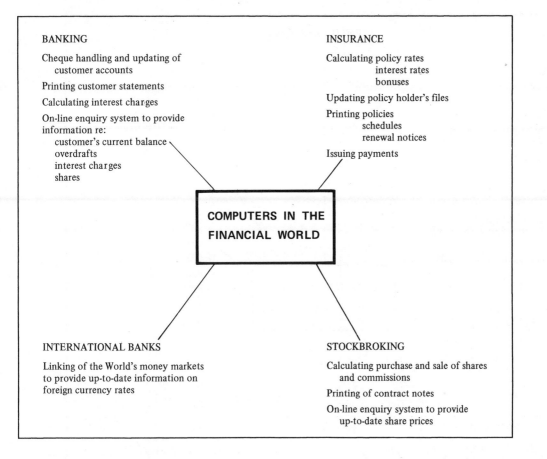

BANKING

Cheque handling and updating of
customer accounts

Printing customer statements

Calculating interest charges

On-line enquiry system to provide
information re:
customer's current balance
overdrafts
interest charges
shares

INSURANCE

Calculating policy rates
interest rates
bonuses

Updating policy holder's files

Printing policies
schedules
renewal notices

Issuing payments

**COMPUTERS IN THE
FINANCIAL WORLD**

INTERNATIONAL BANKS

Linking of the World's money markets
to provide up-to-date information on
foreign currency rates

STOCKBROKING

Calculating purchase and sale of shares
and commissions

Printing of contract notes

On-line enquiry system to provide
up-to-date share prices

the human effort involved in producing them all.

In applications where construction or manufacture is intended, the practicality of a design is of prime importance. Does it meet the requirements and when constructed will it be strong enough to withstand the stresses and strains it will receive in the real situation, e.g. a bridge or an airplane? Computer programs can be written to model or simulate the real situation. This is done by devising mathematical formulae that relate all the factors that need to be considered. Using different data the computer can then test out the design. The computer saves time and the expense of creating a real model.

The application of computers to design is sometimes referred to as computer-aided design (CAD).

Computers in the Financial World

Financial institutions are making ever-increasing use of computers. The banks could not function without them today because of the volume of transactions and customer enquiries that have to be dealt with daily. Processing of cheques at the clearing banks is one task totally dependent on computerization. Typically, a bank branch is linked by one or more terminal devices to a large national or regional centre.

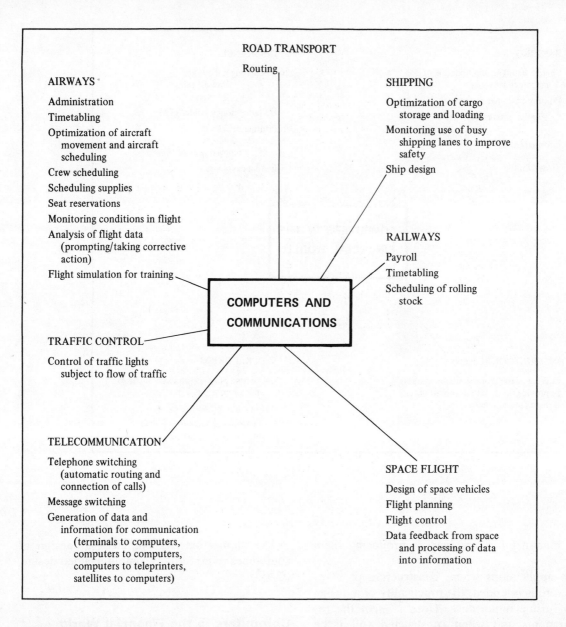

ROAD TRANSPORT

Routing

AIRWAYS

Administration

Timetabling

Optimization of aircraft
movement and aircraft
scheduling

Crew scheduling

Scheduling supplies

Seat reservations

Monitoring conditions in flight

Analysis of flight data
(prompting/taking corrective
action)

Flight simulation for training

SHIPPING

Optimization of cargo
storage and loading

Monitoring use of busy
shipping lanes to improve
safety

Ship design

RAILWAYS

Payroll

Timetabling

Scheduling of rolling
stock

**COMPUTERS AND
COMMUNICATIONS**

TRAFFIC CONTROL

Control of traffic lights
subject to flow of traffic

TELECOMMUNICATION

Telephone switching
(automatic routing and
connection of calls)

Message switching

Generation of data and
information for communication
(terminals to computers,
computers to computers,
computers to teleprinters,
satellites to computers)

SPACE FLIGHT

Design of space vehicles

Flight planning

Flight control

Data feedback from space
and processing of data
into information

Computers and Communications

Great importance is attached to good road, rail
and air traffic communication in the modern
world. Computers play a very important part in
improving the ways in which they are organized, e.g. efficient timetabling, route planning, and scheduling of stock and vehicles. In
traffic control applications, by varying the timing of the lights to reflect the flow, a bigger
volume of traffic can be kept moving. The
computer monitors the movement of traffic
over a given area and automatically adjusts the
lights. A large area of London is controlled in
this way as also is traffic in Tokyo. In the case
of the airways, computers are important to
organization on the ground and are used to
provide a measure of in-flight control. With
space flights and exploration in space computers make it all possible.

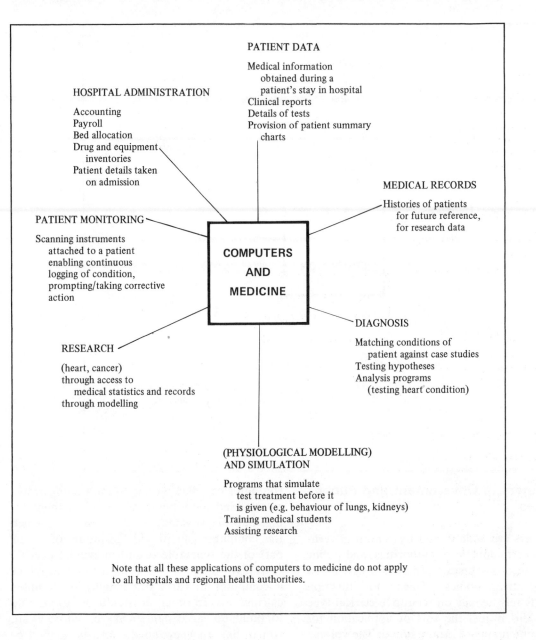

PATIENT DATA

Medical information
    obtained during a
    patient's stay in hospital
Clinical reports
Details of tests
Provision of patient summary
    charts

HOSPITAL ADMINISTRATION

Accounting
Payroll
Bed allocation
Drug and equipment
    inventories
Patient details taken
    on admission

MEDICAL RECORDS

Histories of patients
    for future reference,
    for research data

PATIENT MONITORING

Scanning instruments
    attached to a patient
    enabling continuous
    logging of condition,
    prompting/taking corrective
    action

COMPUTERS
AND
MEDICINE

DIAGNOSIS

Matching conditions of
    patient against case studies
Testing hypotheses
Analysis programs
    (testing heart condition)

RESEARCH

(heart, cancer)
through access to
    medical statistics and records
through modelling

(PHYSIOLOGICAL MODELLING)
AND SIMULATION

Programs that simulate
    test treatment before it
    is given (e.g. behaviour of lungs, kidneys)
Training medical students
Assisting research

Note that all these applications of computers to medicine do not apply
to all hospitals and regional health authorities.

Computers and Medicine

The medical profession benefits from the ability that computer systems have to file and maintain vast amounts of information, and to retrieve information from the files at speed. Complete records can be built up on patients so that all the facts are available for scrutiny when deci-sions have to be made. Doctors can search through data banks of medical information to examine various case histories and to seek out up-to-date knowledge. The computer can be used to assist in the diagnosis of a patient's condition and to watch over the progress of a patient under intensive care. In medical re-search the computer's role is invaluable.

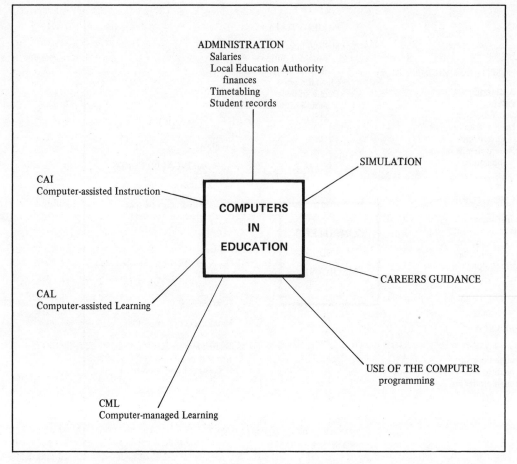

ADMINISTRATION
Salaries
Local Education Authority
finances
Timetabling
Student records

SIMULATION

CAI
Computer-assisted Instruction

COMPUTERS
IN
EDUCATION

CAREERS GUIDANCE

CAL
Computer-assisted Learning

USE OF THE COMPUTER
programming

CML
Computer-managed Learning

Computers in Government and Public Services

Computers are widely used by central government departments, local authorities, and public utilities (e.g. gas board). These are essentially administrative bodies which to function smoothly rely heavily on repetitive clerical type effort. This is just the sort of application for which computers are ideally suited. The volume of information generated and processed is so great that it would be impossible to deal with it all without using computers.

Computers in Education

Computers are beginning to be used more and more in education. Just like any business, the computer can play an important administrative role behind the scenes. As an aid to timetabling, one big advantage is the ease with which the computer can provide printouts of all or part of the timetable to suit individual needs.

In many subjects it is helpful to make use of a computer to carry out lengthy or complex calculations. In others it is valuable to be able to build up large data banks of information, which, like an encyclopedia, can be tapped or referenced when required. The computer can also be used to assist in the actual teaching and learning processes. There are essentially three methods or techniques involved: Computer-Assisted Instruction (CAI); Computer-Assisted Learning (CAL); and Computer-Managed Learning (CML).

CAI concerns programs which are designed to provide instructional sequences on a given topic. Essentially the computer program issues a piece of information and then raises a question about it. The student supplies an answer and, if this is correct, the program moves on to the next step. If the answer is incorrect, the information is presented again and re-tested.

In CAL, the programs are designed to encourage knowledge by finding out and learning rather than by drill and practice. The material is so presented that a student learns by investigation. CAL often uses simulation to achieve its aim.

When a computer program is designed not only to supervise a test but also, as a result of that test, to direct each student as an individual to the next appropriate set of tasks, the application is known as CML. Each student's record is also retained by the computer so that the teacher can find out at any time an individual student's progress.

Simulation allows experiments to be carried out using a model defined by a computer program rather than a real model. The method is particularly appropriate to scientific experiments which in real life might be costly, even dangerous to carry out, or impossible to set up. An advantage of the computer model is that it can be used repeatedly.

It may be that in your own school few, if any, of the suggested applications of the use of computers in education are applicable. They all pre-suppose access to a computer and many of them imply the use of computer terminals. Not all schools have these facilities.

Computers and Information Retrieval

Recovering items of information previously stored in the system is known as information retrieval. In many applications the retrieval of information is the main activity, i.e. little actual computation is involved. The value of using the computer is that a great mass of information can be retained and that any individual item can be found very quickly. Listed on page 138 are some further examples of information retrieval not considered elsewhere in this chapter. Of particular note is the idea of an information

service for the general public, using the television screen in the home as an output device, making it possible at the flick of a switch to find out about such things as travel conditions, weather prospects, shopping details, sporting events, and financial news.

Three such services are offered in the UK. Two, commonly called *teletext*, are presented by the television companies. The BBC version is known as Ceefax, and the IBA as Oracle. The third is more generally known as a *viewdata* service and is offered by the Post Office under the name of Prestel. Unlike the broadcast services, users of Prestel are in direct two-way conversation with the originating computer system. In this sense, Prestel offers more than just an information retrieval facility. However the users will have to pay for the telephone connection to Prestel whereas teletext services are "free".

Computers and Machine Intelligence

For as long as electronic computers have been in existence, man has dreamt of creating intelligent machines, i.e. machines which can think and act for themselves. However, we know that the computer can only perform a number of simple operations but we also know that many clever things can be seen to be done by writing clever programs.

Intelligence is a human quality. We cannot actually give an inanimate machine human intelligence but we can to a certain extent get it to imitate intelligent behaviour and so appear to be intelligent. Artificial intelligence is the name given to the branch of computing research in this area.

Programs which enable the computer to play chess (a thinking game) exhibit a degree of intelligence. Basically, the computer learns as it plays by remembering and by gradually building up a whole encyclopedia of moves and countermoves. The creation of robots to carry out specified tasks is another area of interest in artificial intelligence. Microprocessor technology is likely to increase developments in robotics quite dramatically in the next decade.

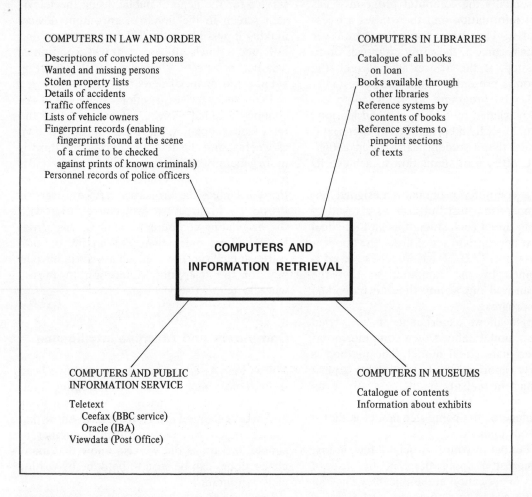

COMPUTERS IN LAW AND ORDER

Descriptions of convicted persons
Wanted and missing persons
Stolen property lists
Details of accidents
Traffic offences
Lists of vehicle owners
Fingerprint records (enabling
    fingerprints found at the scene
    of a crime to be checked
    against prints of known criminals)
Personnel records of police officers

COMPUTERS IN LIBRARIES

Catalogue of all books
    on loan
Books available through
    other libraries
Reference systems by
    contents of books
Reference systems to
    pinpoint sections
    of texts

COMPUTERS AND
INFORMATION RETRIEVAL

COMPUTERS AND PUBLIC
INFORMATION SERVICE

Teletext
    Ceefax (BBC service)
    Oracle (IBA)
Viewdata (Post Office)

COMPUTERS IN MUSEUMS

Catalogue of contents
Information about exhibits

Computing Personnel and DP Organization

Who are the people who work in computing and what are the jobs they carry out? Before looking at the notes which follow you should remember that computers are used to process and support many different types of work. Computer installations vary considerably in size and in the way in which they operate. The number of staff employed may be several hundred or more, each working in one or other of a number of well defined job categories, or no more than a handful of people each performing duties which overlap. The method of operation may be based on an initial card or document input of data involving massive data preparation activity on site, or it may be only concerned with input from numerous terminals situated at various sites removed from the central computer. For these and associated reasons, computer centres or data processing departments may employ some or all of the personnel we now discuss. Figure 5.4 illustrates a large-scale department.

Broadly speaking, staff fit into one or other of the following groupings:

Systems analysts
Programmers
Computer operators
Data-preparation and control clerks.

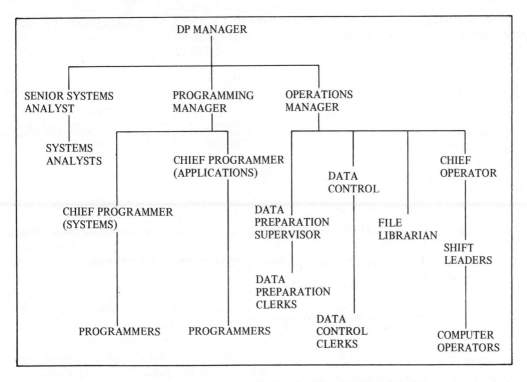

Fig. 5.4   Organization chart of a data processing department (large scale)

Systems Analysts/Designers

The role of the analyst (or system designer) was discussed in some detail earlier in this chapter (pages 128–31). In summary, the analyst is concerned with assessing the suitability of using the computer for a particular application and generally also for designing the computer system to carry out the task.

Responsibilities include:

1) Studying the needs of the organization.
2) Fact finding so that existing procedures can be studied.
3) Defining input and output requirements and file contents, including the equipment needed to fulfill the requirements.
4) Designing forms for input data and results output.
5) Providing overall specifications (plans) for the programming section to follow in developing the system.

6) Providing instructional material for user-departments and data processing staff to enable the system to be used.
7) Supervising the testing of the system.
8) Checking the accuracy and effectiveness of the system once it is working.

Remember that analysts may only be employed to carry out the suitability (feasibility) study. They may also work outside the data processing department, and even be employed on a contract basis from outside the company.

Programmers

The programming section is responsible for the planning, writing and testing of programs, and in general works from plans provided by systems designers. Implementing a system design for any application normally involves the writing of a number of related programs which collectively carry out the task rather than a single large program which does it all.

Responsibilities include:

1) Preparing detailed flowcharts, decision tables etc.

2) Checking the correctness of the logic of the flowcharts.

3) Writing (coding) the program.

4) Testing the program by taking test data through each step.

5) Testing the program on the computer, using different sets of data.

6) Correcting the program if mistakes are revealed.

7) Preparing operator instructions that are necessary for the running of the program.

8) Maintaining the program once it is running.

At a high level (senior programmer), duties may include:

1) Providing the systems designer with advice on the suitability of using the computer.

2) Developing more detailed plans for programming staff to follow.

3) Scheduling and co-ordinating the development of the different programs to more junior programmers.

4) Guaranteeing that programming standards are maintained and that all necessary documentation is produced at all stages of development.

Some programmers are concerned with maintaining the computer operating system and in writing programs to improve it. They are called *systems programmers* as opposed to applications programmers who write the programs which the computer processes. Systems programmers normally write in the assembly code appropriate to the design of the computer they use. Applications programmers write in a so called high-level language such as Cobol, Basic or Fortran.

Programmers are also required to maintain, that is watch over and keep up-to-date, existing programs as well as to create new ones. Acting in such a supporting role may be their main concern. Increasingly, use is being made of program packages provided by computer manufacturers, consisting of sets of related programs designed to carry out standard tasks on their machines. Programmers are required to ensure that a package is working correctly, and to maintain it in working order thereafter.

Computer Operators

Operators are required to supervise the running of the computer installation and to operate, where necessary, the individual pieces of equipment.

Responsibilities include:

1) Powering up the equipment.

2) Loading the system (i.e. setting up the operating system and the various supporting programs which must be resident to enable the user/application programs to run).

3) Mounting (putting on) magnetic tapes and disc packs on the drives.

4) Loading input and output devices, e.g. lineprinters with paper or pre-printed forms, the card punch machine with cards.

5) Observing and acting upon messages received from the computers operating system via the operators own console display screen.

6) Recording (logging) the performance of the computer, particularly any unusual behaviour, in log books.

7) Cleaning on a regular basis equipment sensitive to dust, e.g. tape drives.

Cleanliness in a computer room is important. Dust particles can distort information held on magnetic tape and disc. The surface of the media can be scratched and damaged irretrievably.

8) Checking the performance of air-conditioning units required to control the working environment.

[Computer equipment uses much power and generates much heat. Some devices malfunction if they get too hot or the atmosphere becomes too humid.]

Computer installations generally operate for longer hours than the normal eight-hour working day, often for twenty-four hours a day. Operators are therefore required to operate in shifts and these normally overlap to ensure continuity of work.

Operating staff are supervised by a shift

leader who is responsible for training and maintaining operational standards as well as for allocating individual duties. It can take several months to learn how to operate the equipment and to master the operating system. The shift leader or chief operator is also responsible for calling in a systems programmer in the event of a systems failure or an engineer in the event of equipment (hardware) failure which cannot otherwise be resolved.

Engineers are normally provided by the computer manufacturer as part of the maintenance contract. They specialize in one series of computers, or in one piece of equipment.

Data Preparation and Control Clerks

Data preparation clerks are concerned with preparing data in a machine-acceptable form. Traditionally this involves punching and verifying cards or paper tape. However, these media are being used less and less as more and more data is collected at source in a machine-readable form, e.g. by using computer terminals, or input by direct methods, e.g. key-to-disc systems. People are of course still concerned with preparing or inputting data, but they may not necessarily be employed within the data processing department. They can now do so within their own working environment, that is at their own desk.

There may be data to handle within the computer installation, e.g. decks of cards, sheets of documents, and also printed output forms to be distributed following processing. In these circumstances, data control clerks are employed. Their responsibilities may extend to checking the accuracy of material for input and assessing the reasonableness of output, and even arranging for the correcting and re-running of work. The work ranges from distributing output to user departments within the organization to mailing invoices, statements, etc. to customers and clients.

An installation may have a file librarian responsible for the safe-keeping of all computer files. These files may be retained on magnetic tapes, discs or even punched cards or punched tape. The librarian is responsible for retaining an index or catalogue of all the files, for their physical storage, for issuing files for use when required, for replacing files that are showing signs of wear and tear, and for keeping duplicate copies for security purposes.

In a business, commercial or government organization, the head of the computer centre is more commonly known as a data processing manager. The DP manager is answerable to top management for introducing new information systems, for meeting the data processing needs of the organization, and for planning for future needs.

Important Words and Terms in Chapter 5

analysts
applications programmers
artificial intelligence

business systems

commercial data processing
computer bureaux
computer-aided design
computer-assisted instruction
computer-managed learning
computer operator

data bank
database
data capture
data control clerks
data preparation clerks
data processing
DP manager

EDP electronic data processing

feasibility study
file librarian

humanities

information retrieval
interactive displays

machine intelligence
management information systems

on-line enquiry system

packages
point-of-sale terminals
process control
programmer

robotics

security of information
simulation
systems analysis
systems programmers
systems specification

telecommunication
text analysis

updating of files

viewdata system

word processing

Exercises 5

1 Describe briefly what is meant by commercial data processing.

2 *a*) Name *four* uses to which computers are put in science and engineering.

b) Write notes on *two* of the applications you choose, explaining briefly the purpose of using computers.

3 *a*) Name *four* uses to which computers are put in business and commerce.

b) Write notes on *two* of the applications you choose, explaining briefly the purpose of using computers.

4 Draw a simple chart showing the staff structure of a typical data processing department of a commercial organization. (You should include at least four different personnel.) Briefly describe the work done by each person. (*WJEC* 1976)

5 For each of the following give an example of a computer application (e.g. airways seat reservations): *a*) banking *b*) law and order *c*) engineering
d) humanities   *e*) space flight   *f*) shipping
g) medicine   *h*) gas board   *i*) education
j) libraries

6 Write notes on three of the following:
a) computer-aided design   *b*) process control
c) word processing   *d*) simulation
e) information retrieval   *f*) machine intelligence

7 What are packages and why have so many been developed?

8 Make brief notes on the uses of computers in
a) *either* medicine *or* education
b) *either* science and engineering *or* commerce.   (*OLE*)

6 Computer Systems and Operating Systems

A Computer System

When a company talks about owning a computer, it does not simply mean the central processing unit together with the various associated input/output and secondary storage devices. These pieces of equipment form the **hardware** of the computer, those parts which can be seen and touched when walking around any computer installation. On their own they remain pieces of electronic and electro-mechanical machinery rather like a car without a driver. The I/O and the secondary storage devices may be linked by wires to the CPU but, without something else, they can but remain stationary or inoperative. As a car needs a driver to make it function and move from one place to another, so the hardware units of a computer need special programs to make them function. These special programs are collectively known as the **operating system software programs** or just **system software** or **system programs**. These operating system programs are supplied by the computer manufacturer, not free of charge but included in the price of the computer itself. The hardware units and the system software are known as a computer system, a collection of individual pieces of equipment and system programs which when linked together form a working computer.

When a car has a driver it then becomes functional and can do the job for which it was designed. But drivers are human beings and have individual personalities. One person may drive faster than another, one may be more cautious than another and more considerate of others who also use the streets. Thus, depending on the driver, the car itself can be turned into different machines, one safe, one a danger to other road users. In a similar way, depending upon the type of operating system software, the same computer can become one of several different types or *systems*.

In this chapter we are going to take a look at computer operating systems and discuss how this software can turn a computer into one of several different computer systems, namely a *batch processing system*, a *multi-programming system*, a *time-sharing system*, and a *real-time system*. Since all these systems evolved as a result of changes in computer technology, we shall adopt an historical approach and begin our study at the early days of computing.

The Early Days of Computers

During the first years of computing when machines such as ENIAC and EDVAC were first built (see Chapter 8), the machines were very simple. Programs and data were read straight into the CPU memory via an input device such as a paper-tape reader or punch card reader. Output from central memory was punched onto paper tape or punch cards or onto a printer similar to an electric typewriter. The programming language used had been invented by the designers of the computer who were in fact also the users or programmers of the machine itself. Once the program had been loaded or read into memory, a switch was depressed which would cause the program to be executed. The data for the program would be read from whatever input device was available. Once the program had completed its work, the computer would be switched off and not used until another program had to be *run* i.e. executed, probably on some other day.

In such a simple environment there was no

real need for any operating system nor for any language translator since the programs were written in the language which the computer had been designed to recognise. It was later on, when computers became more common and were used by more than just a few people, that difficulties arose. It was in the early 1950s that commercial organisations began to realise that computers were not simply very fast calculating machines useful only to a scientific world but machines which could perform many routine clerical tasks such as payroll and invoicing. Machines such as LEO and UNIVAC I (see Chapter 8) were the first of the so called *general purpose* or business computers, designed to carry out not just one or two specific scientific tasks but which could be used for a variety of jobs common to commercial organisations. This period saw a substantial growth not only in the number of computers but also in the number of programmers. Whereas in the early days Universities like Cambridge and Harvard in the United States and Cambridge and Manchester in the United Kingdom "manufactured" computers, now computer manufacturers began to establish themselves.

With this situation in which more and more use was made of computers, the old system whereby few programs were processed each day was no longer viable. Many more programs were being written and of course they had to be tested and corrected. While one programmer was correcting his program via the computer, other programs in the queue could not be processed. The solution to the problem was temporarily solved by the introduction of a batch processing system.

Batch Processing

Figure 6.1 illustrates the problem which led to the introduction of batch processing. With the very early computers designed to solve a specific problem, there were few programmers to make use of the computer. If a program was to be tested, the programmer would do so by sitting next to the machine, watching the pro-

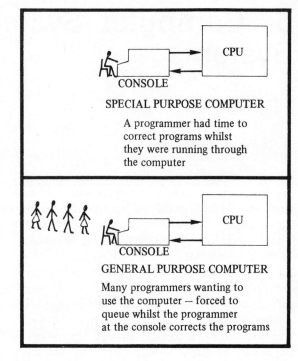

SPECIAL PURPOSE COMPUTER

A programmer had time to correct programs whilst they were running through the computer

GENERAL PURPOSE COMPUTER

Many programmers wanting to use the computer — forced to queue whilst the programmer at the console corrects the programs

Fig. 6.1

gress of the program via the CPU control panel, and by checking the results which the program was producing. If an error occurred, the programmer could correct the error there and then by entering the corrected machine code directly into the memory locations via the console switches (see Figure 6.2). Time was not so important since no one else would be waiting to use the computer. However, with the proliferation of general purpose computers (that is those

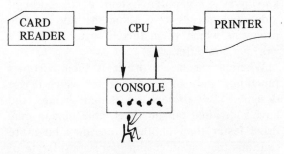

Fig. 6.2 The programmer correcting the program via the console desk, which allows the programmer to read from any memory location and to alter its contents

144

designed for use by both scientific and commercial personnel to solve a variety of problems) this situation became intolerable. Not only were programmers queuing up to use the machine, but the computer was being inefficiently used.

One satisfactory solution was to collect all the programs at set times during the day, e.g. at 10.00, 12.00, and 14.00 and then to process all the programs in sequence. Thus, all programs submitted up to 10.00 would be processed between 10.00 and 12.00 and the programmers could collect their output after 12.00. The collection of programs was called a *batch*, hence the term **batch processing**. This approach in many instances improved the number of processed programs by as much as 60%. This was due to the very important point that individual programmers no longer had direct contact with the machine. They could no longer monopolise the computer while they corrected their program during its progress through the computer. Instead, they now had to return some time later and look at their program results. If these were wrong, they would correct their program back in the office and re-submit the modified version at one of the other times later in the day. Once the program had been thoroughly checked it could be used to process real data and the program would be submitted along with other programs in a batch.

However, since programmers no longer ran their own programs, someone else had to, someone who was solely responsible for running all programs, returning output to the correct programmer and, of course, operating all the computer hardware. The people who had this responsibility became known as *computer operators* and the following list gives some of the duties they had to perform:

Running a batch of programs at the publicised times.

Checking that the programmer was authorised to use the computer.

Operating the computer equipment.

Making a note of the names of the programmers so that output could be returned.

Noting how many programs were run by each programmer.

Making a note of all programs run through the computer so as to monitor its performance.

Noting the length of time each program monopolised the computer, and how much paper or punch cards were used for output in order to charge the relevant department.

Marking in some way the beginning and end of a program and its data from the next in the batch.

Watching the console panel to see when a program had finished.

Watching the console panel to make sure that because of some program error the program was not caught in an infinite loop, thus unable to stop itself.

Making sure that the printer had sufficient paper and the card punch machine enough cards.

Cleaning the machines and the machine room.

The above duties involved the operator in some paperwork and record keeping. It was not long before it was realised that the computer could perform a certain amount of this work more quickly and efficiently than the operators. To illustrate this let us take the case of an installation using punch cards as the input medium, which in fact was a very common form especially in a data processing environment where punch cards had been the normal means of recording information.

It was mentioned that one of the operators duties was to separate somehow the program from the data. In the early days different coloured cards could be used so that the operator had a visual means of identifying the two. However, if a special card was placed at the beginning of the program with some set of unique characters, and another at the end with some other set of unique characters, then the entire program would be in between these two special cards. The second one could denote the end of the program and the start of the data. A third special card at the end of the data could signify the end of one particular program and data. When this approach was adopted the block containing the program, data and the special cards inserted at the places described was known as a *job*.

The unique set of characters for each of the special cards varied from one computer manufacturer to another. A typical example was that used by IBM for their 7094 computer. A £ symbol punched in column 1 of a card signified that this card was a special card as opposed to a program card containing some instruction or a data card containing one or more items of data. Other characters followed the £ symbol to denote which of the three special cards it was. Thus card 1 often had £JOB to mark the fact that it was the start of a new job; card 2 often had £DATA to denote the end of the program and the beginning of the data; £EOJ on the third special card meant the end of the entire job itself. This is shown in Figure 6.3. If other jobs followed, as they would when more than one job was batched together, the next £JOB would inform the computer that another entire job had to be processed. Furthermore, if each programmer was given a unique number (e.g. AB123), this number could be punched on the £JOB card (£JOB AB123) and the computer could make a note that programmer AB123 had submitted another job and accumulate in this way the total number of jobs run by this programmer each day, each week or each month. Again, the computer could count the number of cards each job contained, how many lines of output were printed, and how much computer time each program used, so that every month the programmer's department could be charged for the use of the computer and the amount of printer paper used. The computer could be given a list of all valid programmers' numbers. Every time a £JOB card was encountered the number would be checked against this list. If the number was false then the computer would not process the program. It would simply go through the job looking for the £EOJ and then begin on the next £JOB card in the batch. By using the computer to perform these and similar tasks the whole process of running jobs became faster and more efficient.

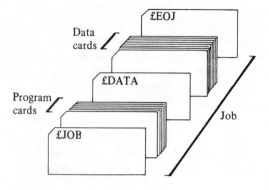

Fig. 6.3 Note that Basic is able to combine both program cards and data cards within one unit via its DATA statement

The Batch Operating System

When one first begins to learn about computers and to use them to run programs, it is common to become mystified by how computers perform all this checking and by the use of the special cards. To understand exactly how they perform the logging procedures (i.e. the duties given above) would entail a study of systems programming, a subject which requires full-time practical experience of one particular computer system. At our level of appreciation, and for the vast majority of programmers who only wish to *use* a computer, we need only to understand that, since a computer can do nothing unless a program tells it precisely what to do, then these systems programs are programs which tell the computer how to perform the logging and accounting procedures, validating programmers' numbers, counting the number of cards read in, lines printed, CPU seconds used, etc. Systems programs are no different to the everyday programs which any programmer can write except that the application is towards a computer rather than some scientific or commercial problem. The systems programs are usually also written in the assembly version of the computer's machine code.

The systems program can very simply tell the computer to look for a £ symbol in column 1 of a punch card and if it is followed by JOB then a

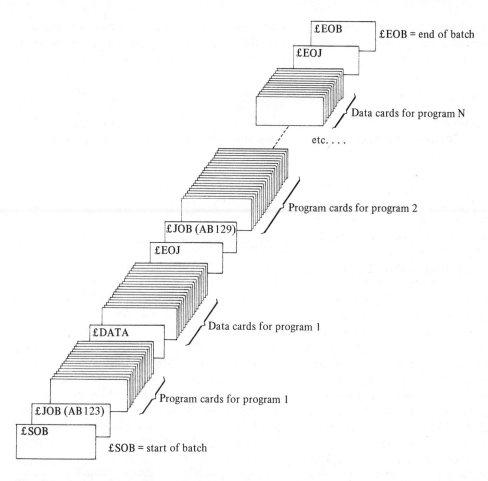

£EOB = end of batch

Data cards for program N

etc. . . .

Program cards for program 2

Data cards for program 1

Program cards for program 1

£SOB = start of batch

Fig. 6.4   Batch of jobs complete with control cards

new job is beginning. Next the programmer's number can be matched against the internal list of valid user numbers. If the £ symbol is followed by the characters DATA, then data follows. If the characters are EOJ then the end of a job has been reached and the next card in sequence can be checked to see whether it is a £JOB card. If yes, then the cycle repeats itself. If not, then either it is the end of the batch or someone has forgotten to put in the £JOB card, and the computer can issue a message and skip over the cards until an £EOJ is found or another £JOB card. There is nothing magical about this. A £EOB card could be placed by the operator at the end of the last program in a batch to inform the computer that the end of the current batch had been reached (see Figure 6.4). The computer would then begin to execute the system accounting routines which produce the totals of jobs run, lines printed, and so forth. These figures can be given to the person responsible for the overall running of the installation, i.e. the computer manager or the Data Processing Manager if the organisation is a commercial company. From these figures he can work out how much paper and cards need to be ordered; how many jobs (and the size of programs) are processed each day or each week or each month; whether the system is running efficiently or needs to be improved, etc.

The special characters on the card are commonly called *control commands* and, if punched onto punch cards, the cards are called *control cards*. We shall return to these later but first we need to be aware of other developments which were taking place while these early and rather primitive systems programs were being used.

Other Developments: Assembly Languages, Translators, Library Routines

Before the advent of general purpose computers, the people using the special purpose computers of the first days, i.e. the programmers, were those who had either designed the machine itself and therefore the machine language, or those who were closely associated with the design stage. In other words people who had a very clear understanding of the machine language and in some cases they actually wrote programs directly in binary format. We have seen in Chapter 2 that any given computer can only recognise and obey the one language which it was designed to understand. But with the growth of general purpose computers, a second generation of programmers were in demand, people who did not have a close association with the machine code of the computer for which they had to write their programs. To make their work easier, assembly level languages were developed and later high-level languages. As we have seen, an assembly or high-level language program has to be converted into the machine code by a special translator program—the assembler or the compiler (again see Chapter 2).

Furthermore, certain mathematical routines (short programs) such as square root and cosine which were used frequently by programmers were constantly being re-written time and time again. This led to the idea of a *library* of routines. The routines would be written once and thereafter could be used by other programmers, saving them the effort of having to write such routines every time they were needed.

Now when the programmer submitted a job for processing, not only were the program and data handed over but also any of the pre-written routines as well as the language trans-

lator. This is illustrated in Figure 6.5 and note that the language translator had to precede the program. The result was that many more cards (or paper tapes) had to be read through the card reader (or paper tape reader), thereby increasing the time spent on inputting information into central memory. Thus, although the programs were easier and faster to write, the input phase was taking up much more time. Consequently, some faster means of reading information into memory had to be found. The first solution was in the use of magnetic tape.

Magnetic Tapes

We shall go into detail later in the chapter about the comparative speeds of I/O and secondary storage devices but for the moment we must accept that magnetic tapes transfer information far more quickly into memory than either paper tape readers or punch card readers. This fact led to the increasing use of magnetic tapes and each installation organised their use in different ways. Let us see how they could be used in the case of one program and then relate this knowledge to a batch processing system.

Essentially, the language translator, or in many instances two or more translators, would be kept on one magnetic tape whilst the library routines would be kept on another. When a program was submitted, the programmer would now have to include two other special cards. One card would contain the control command informing the computer which translator the program required; the other, if present, would indicate that the program required access to the library routines. Figure 6.6. illustrates this but now includes yet another card to signify the end of the control commands and the start of the program.

Obviously, the original and rather simple operating system becomes more complex since now not only does it have to identify the £JOB card but also the language translator. £FORT, for example, could indicate the Fortran translator, £COBOL the Cobol translator, etc. Once

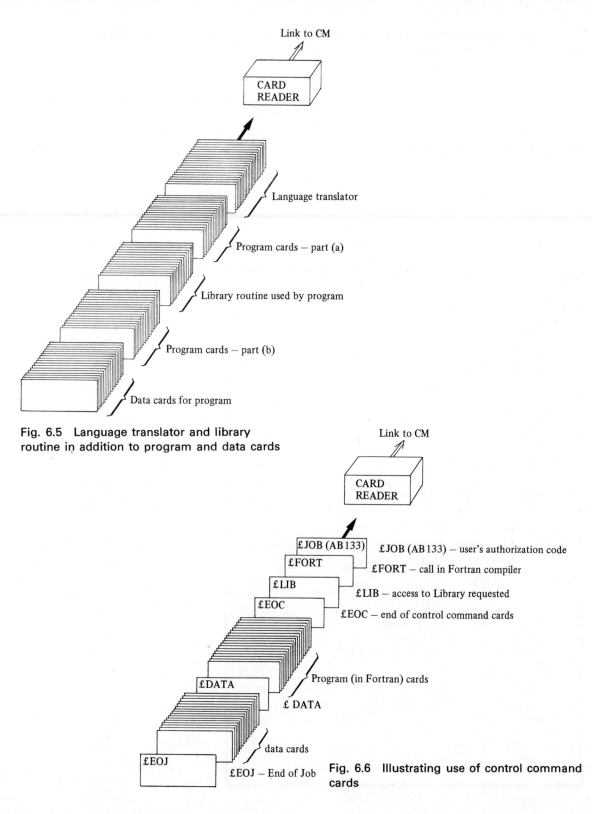

Fig. 6.5 Language translator and library
routine in addition to program and data cards

Link to CM

CARD READER

Language translator

Program cards – part (a)

Library routine used by program

Program cards – part (b)

Data cards for program

Link to CM

CARD READER

£JOB (AB 133)

£FORT

£LIB

£EOC

£DATA

£EOJ

£JOB (AB 133) – user's authorization code

£FORT – call in Fortran compiler

£LIB – access to Library requested

£EOC – end of control command cards

Program (in Fortran) cards

£ DATA

data cards

£EOJ – End of Job

Fig. 6.6 Illustrating use of control command cards

149

the operating system knows which translator is required, it then has to find that translator on the translator tape. Since the language translator is a program, it can only do its work when it is inside the central memory. Consequently, the operating system not only has to find the correct translator on the tape but also has to load it off the tape and into CM. (At this point it is worth mentioning that only a copy is transferred from the tape, i.e. the original translator is still left on the magnetic tape for some future occasion. The advantage of this is that it does not have to be read back onto the tape!)

If the program written by the programmer (the *source program*—see Chapter 2) was in Fortran, then the translator or, more technically, the compiler, would be loaded into CM and then the operating system would load the Fortran source program into memory. The compiler would convert the source program into the machine code of the computer, so that the source program now becomes the *object program* (see Figure 6.7a).

If any library routines are required by the program, indicated on the control card by a command such as £LIB, the relevant routines,

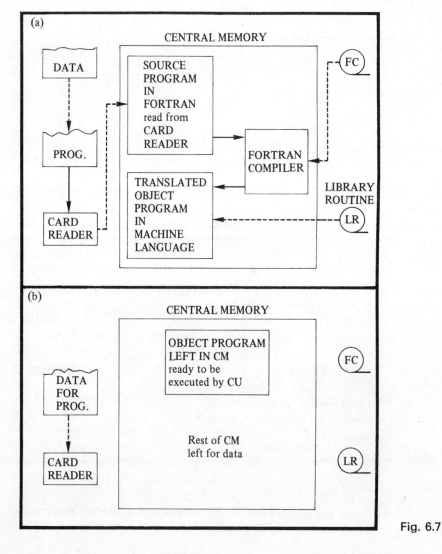

Fig. 6.7

which would be mentioned within the source program itself, would be inserted into the object program by a part of the operating system called the *library loader*. Once the object program has been completed, the translator is no longer needed and the area in CM which it occupied could be left for the data. Similarly for the source program which, again, is redundant because it is the object program which the computer will execute. Thus at the end of this stage only the object program is left in CM and the rest of the locations can be used for data (see Figure 6.7*b*).

Because information can be read from magnetic tape far more quickly, the whole process of inputting the language translator and library routines was a much faster process than when these had to be input via a card reader or paper tape reader.

The Supervisor Program

So far we have said that it is the function or duty of the operating system program to check the validity of the programmer's number, perform accounting and logging procedures, to load the correct language translator, to begin the execution of the object program instructions, etc. Since this operating system is a program it can only do its work, as with any other program, if it is in CM. Different computer manufacturers give different names to their own operating system. Some call it the *monitor*, some the *executive*, others the *traffic controller*. One name that is generally recognised by most computer people is the term **supervisor** since the operating system supervisor is really supervising or monitoring or controlling the progress of a user's program through the computer system. In Figure 6.8 we see that the supervisor program occupies a certain amount of memory from location 0 to some location m. The remainder of memory, i.e. from location m + 1 to the last location (n) is reserved for the language translator and source program, and, eventually, just the object program and data.

In an uncomplicated system, it is very simple

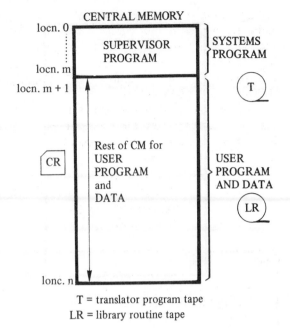

T = translator program tape
LR = library routine tape

Fig. 6.8 Supervisor program in CM

for the supervisor to "know" where to begin loading the language translator program and the source program. The supervisor knows the exact address of the last location which it occupies. If this is address m, then the translator can begin to be loaded into address m + 1. Since the translator program has a fixed length, it will in turn occupy a fixed number of locations, let us say from m + 1 to location j. Therefore, where does the supervisor begin to load the source program? Obviously, in location j + 1.

Of course, user programs vary in length but it is not difficult for the supervisor to make a note of the last location occupied by the source program, address k in Figure 6.9. This address can be passed to the translator by the supervisor so that the translator knows where to begin loading the converted source program instructions, namely at location k + 1. Once the translation has taken place, the translator informs the supervisor which can now begin to transfer the object program from location k + 1 into the area formerly occupied by the translator, i.e. location m + 1. The rest of the memory can be left for the data on which the

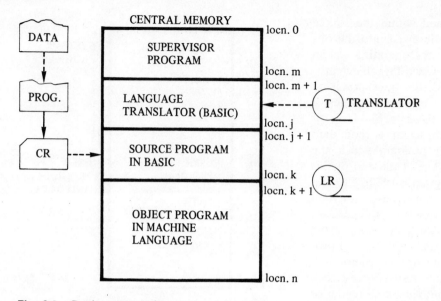

Fig. 6.9   During translation

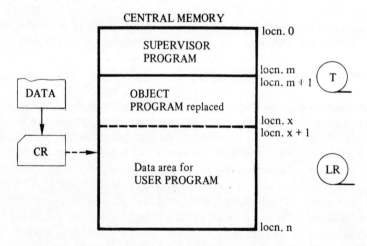

Fig. 6.10   After translation

program has to work (Figure 6.10). An alternative method would be to leave the object program where it is and to use the locations formerly occupied by the translator and the source program for the data. This would save the time of transferring the object program back to $m + 1$.

Systems Programs

We should note that, unlike user programs, systems programs such as the supervisor and the language translator should not have to be translated every time they are used, otherwise this would result in a serious increase in the time spent in processing a user's program. Systems programs are usually written in the assembly version of the machine language and are translated once into the machine code itself. From then on they can be loaded into memory in machine code without the need for any intermediate translation phase. They are written by specialist programmers called *systems programmers* who know a great deal about the computer and the computer system for which their programs are written. They know the exact number of locations which each system program will occupy and in consequence can make use of these numbers in the supervisor and translator programs. Thus, there is nothing mysterious about how the supervisor program "knows" where to begin to load a translator or how many locations it will occupy. It has all been worked out in advance by the very people who wrote those programs.

Another point to mention is that the supervisor program must be carefully written so that it does not occupy too much of central memory and leave too little space for other programs (see Figure 6.11). We must never forget that the important thing about computers is that they are there to process *user* programs, not *systems* programs. The system programs are only written in the first place to help the running of users' programs. Sometimes, this point seems to be overlooked by the systems programmers.

Thirdly, we should note that computers can only execute one program at a time whether that program is a user program or a systems program. Thus, whilst the supervisor program is performing its work (by being executed by the computer) no other program can be executed. Again, therefore, systems programs should be written so that they do not take too long in performing their tasks, otherwise the user program will never get much of a chance to be executed. From these comments we see that a good systems program particularly in the case of the supervisor should have two characteristics. It should take up as little room as possible and should execute as quickly as possible.

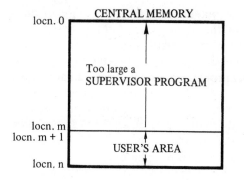

Fig. 6.11 Impractical supervisor program leaving too small an area in CM for user program

A Batch Supervisor

We can now return to the batch processing system previously outlined and discuss the type of supervisor required, i.e. we shall now examine a batch supervisor program. The main objective of a batch processing system is to speed up the process of executing a number, or batch, of users' programs. We have already seen that, with the advent of the magnetic tape, the language translator and library routines could be resident on these tapes. This enables a faster transfer of these programs into CM by reducing the number of cards or paper tapes to be read via the comparatively slower card and paper tape readers. By extending the use of magnetic tapes, it was realised that an entire batch of programs and data could be read onto a magnetic tape so that, instead of the computer having to read programs and data from these readers, it could read directly from the magnetic tape. This meant that programs and data punched onto cards would first have to be read onto a magnetic tape. This led to the idea of overlapping batches of jobs.

If we stop and think about the steps involved in processing a program, we come to the conclusion that there are only three broad stages. The first stage is to input the program into memory, secondly to process that program, and finally to output the results. Any program then goes through an *input-process-output* stage.

It became possible to carry out these distinct phases at the same time if three batches of programs were available. Technically this approach became known as **overlapping batches**. The only problem was how to read a batch onto magnetic tape (the input phase) or to output a batch of results from a magnetic tape onto the printer (the output phase), whilst the computer was in the middle of processing a batch of programs (the process phase).

The cause of the problem is that the computer itself is needed in order to read a batch onto magnetic tape or to output a batch of results. A simple solution would be to have three computers, one to perform the input phase, a second to perform the processing phase, and a third to perform the output phase, so that all three phases could be carried on at the same time. However, since computers were very expensive it was a sheer waste to have one committed solely to reading programs from a card reader onto a magnetic tape, similarly for the output to a printer. The solution was to design a special

and very limited "computer" whose sole task was to channel information from a card reader onto tape or to channel information from a tape onto a printer. These limited "computers" were called **channels**.

Figure 6.12 depicts a typical batch processing system involving the use of an input channel and an output channel with one main computer which performs the processing of a batch of programs directly from magnetic tape. With such a system three individual batches can be overlapped. One batch of programs is being read from the reader onto the magnetic tape via the input channel, while a second batch which has already gone through this stage is currently being processed by the central computer. All the programs and data are being placed in sequence into the CM at the faster transfer rate of the magnetic tape. All results from these programs are written to the output magnetic tape, again at the faster transfer rate. Meanwhile, a third batch, which has undergone the input and the process phases, is currently in the

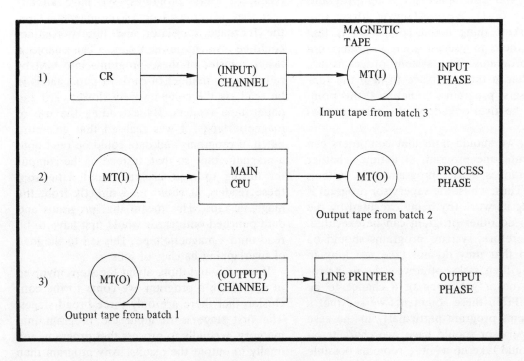

Fig. 6.12 Overlapping three batches of user programs

output phase where all the results are transferred from the output magnetic tape to the printer by the output channel.

The above method was in use at Imperial College, London, during the late 1960s and the very early 1970s to run students' programs. A commercial organisation would not have had so many programs to run each day but the programs they would run would be much larger than typical student programs. Obviously, each computer installation would have to vary the basic idea of batch processing with magnetic tapes and the use of channels to suit its own individual requirements. Perhaps, one channel would be sufficient and could be programmed to perform either the input or the output phases. Whatever variation was used, the overlapping of batches increased the number of programs executed each day.

The batch supervisor program used at Imperial College was similar to the one outlined in Figure 6.12, where the input came from a magnetic tape via a card reader, and output was transferred to magnetic tape and later direct to a printer. Naturally, the systems programmers at Imperial had to be familiar with the actual computer as well as the requirements of the installation before they could begin to write the supervisor.

We have not wasted time by discussing *how* operating system supervisors are written, although several hints have been given because the important point to grasp is *what* the supervisor have to do and *why* they were written in the first place.

Summary of the Batch Supervisor's Duties

1) To process an entire batch of programs.

2) To detect the £SOB card—start of batch—and set totals initially to zero.

3) To detect the £JOB (ABnnn) card and to check validity of a programmer's number.

4) To detect £FORT, £BASIC, £ALGOL, £COBOL, etc. card which identifies the language in which the source program is written.

5) To locate the language translator on magnetic tape and to load translator into CM starting at location $m+1$.

6) To look for a possible £LIB card: if present, *inform* language translator that some library routines are to be used by the program. The translator will supply a list of wanted routines which have to be located and which will be loaded into CM *after* the translation phase.

If not present then ignore this procedure.

7) To read in the program (from magnetic input tape if batches are overlapped—from card reader or paper tape reader if batches not overlapped).

8) Allow language translator to convert source program into machine language, i.e. produce an object program (and to load in any requested library routines).

9) If necessary, after translation swap object program into locations formerly occupied by language translator (see Figure 6.10).

10) Process program—reading data as required by program and writing results to magnetic output tape or line printer as appropriate. If £EOJ card encountered before all the data has been read in by program, inform user via a system message that the £EOJ card has been encountered and that a programming error has occurred.

11) Stop execution of program when program says so.

12) Complete totals for this job, i.e. for lines printed, cards read (or card images if magnetic tape input is used), CPU time used, etc.

13) Read next control command:

if this is a £JOB repeat process from (3) above

if this is a £EOB no more programs to process and go to (14) below.

14) Log the entire totals for this batch (cards read, lines printed, jobs processed, CPU time used) for information for Computer Manager.

Input/Output Speeds

Before moving onto the next development in computer systems, it is necessary to discuss the speeds of the I/O devices compared to the internal speeds of the computer's CPU. Chapter 2 has already given typical speeds at which a card reader can read punch cards, between 100 and 2000 cards per minute. If an 80-column card is used which contains 80 characters, then in one minute the slower card reader could read

$$100 \times 80 = 8000 \text{ characters per minute}$$

$$\text{or } \frac{8000}{60} \text{ characters per second}$$

i.e. approximately 133 characters per second. The faster card reader could read

$$\frac{2000 \times 80}{60} = \text{approx. } 2666 \text{ characters per second.}$$

Line Printers

A line printer has typical printing speeds of between 200 and 2000 lines per minute and, if 130 characters can be printed on one line, then a fast line printer can print

$$2000 \times 130 = 260\,000 \text{ characters per minute}$$

$$\text{or } \frac{260\,000}{60} = \text{approx. } 4333 \text{ characters per second.}$$

These speeds are very impressive. If an average word contains six characters and a page of a "typical" book contains 450 words, then a line printer printing at 2000 lines per minute can print a page and a half in one second or a 200 page book in about two minutes.

On the other hand, information inside a computer can be transferred from central memory to the control or arithmetic unit and back again at a much faster rate, since the speed of transfer is at electronic speed rather than at the rate of electro-mechanical devices such as I/O units. One example is the CDC 6600 computer which can move internally ten million characters per second. A little more arithmetic will demonstrate what this means in reality. Let us take the example of the CDC 6600 outputting information to the fast line printer. To keep the line printer going at full speed the computer must output 4333 characters per second. However, from the following arithmetic we can see that the computer can achieve this without any trouble at all, since it can perform many more operations within the space of one second:

$$\frac{10\,000\,000}{4333} = 2300 \text{ approx}$$

In other words, whilst the line printer is handling just one character, internally the computer could be doing $(2300-1)$ operations or 2299 more operations. This ratio of 1:2300 demonstrates the difference in speed of CPU and output devices. This ratio is even greater if the I/O device is a card reader. Even with the fast card reader the ratio is approximately 1:3750. In computer terminology, this difference in speed is called the **speed mis-match** between the CPU and the I/O devices. We must remember that it is the CPU which controls these I/O devices, i.e. the passage of information to and from the CM and the I/O devices.

With magnetic tapes and later with magnetic drums and discs, the speed mis-match was reduced but still present. These magnetic devices tend to have a transfer rate measured in terms of milliseconds (thousands of a second) or sometimes even in microseconds (millionths of a second) but the internal speeds of the CPU are measured in terms of nanoseconds (thousand-millionths of a second) or even today in terms of picoseconds (million-millionths of a second). In other words the mis-match is still present even between these faster devices and the CPU.

It was an appreciation of this mis-match which led to the development of the next computer system, the *multi-programming system*.

A Disadvantage of Batch Processing

The batch processing system was devised early on in computing to speed up the processing of programs and, with the advent of magnetic tapes, to overlap batches so that input and output stages could be speeded up. But only one *user* program could be resident at any given time within central memory. For this reason the traditional batch processing system is sometimes referred to as a single or **mono-programming** system. One user program would be loaded into CM and would be totally executed before the next user program could be brought into memory by the batch supervisor.

Individual programs however vary in size. Consequently, one program may occupy only one thousand memory locations whilst another may occupy eight thousand or more. The result is that, with a mono-programming system, some portion of memory might not be used at all. In Figure 6.13, for example, the storage locations i+1 to n are not used by either the object program or the data. Since the CM forms a major proportion of the overall cost of a computer system, the fact that some programs might waste or not use this expensive main memory meant that the computer as a whole was not being used to its full potential.

A second situation was also recognised in those early days, namely that programs typically fell into one of two major categories. There was the scientific type of program which by its nature spent much time performing calculations with relatively little time spent on reading data and outputting results. The other category was the typical commercial program which spent, by comparison, little time in performing calculations but a great deal of time in reading data records and outputting lists. The first class of program in computer terminology is called a **computation bound** job, whilst the other class is called an **input-output bound** job.

The previous section on I/O speeds pointed out that, even when magnetic tapes are used for input and output operations, there is still a speed mis-match with what the computer could be doing internally if only it was not slowed

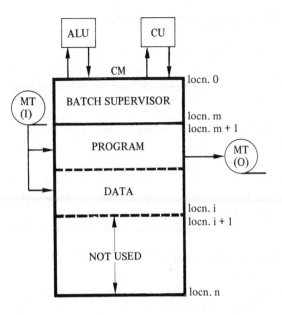

Fig. 6.13 Mono-programming computer system illustrating waste of CM locations

down by the comparatively slow speeds of I/O and secondary storage devices.

So the traditional mono-programming batch system had a serious drawback in that two valuable resources were frequently under-utilised—the CM and the computational ability of the CPU. In passing it is worthwhile to note that these two resources or features determine the **power of a computer**. Often one wishes to know "how powerful a given computer is". Really one is asking "how fast can it perform calculations and how large is the CM?"

This drawback became even more obvious as computer memories became larger and computational speeds faster due to the continuous advances in computer technology. A solution had to be found and came in the guise of multi-programming systems, one of the hall-marks of the third generation of computers. As this new system increased in popularity so the traditional batch system became outdated, so much so that today very few computers make use of the mono-programming batch system.

157

Multi-programming Systems

A very simple alternative to having only *one* user program in CM at any given time was to have two or more user programs in CM at the same time. This became feasible as the size of CMs increased. This is the basic idea behind multi-programming as the name itself implies. Figure 6.14 illustrates this concept. The CM was divided or partitioned into several areas or more commonly **partitions**. One partition had to be reserved for the multi-programming (MP) supervisor. Note that a traditional batch supervisor could no longer be used since it would expect only one user program to be in CM. The other partitions would be reserved for individual user programs and data. In Figure 6.14 we have four partitions, partition 0 for the MP supervisor, and partitions 1 to 3 for three user programs and data (areas A, B, C). In order to hold two or more user programs, the CM for a multi-programming must be at least 64K with a word length of 32 bits or more.

To appreciate how such a system works we need to recall two facts. The first is that the CPU can only execute one program at any instant in time, whether the program is a system or a user program. The second fact is that, because of the speed mis-match, it is possible for many internal operations to be going on whilst the CPU is passing one character and the next to an I/O device or a magnetic storage device. Since this latter point is so crucial to the appreciation of the MP system, let us just dwell on the point a little longer. If we return to the fast line printer, we remember that the mis-match was in the ratio of 1:2300. Thus whilst the line printer is handling just one character, the CPU could be doing 2299 other internal operations *before* it needs to pass the next character to the line printer. To put this another way, to keep the CPU fully occupied, it could service many line printers, almost 2300. Clearly, this would not be practical since no other device could be used but, because of the speed mis-match, the one computer could easily service a line printer, a card reader, a card punch, one or more magnetic tapes and discs,

CENTRAL MEMORY

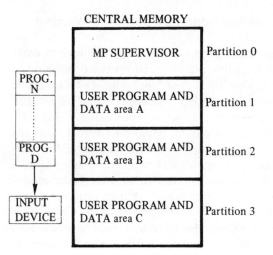

Fig. 6.14 Multiprogramming computer system

and still have time to carry out some internal computations, all within the space of one second. This is the secret of multi-programming systems.

Let us assume that programs A, B and C have been read into the three user partitions. The MP supervisor will allow program A to be executed. At some point this program will become involved in an input or an output operation. The operating system is designed in such a way that, as soon as one program becomes engaged in I/O operations, the MP supervisor is informed. Suppose program A is outputting information to a line printer. Between passing one character and the next the MP supervisor can perform many other operations and, consequently, it can quite easily begin to execute part of another program in CM, say program B. If this becomes engaged in I/O activity, then part of program C can be executed whilst both programs A and B are performing I/O operations. When program A has completed this output, the MP supervisor is informed and it can stop executing the computational activities of program C and return the control unit to the execution of program A. In this way, parts of all three programs can be executed *not* at the same time but in succession. If program B happens to complete execution before the other two because it is a very short program, the supervisor can now permit the next program, program D in Figure 6.14, to be brought into CM from the queue of jobs awaiting execution on the input device. It will be placed in partition 2 previously occupied by program B. In due course, this program will be executed when programs A and C are involved in I/O operations.

Once this basic idea is appreciated, many variations on the theme can be explored. For example, some installations may have to run fairly short programs as well as larger programs. This is especially true in a university or college environment where short student programs have to run alongside large research programs. One partition may be too small for the larger class, and consequently the MP operating system can be made more flexible to allow the use of two partitions for the larger program (see Figure 6.15).

In turn this implies that the user must inform the operating system of the type of job being submitted. There are many ways of doing this. One method is to include this information on the £JOB card after the user number, thus: £JOB (AB123, J1), where J1 indicates a smallish program requiring only one partition. A J2 could indicate that the program needed more memory space than one partition allows. In this case, when the MP supervisor "sees" a J2 on a £JOB card, the supervisor will wait until both programs in partitions 2 and 3 have completed execution before being able to allow the large program to run in those two partitions. Other programs which may require the total amount of available memory space, i.e. all three partitions, might be run at a time of the day when the J1 and J2 class of programs are not being submitted, for example overnight between the hours of 21.00 and 09.00. This also implies that these very large jobs will have a J3 category on their job-cards.

Today many large computer installations work on a 24-hour basis in order to make the most of the computer system. The MP supervisor would have to be written in such a way that, if a J3-class is submitted during the daytime, it will not execute that program but in-

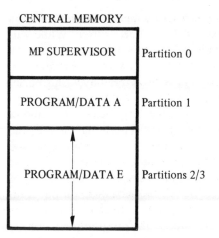

CENTRAL MEMORY

MP SUPERVISOR — Partition 0

PROGRAM/DATA A — Partition 1

PROGRAM/DATA E — Partitions 2/3

Fig. 6.15 Two partitions for a large program

stead issue a message to say that "J3 jobs can only run between 21.00 hours and 09.00 of the next day". Thus, another duty that the MP supervisor has to do is to keep track of the time of day. This is a simple matter. When the daytime MP supervisor is set up by the operators each day, they can enter the time of day (and the current date, for that matter). Then the MP supervisor can add to this time every second and include, on the output of each program, the time and date when it was processed.

The ultimate aim of the MP system is to avoid the wastage of two of the computers most valuable resources, CM space and the CPUs computational ability, by not allowing the CPU to idle or waste time between the passing of one character to some external device and passing the next, or between receiving one character and the next from some external device. Obviously, a secondary effect of this procedure is to increase the number of jobs which the computer can process during a given time period.

However, MP systems only became a practical procedure with the introduction of magnetic drums and discs. This was not solely due to the fact that these devices were faster than magnetic tapes but to the much more important fact that these devices allowed *random* or *direct access*. To illustrate this point, let us suppose that program A in Figure 6.14 becomes involved in some output of information via a

WRITE or PRINT statement. This information may be destined for a line printer. While this activity is going on, the MP supervisor will begin the execution of the next program in memory, program B. This too may wish to print some information for the line printer. Meanwhile program C may begin execution and it too may want to print something on the line printer. Thus a bit of output from all three programs will appear on the line printer paper, scattered at random. Imagine the problem of having to sort out all the mixed-up output from three or more programs in order to return the output to the individual programmers. Obviously, this approach is totally useless. But with random devices the problem disappears. For now each program can be given a separate area on the drum or disc. In a simple system this could be one complete track.

Now when program A is outputting information destined for a line printer, it will first go to a particular track, track 10 in Figure 6.16. Eventually, when program A has completed its work, all the output on track 10 can be passed to the line printer as one complete unit, likewise for the other programs. Program B has its output built up on track 11, program C on track 12, etc. Thus, each program has its own output on separate tracks. A part of the operating system will be responsible for building up individual program output onto its output track. The programmer could do this, of course, but that would mean acquiring an intimate knowledge of the computer system, the I/O devices, and the various random access devices. The program too would become very large since all the I/O operations would have to be programmed.

Fortunately, the operating system does this for the programmer. A special set of program routines will send a program's output to a track on disc or drum and, when the program has completed all its work, will automatically print from that track all the information onto the line printer, so that each programmer has all their output in one complete unit. The track which contained this output can now be re-cycled to some other program. The set of system routines

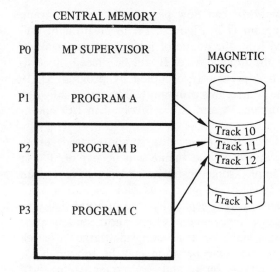

CENTRAL MEMORY

Fig. 6.16 Individual tracks on disc for individual programs

which performs this work has various names. We shall call it the **I/O handler** and it is common practice to reserve a partition entirely for these routines. A more realistic organisation of CM partitions is shown in Figure 6.17a. Now we see two user programs A and E in memory

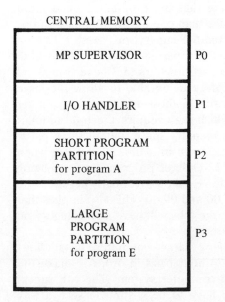

CENTRAL MEMORY

Fig. 6.17a Allocation of partitions in multi-programming

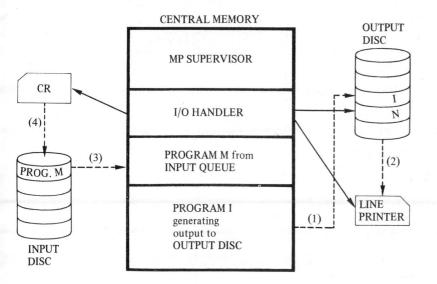

Fig. 6.17b Numbers in brackets relate to the four duties of the I/O handler. (Output from track N going to LP. Program M being read into CM from input disc. Program I generating output to track I of output disc.)

in partitions 2 and 3, the I/O handler in partition 1, and the MP supervisor in partition 0.

The I/O handler has more to do than just pass parts of program output to output tracks. The following list describes its duties (see Figure 6.17*b*):

1) To build up, onto individual tracks, output from executing programs.

2) Once programs have completed their tasks, to transfer the output from the output tracks to the output device, e.g. the line printer. In Figure 6.17*a*, since programs A and E are still in memory, we can assume that programs B, C and D have finished. Their output will be on tracks ready to be transferred to the line printer, one by one.

3) To bring into CM other jobs awaiting execution.

4) To create an input queue of jobs onto separate tracks for eventual transfer from the track onto CM.

This last point needs to be explained in more detail. We have already seen in the batch pro-

cessing system how effective it was to read an entire batch of jobs from a card reader onto a magnetic tape, and for these jobs to be read into CM from this faster medium. The same idea is applied in MP systems. As programs are submitted at the card reader, the I/O handler transfers them onto separate tracks of a disc or drum and, when a partition becomes free, one job can be read from the disc into CM.

Let us now follow the passage of a few programs through an MP system. We assume that the programs are punched onto cards and that the computer system hardware consists of a card reader, a line printer, three discs (one for the input queue of programs, one for the output queue of results, one to contain copies of the operating system software, language translators, library routines, etc). This hardware system is shown in Figure 6.18.

It is the beginning of the day, 09.00 hours and the time and date have been entered by the operator via the operator console. Three users are queuing up at the card reader with their programs and data. The MP supervisor notes that no programs are in CM apart from itself in partition 0 and the I/O handler in partition 1. Thus, it allows the I/O handler to activate the card reader. The three programs are read onto separate tracks, 10, 11 and 12, and the first program A is then loaded into partition 2. It is

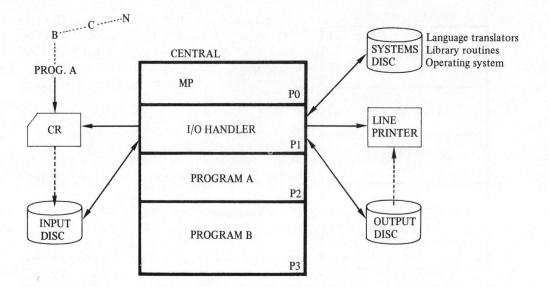

Fig. 6.18 Typical hardware system required for multi-programming

of course translated into the object code of the machine language and is now ready to be executed. The MP supervisor allows program A in partition 2 to be executed.

As soon as this program becomes involved in some I/O operation, the supervisor is informed and passes control over to the I/O handler. If the program requests data, then the handler will execute a routine which will bring data into partition 2 for program A to work on. If the program is outputting information, the I/O handler will control the transfer of the data to the output track reserved for program A. Whilst this is taking place, the I/O handler can begin to read in the next program, B, into partition 3. In due course both program A and program B will be executed and perhaps at some time both engaged in I/O operations. At this point the I/O handler can read into the input queue some other program from the card reader. And so the cycle goes on all day. Should the input queue, i.e. the tracks reserved on the input disc for programs being read at the card reader, ever become full, then the I/O handler can send a signal to the card reader to switch itself off temporarily. It will restart the

reader when a given number of tracks on the input disc become free.

Clearly, the I/O handler has a great deal of work to do and in order to do it effectively it must be given more opportunity to execute than any of the user programs, i.e. it will have to be given a higher **priority** to execute. It is the function of the MP supervisor to organise the execution of all the programs in CM including itself and the I/O handler. In Figure 6.17*a* there are four programs in CM: the MP supervisor, the I/O handler, and two user programs. The program with the highest priority to execute must be the MP supervisor itself, then the I/O handler, and then the two user programs. It would not do for either of the systems programs to be too long otherwise the user programs would not get much of a chance to be executed.

Sometimes, people refer to an MP system as a batch system. If we think of the traditional mono-programming batch system, this can be a misleading use of the phrase. However, what people really mean is that a batch of jobs can be submitted to an MP system where they are read onto the input queue at one time and thereafter dealt with in the manner outlined above. Alternatively, a card reader may be placed at some convenient location and any authorised programmer can read his program through the reader at any time. The essential point about the MP system is that two or more programs are resident in memory at one time although at any given instant only one program can be executed.

Let us now move on to a discussion about *time-sharing systems,* sometimes referred to as *multi-access systems.*

Time-sharing Systems

Although the MP system executes programs at a faster rate than the traditional batch processing systems, programmers, nevertheless, have to wait their turn in a queue. A certain amount of time will elapse between reading in a program and actually receiving the results. This period of time is referred to as the *turnround* or **turnaround time** and may take minutes or even hours, depending upon how the installation is organised. Furthermore, once the program has been submitted, the programmer can do no-

Fig. 6.19 TT user 1 inputs command to place program X into CM. TS supervisor informs I/O handler to load program X into CM.

thing about it until the results are seen. Thus, if the language translator detects some grammatical error and issues an error diagnostic, the programmer cannot alter the program until the output is looked at and the error message is read.

Some programmers want to have instant results and to be able to correct any programming error as soon as it is diagnosed by the translator. With the advent of teletypewriters and VDU terminals, this became a possibility but the type of operating system for such an environment differs from either of the two already discussed. How does it work?

A programmer will sit down at the terminal and type in a program, or if the program has already been typed in and stored for later use on the secondary storage device, the programmer can call up the program and ask for it to be placed in the central memory (Figure 6.19). Once the program is in CM, the programmer can ask the **time-sharing operating system** to execute the program. This means that the program is first translated and, if any programming errors are detected, diagnostic messages can be issued via the translating program. The programmer can now correct the errors and ask for

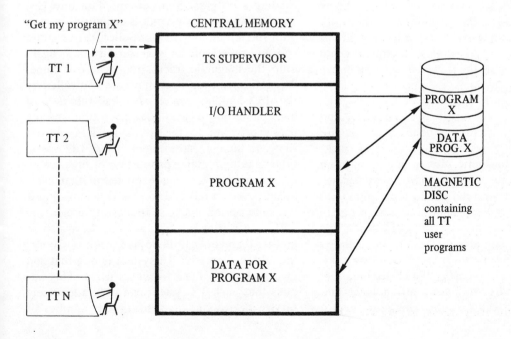

"Get my program X"

CENTRAL MEMORY

TT 1

TT 2

TT N

TS SUPERVISOR

I/O HANDLER

PROGRAM X

DATA FOR PROGRAM X

PROGRAM X

DATA PROG. X

MAGNETIC DISC containing all TT user programs

the program to be re-executed. If the program requires any data, this may be typed in at the terminal keyboard as soon as it is required, or, alternatively, the data may already be stored on the secondary storage device and can be accessed by the program through the help of the I/O handler. The point is that the program can be executed and can produce results straightaway, with the turnaround time measured in seconds rather than minutes or hours. However, typical time-sharing systems have many more than one terminal user to deal with, all of whom wish to see their program results within seconds.

Again, the secret lies in the amount of work the CPU can do in one second compared to the speeds of the I/O devices, in this case very slow terminals. A teletypewriter or VDU has a speed of about 30 characters per second, sometimes even lower. Note how very much slower this is compared to even the slowest card readers or line printers. The real speed of these devices when inputting information depends simply on how fast the user can type. 10 characters per second is usually a very fast speed for most users. Often it is far less because the user has to look for the key with the correct character on it, and very often the user becomes involved in relatively long "thinking" spells especially if a piece of program is being corrected. Bearing this in mind, together with the knowledge that two or more user programs can be resident in CM at the same time, it is not difficult to see how the time-sharing system can work for many users.

Suppose 30 terminals exist in a building, all of which are linked up to the computer, and that twenty of them are being used (Figure 6.20). Each user has a given number of tracks on the input magnetic disc for their program and data. The time-sharing (TS) supervisor will permit the first terminal to run a program, and the TS I/O handler can read in the program from the fast input disc to CM. When the program and data are in CM, the I/O handler informs the TS supervisor which will now allocate a period of typically 10 milliseconds (i.e. about one-hundredth of a second) in which that user's program can execute. This may seem a

very short time but remember that many computational statements can be executed in this time, (arithmetic, logic, comparison type statements). Once this time period is finished, the next terminal user will be allocated another 10 milliseconds, and so on for the 20 users. The 10 millisecond time period is frequently called a **time-slice** and is given in strict sequence to each of the twenty users. When the last user has had a time-slice, the TS supervisor goes back to the first one again and repeats the whole cycle. If one of the users is engaged in a "thinking" spell, and therefore does not need the CPU at that time, or if a user is still typing in a program instruction, then the TS supervisor will pass on to the next terminal in sequence. The former user will have to wait for the next cycle to be given a chance to use the CPU. This cycle is called a **polling system**, whereby each terminal is polled in turn every two seconds or so on a strict **round-robin** basis. In practice, very few of the terminals will need the CPU within the same second. In the meantime, any new user starting up one of the free terminals, i.e. becoming terminal user number twenty-one, will get a turn in strict sequence with the other twenty users.

In computer terminology, the process of reading a program and perhaps data into CM from the magnetic disc unit is called **roll-in** and, after the ten millisecond time-slice, the program will be **rolled-out** or transferred back again onto the magnetic tracks from where it came. The roll-in/roll-out operations are controlled by the I/O handler, which also has the task of controlling output generated by a time-sharing user's program to the user's track and from there to the correct terminal. These I/O operations take up a major proportion of time. From tests carried out, it has been learnt that users begin to get bored and to lose concentration if the time period between requesting use of the CPU and getting a response from the system is greater than about three to five seconds. Consequently, a successful TS system is one that can give such a response to *all* its users. This implies that each TS system can only adequately service or respond to a maximum number of

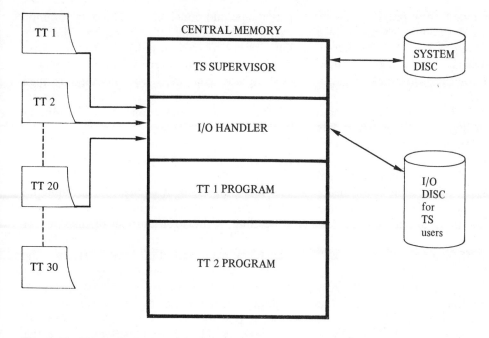

Fig. 6.20 Time-sharing computer system

terminals. It is the duty of the computer manufacturer to work out in advance exactly how many terminals can be serviced within a three to five second period.

Both the TS supervisor and the MP supervisor are far more complex system programs than the comparatively simple monoprogramming batch processing supervisor. Indeed, the control of I/O between the various I/O and secondary storage devices alone deserves to have a dedicated system program in the guise of what we have called an I/O handler. However, the important point for us to note is *what* these various computer systems do rather than *how* they do it, which is better left to those who specialise in systems programming.

Some installations prefer to have a mixture of both MP and TS. This enables users of such a computer to choose the method more suitable to their own application. Usually, it is more convenient to have two computers, one to perform the MP tasks, the other to perform TS tasks. However, such systems are organised so that if one of the computers develops a fault,

the other can take on both tasks but at the expense of degrading (i.e. slowing down) the response of both systems. This can be tolerated for a short period, say a half a day, whilst the faulty computer is being "repaired". Universities and computer bureaux are typical environments where such a mixture of systems is particularly useful because of the varied requirements of their users.

Real-time Systems

A final type of computer system, the **real-time system**, is easy to confuse with time-sharing systems since both use teletype and/or VDUs and both systems are frequently called *on-line systems* (see below). However, it is the application area which lies behind the different philosophy of these two systems. A real-time system is usually devoted entirely to one application such as banking, air-line reservations, hotel-room, or theatre bookings, etc. In other words, the user of a real-time system does not write programs or modify any previously written program. He or she is only interested in a quick answer to a given enquiry, e.g. "is there a free seat on the British Airways flight at 09.30 hours from Heathrow to Montreal on 15th September?" If the reply to this enquiry is affirmative, then the BA agent can use the system to reserve a seat for the customer. The terminals used are often special-purpose ones in that the keyboard is slightly different to standard teletypes and VDUs, having special buttons or keys which make their work easier by being orientated to the application. But first let us go back to the point about on-line.

On-line Versus Off-line

The distinction between the two is really very simple. The term **on-line** refers to the fact that I/O devices, data files and secondary storage devices are all connected to the control unit of the CPU so that any device may be used by the computer at any time. By being connected to the CU we mean that, via the I/O handler, any of the devices may be controlled directly by the computer system. This is the case with the time-sharing system as well as the multi-programming systems where the I/O devices and the secondary storage units may be activated at any time.

This is contrasted with the **off-line** situation where the computer has no immediate contact with such devices as in the case of the mono-programming batch system when batches are being overlapped. In the input phase, it is the input channel which controls the transfer of information onto the magnetic tape, not the central computer. The same applies to the printing phase where the output channel controls the transfer of information from the output tape to the printer. The only on-line connection is in the process phase where the computer has direct control over the input and output magnetic tapes. Another example of off-line is the case where cards are punched via a punch card device for eventual use on a card reader. Today there are very few examples of off-line procedure, except in the punching of paper-tape and punch cards. The only common example today is the off-line graph plotter. The information to be assembled in a graph form has been previously prepared onto a magnetic tape by the computer, but the tape is then connected directly to the graph plotter system and has no more connection with the computer system.

Real-time Enquiry System

The real-time element comes into prominence because the customer making the enquiry about a possible flight to Montreal or his or her current financial situation will only be willing to wait for a given period of time. Therefore, the response to a query *must* be given within a definite time period. Also it is important to update any transaction that may take place as soon as possible. For example, let us suppose that there is only one seat available on the BA flight, yet two potential passengers make an enquiry at about the same time. One could be in Paris, the other at Heathrow itself. If the Paris customer makes the enquiry first, they will be told that only one seat is left. The Paris customer accepts the seat and the agent makes out the reservation via the real-time system. The reservation file has now to be updated to say that all seats have been taken *before* the second agent at Heathrow is allowed to access that reservation file. If this did not happen it is obvious that the one seat could easily be given to the two customers and the error would not be noticed until two passengers turned up on the 15th September for the one seat.

Figure 6.21 shows a similar illustration as for a time-sharing system but includes the all-important transaction file containing the relevant files for the application in hand. Some of the more distinct features of the four computer systems discussed in this chapter are catalogued in the table opposite.

Systems Programs

In this chapter we have mentioned several system programs, we now summarise these.

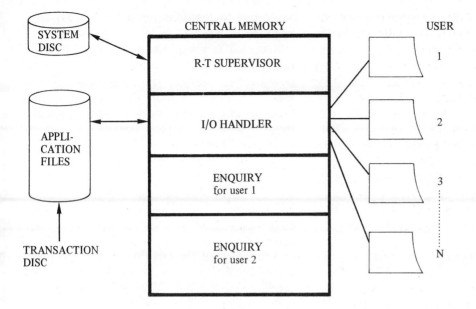

Fig. 6.21   Real-time computer system

Batch Processing

One user program in CM at one time
  —a mono-programming system.

May use any secondary storage device
  such as magnetic tape, disc or drum.

Fairly simple operating system required.

Multi-programming

Two or more user programs in CM at
  at one time.

Only magnetic discs or drums suitable
  because of *random* access.

Complex operating system required.

Real-time

Usually devoted to one application.
User makes enquiry only and cannot
  be allowed to write or modify programs.
User *must* get a response within a given
  time period, depending upon the
  application.
Transaction files *must* be updated before
  another enquiry using those transaction
  files can be serviced.

Time-sharing

Many different applications.
User can write and modify programs.

Users *should* get a response within
  3-5 seconds but not disastrous
  if not.
Transaction files are updated but the
  time in which this is done is not so
  critical.

The **operating system** is responsible for directing a given computer into a batch mono-programming system, a multi-programming system, a time-sharing system, or a real-time system.

Language translators are supplied by the manufacturer for translating user programs written in Fortran, Basic, Cobol, or Algol, etc.

The **I/O handler** is responsible for the on-line control of all input/output and secondary storage devices.

Many **utility programs** exist for the benefit of users, such as *library routines*; the *edit* programs, which allow a user to correct any program or data file by adding lines of instructions or data, and deleting unwanted lines; *sort and merge routines* for typical commercial applications (see Chapter 4), etc.

Important Words and Terms in Chapter 6

hardware, software
operating system software programs and systems programs
general purpose and special purpose computers

batch processing system
  batch
  computer operators
  job
  user
  control commands, control cards
  library routines, library loader
  source program, object program or object code
  supervisor program
  input-process-output phases
  overlapping batches
  channels
  speed mis-match
  mono-programming

multi-programming system
  computational bound programs
  input/output bound programs
  power of a computer system
  partition
  random or direct access
  I/O handler
  priority

time-sharing systems
  multi-access systems
  turnaround time
  time-slice
  polling system
  round-robin system
  roll-in, roll-out

real-time systems
  on-line, off-line
  enquiry

Exercises 6

1 Multi-programming is
a) writing many programs at once.
b) incorporating many programs in one program.
c) using many backing stores in one program.
d) using many programs to solve a problem.
e) the processing of two or more programs in the computer at the same time. (*YREB* 1977)

2 Explain what is meant by the terms: batch processing; multi-programming; on-line working. (*JMB* 1975)

3 Which is the correct answer to the following statement: "An essential requirement of a computer system supporting many on-line terminals is ..."
a) a line printer *b*) a graphics display *c*) an operating system *d*) card punch equipment *e*) Basic.

4 Explain why a program written by you *cannot* occupy the entire main memory store of a computer. (*AEB* spec.)

5 What is meant by a real-time system? Name two applications in which real-time computing systems are used. (*EAEB* 1977)

6 Choose two of the following list which are "real-time" applications:
designing a motorway; traffic light control; stock control for a supermarket; airline seat booking; preparing electricity bills.

7 Early computers could only handle one program at a time. Modern systems can handle several programs at once. What is this facility called? (*SWEB* 1976)

8 List and describe the functions of the executive (supervisor) program in controlling the operation of a multi-programming system. Your answer should include those functions which are also required in batch processing. (*SWEB* 1977)

9 Describe the various methods that are available to increase the efficient use of the central processor time. In your answer you should consider batch-processing, multi-access, and multi-programming. (*EMREB* 1977).

7 Computers and Society

Technology and Society

Major technological innovations have a habit of affecting the lives of individuals. A society is composed of individuals, and there is a tendency to use this somewhat impersonal term "society" when really we mean ourselves and our families and friends. On balance, technology has helped the human race to become the superior member of the animal kingdom, and as a result we have attained a more "comfortable" and higher form of existence than other members. A classic exåmple is the *wheel* which allowed heavy goods to be transported more easily and quickly and, when the superior pulling power of an ox or a horse was enlisted, with far less effort for humans.

The invention of primitive tools, especially of iron implements, enabled people to manufacture goods, cut stone, and dig channels in the earth to irrigate formerly barren land. The fact that iron swords and the deadly horse-driven chariots used in battle caused mutilation and death is more a reflection of "man's inhumanity to man" than a bad side-effect of primitive technology.

Printing resulted in the opening up of knowledge to the whole of society and raising its mind to a higher intellectual level, so that knowledge was no longer the preserve of the few. The harnessing of water, steam and electricity to create power greater than the muscle of man led to faster movement from one place to another over land, sea and air, as well as to the mass production of goods and greater employment prospects for the majority. However, such advances or progress can bring in their wake a certain change in the lives of individuals and a re-organisation of society which many claim is not totally beneficial.

A history of human evolution suggests that people are shaped anew by each major technological advance. A new invention leads people and society to view the world through new eyes and to accept new values. For example, the telescope permitted us to see beyond the confines of our eyes but in turn changed our conception of the universe and our place in it, and in time led us to explore outer space. Printing led us to think for ourself and encouraged individualism which in turn led to a change in attitude to art, religion and science. The obvious benefits derived from harnessing steam and electricity as a form of power have undoubtedly made our present society increasingly materialistic and acquisitive. The splitting of the atom has brought fear of nuclear warfare resulting in the protest marches of the 1960s. Certainly the television has had an affect on our lives and, in one strange way, may almost reverse the impact of printing by promoting ideas which can be absorbed by a mass audience. Alexander Bell one hundred years ago could not have foreseen the re-organisation in society as a result of his invention of the telephone. Who could have foreseen the problems raised by the combustion engine which led to the motor car? It has divided the family into smaller units so that often adults, children, their parents and grandparents live separate lives in different towns or counties. Furthermore, the countryside has become scarred with motorways and the air in towns polluted.

Thus, apart from benefits, many technological advances have side effects which can be as harmful as the side effects of many drugs prescribed by our family doctors. Yet humans by their very nature will not, or perhaps cannot, stand still. We are ever hungry for new inventions and must learn to adapt to them in order to survive.

In addition to all these, we have the current technology which led to the development of the computer. It would be naive of us to believe that this technology will be all good or all bad. If history repeats itself as it has done throughout the past, then we can expect our lives to be affected in some way. Hence, the purpose of this chapter is to encourage you to think about this.

Computers in Society

In trying to assess the impact of computers on society, there are two points worth noting. The first is that of the incredible speed with which this form of technology has made itself felt in so many areas of everyday life. It is just thirty years ago that the first computer was built, yet today there are many hundreds of thousands of computers being used (see Figure 7.1). So entrenched in our society are computers that, if they could be swept away overnight, the entire financial world of the West would collapse. This may serve to illustrate the second point, namely that computers have penetrated our society far more deeply than the average person realises. It may be difficult for the average man or woman to appreciate the benefits of computers to the commercial world, especially when they are sent repeated reminders for an invoice already paid, or their driving licence is delayed because of "teething problems" of the new computer system. Nevertheless, for better or worse, industrial societies have become dependent upon computers in a similar degree to their dependence upon electricity or the telephone system.

Dependence of Society on Computers

The use of the term "society" above needs more explanation. What we really mean is the organisations within society for which individuals work, for example the teaching organisations, the commercial organisations, the industrial organisations, the administrative and transportation organisations, etc. All are dependent

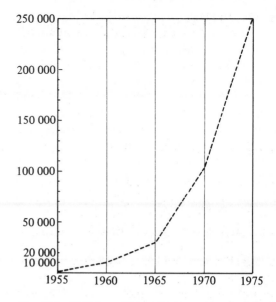

Fig. 7.1 Total number of computers installed in USA, Japan, Germany, France, and UK.

upon the help of computers to one degree or another.

a) COMMERCE It is the commercial world—the shopping centres, the financial world of banking, insurance and credit companies—which would most suffer without computer centres. They form the majority of users. Indeed, it is doubtful whether the financial world in particular could even survive today without assistance from computers. This dependence can only become greater as time passes.

b) INDUSTRY Many industrial organisations such as the steel, chemical and oil companies, rely on computers not merely for their own internal administration but for the actual control of the plant processes. This trend can only increase, more so now since the coming of the microprocessor. It is cheap, reliable and robust. It can be used in environments in which the traditional computer could not be used: in extremes of cold, and in dirty and noisy atmospheres. Many of the tasks involved in assembly work, as in the motor-car, washing machine and television industries, could be undertaken by processes controlled by micro-computers.

171

c) EDUCATION Although little impact has been made at secondary level education, the day will come when much of the traditional teaching will be performed through the help of computers. This form of teaching is known as *computer-assisted instruction* (CAI) and *computer-assisted learning* (CAL). Technically this is possible and indeed already exists in a few instances in the UK. The main reasons for it not being already widespread are lack of funds to purchase the necessary equipment at a national level, the almost total absence of suitable software and teaching material, as well as the current crisis within the teaching profession in the UK where officially there are too few teaching posts for too many trained teachers.

Interestingly enough this last point results from the drop in the birth rate and underlines that what may be technically possible does not always occur because of other social influences. However, at the tertiary level of education, especially in universities and polytechnics, the computer has become an indispensable tool for undergraduates and postgraduates, mainly from the science and technology departments. Many of the current projects under-taken by postgraduates would be impractical without the help of the computer.

d) ADMINISTRATION Every organisation has its own internal administration to look after but some specialise in administration itself. In the UK for example, the Civil Service aids the government in applying the laws of the country; local County Halls manage the administration of street lighting, refuse collection, housing, road maintenance, local laws, etc.; local education authorities are responsible for the administration of primary, secondary and some tertiary level education. Many of these administrative tasks are performed by computers. The Post Office is another example.

e) TRANSPORTATION Many forms of land, sea and air transportation rely on computers. Some road haulage companies use them to prepare optimised routes for their vehicles.

Many sections of the British Rail and the London Underground service rely on computers to help in the formidable task of routing railstock. There is a growing dependence in major cities on computer-controlled traffic systems, as well as, in the UK, for a computerised signalling system for motorways. Without computers, air traffic control would be virtually impossible to regulate at current traffic volume. It is now becoming necessary to have some form of control in congested shipping lanes, such as the English Channel. Not only are we becoming more dependent on computers in these areas but we need the computer in order to cope.

f) OTHER PROFESSIONS The law, medicine, libraries, the armed forces and many other professions and working environments are gradually making use of computers and thereby building up a greater dependence upon computers. It is no exaggeration to state that over 70% of children at school today will be working directly or indirectly with computers after they leave school. Hence the necessity to understand computers while at school or college.

g) INDIVIDUALS Even if we are not directly concerned with computing in our everyday work, as individuals we are affected by them. The motorist, the air passenger, some hospital patients, the shopper in any large store are some of the people for whom computers process information. Everyone who pays for rates, electricity, telephone or gas has their bills processed by computers. Most people who receive a weekly or monthly salary have their salary slips generated by computers. Indeed, it is becoming increasingly difficult to find anyone who in some way or another does not have some information concerning them processed by the ubiquitous computer.

Why Society is Dependent upon Computers

It should be evident by now that not only are computers here but they are certain to stay.

Perhaps we should consider why they have become so entrenched in our society?

a) *Ability to Calculate* (*compute*) Computers were invented primarily to perform calculations at a speed beyond human ability and with an accuracy and consistency which people could never match. The early computers processed the calculations necessary for producing firing tables for ballistics and navigation tables. This calculating ability is still valid today to the extent that some of the knowledge we possess would still be unknown were it not for the computational ability of computers.

b) *Processing Information* Without doubt, it is the ability to record and store information, process that information, and reproduce the information in a variety of ways that makes the computer such an indispensable aid to society. It came at a time when information was being generated in such volume that administrative departments were unable to cope by conventional methods. This is sometimes referred to as the *information explosion*. More and more paperwork was being produced and it was taking longer to sift through it and to gather the relevant information. Prototype commercial computers such as LEO and UNIVAC I had already shown that computers could be used to perform certain information processing tasks more quickly and more efficiently than human beings. In turn, this meant that management could be given relevant information from which to take decisions more quickly and effectively. The processing capability of the computer was recognised at a time when it was most needed, hence the dramatic increase in the purchase of commercial computers since the late 1950s.

Benefits versus Disadvantages

Having discussed just how much society depends upon the computational and information processing skills of the computer, let us consider some of the effects of this. The benefits are obvious and have been discussed above but now a growing number of people are worried about this efficency at gathering information. Their fears are summed up in the current phrase "the privacy issue".

Privacy Issue

Today, certain information about individuals exists in many separate computer files and, if this trend continues, it will not be too long before fairly comprehensive records on every person could exist in different filing systems, e.g. information about one's driving licence, criminal records, medical records, social security payments, work records, tax records, credit ratings, mailing lists, shopping accounts, and even a complete school record from the age of five. Many of these already exist but the next step would be to collect all the separate information and to combine them into a complete life history of each individual. Is this desirable? Should people be allowed to know what information is held about them on computer files? Should they be allowed to check the details and to report any errors? Most important however is the issue about who should be allowed to access all this information? These are just some of the points being debated.

An example may help to illustrate current anxiety. In the USA in particular, credit rating systems are very common. A substantial number of people have already had their reputations tarnished because incorrect data had been recorded about their credit worthiness. An even more terrifying situation is that an unscrupulous government could have access to all known information about any individual, even details about eating habits and the journals and magazines subscribed to. Another undesirable result of pooling information is that individuals would become a mere statistic in the eye of the record keepers. Few would like to think of themselves as being a number, as something impersonal. But against these fears must be balanced the benefits derived from computerised information.

Unemployment

The fear in many people's minds is that computers will take away their jobs. Clerical workers, factory floor workers, tube train drivers, even teachers are but a few. The unemployment fear was quite the fashion in the late 1960s and early 1970s. In fact it never became a real problem. It is true that computers did perform many aspects of people's work but it tended to perform the more dull and repetitive tasks and in some instances freed people to concentrate on more creative and challenging work. However, the social problem here is not with those who have the intelligence to perform the more challenging work but with those who cannot do anything else but unskilled manual and low-skill tasks. There is no easy answer to this. With the current possibility of yet another widespread increase in the use of computers through the micro-electronic revolution, the unemployment problem has again been raised, especially for those engaged in any form of assembly work.

In the past, the computer industry was able to create many jobs which had previously not existed, for example, computer manufacturers, computer operators, programmers, systems designers, systems analysts, data preparation staff, etc., and this helped to solve the problem. Perhaps, a similar growth in new jobs may arise as a result of micro-electronics, but it is not easy to be sure at this stage, hence the concern especially amongst trade union leaders.

Correct Information

We have already alluded to the problems for individuals whose information stored in computer storage systems is incorrect. But another problem awaits those who are responsible for securing correct information in the first place. It seems likely that, with continued dependence on computer-stored information, future governments will be involved more and more in creating legislation to protect the individual. However, to implement such laws much time and money will be needed. The price of privacy, the price of ensuring correct data, the price of preventing unauthorised access to information will have to be borne to some extent by the owners of the computer information. Very likely they will have to apply for a licence and become registered (in the UK) with the Data Protection Authority. Failing to register may well have to become a criminal offence.

Technology Gap

At the present time, it is the industrialised societies which possess the capital to invest in technology. The poorer countries cannot afford to invest money in high technology, with the result that the gap between the two is widening each year. Even with the USSR where industrial production is larger than in the USA, the gap in computer technology is in favour of the Western World. This is due not so much to lack of money but to a slow start in this field, to the ideology of self-sustenance which prevented any interchange of development between the Soviet block and the West, and to the lack of competition between manufacturing companies which the capitalist countries favour on the grounds that it promotes faster development and encourages new ideas. It seems impossible for those on the other side of the gap to catch up. Not only would an immense amount of money have to be invested but the technology is developing at such a rate that to be even a few years behind, let alone a few decades, is enough to keep the gap ever open.

Yet, with the development of micro-electronics, computing power could be something attainable for any country, even the poorest. The Prime Minister of China, in 1978, stated that micro-computers could well be the bridge which would close this gap. This is most encouraging for the world as a whole since, like human beings, no country likes to be always reliant upon the charity of others and to become a pawn in the political games of the superior powers.

Micro-electronics

As a result of the technological advances made in electronics, we are witnessing today the advent of the micro-computer. It is too soon yet to pronounce with any certainty how these latest computers will affect our lives. It was only in 1971 that the first microprocessor (the equivalent of the CPU of a traditional computer) was produced by Intel, the INTEL 4004. Its significance is that it could be contained on a single chip of silicon less than 6 mm square. But already microprocessors are being used in a variety of applications: for example, in washing machines to control the selected programme wash; in taxi-meters, microwave ovens, petrol pumps, pocket calculators, digital watches, refrigerators, word processing machines, point-of-sale devices, many computer peripherals, in military and space applications, and in aircraft where very small and reliable processors are vital.

Their current impact is due to their very small size and, when produced in vast quantities, their very low cost. They tend to have a high degree of reliability and are not affected as much as the traditional mini-computer in noisy, dirty and very cold atmospheres. Although micro-computers are true computers, that is the microprocessor has necessary input, output and auxiliary storage devices attached to it, they cannot yet compete effectively with the larger and more traditional computer. Future technology promises to reduce the gap and to provide effective micro-computer systems at a fraction of the cost of traditional mini-computers. Where this will lead us is difficult to predict but it should bring about a further increase in the use of computing power in many areas where formerly it was not economically viable to use traditional computers.

Some Applications of Micro-computers

Very Small Organisations The very small business which either has to do without computer access or has to hire time from a computer bureau can now afford to think about buying its own micro-computer system. Individual schools can purchase small micro-computers for less than £2000, capable of processing Basic programs and of storing programs on cassette tapes or floppy diskettes. Individual doctors are being offered micro-systems which will produce lists of patients into age and sex groups, and which compute capitation fees provided by the National Health service (in the UK) for each of their patients and according to the type of patient. Accountants, lawyers, estate agents, surveyors and many other professional people may well find that micro-systems provide an ideal solution for the information which they handle but for which traditional computers have proved to be far too expensive. Micro-computer manufacturers are preparing for a substantial increase in sales over the next ten years. If this becomes a reality, then society is set to become even more deeply committed to the use of computers in areas as yet unaffected.

Industry Another major area in which micro-computers are expected to play an important role is in industrial and manufacturing companies where currently computers are too expensive for automatic assembly processes. But with the low cost of microprocessors this could soon change. Indeed, it has been stated that few companies will survive the 1980s unless they do change over to automated process control.

Robotics for the Disabled For any of us who have relatives or friends seriously handicapped by paralysis, the promise of micro-computer-controlled arms must be a happy outcome of micro-electronics. A prototype of a micro-controlled robot arm for the severely handicapped has been developed at Queen Mary College, London. This differs from the so-called bionic arm already available which requires patients to have some existing muscle movement. The micro-controlled arm can be programmed to carry out any type of function independent of the patient, and a demonstration has been given as to how it might be used by a patient who can do nothing but move his head and hold a stick in his mouth.

The Future

If we succumb to the temptation of forecasting the future based on likely technological advances alone, and without regard for other factors which also play a part in shaping our future (such as public opinion, human psychology and political issues), we could foresee a society totally different to our present one. Technologically, it is possible that in the near future every home could have its own computer based on micro-electronics. It could be trained to respond only to our voices and those of our immediate family. Thus, when we come downstairs in the morning we could say "Hallo" to it, whereupon it would greet us in turn and ask us what we wanted for breakfast. Of course, we would have to put the bread in the toaster to which the micro would be connected and the other foods in the pots and pans, but the *family micro* would do the cooking.

It would remind us over breakfast of any appointments we had to keep or birthday presents to buy. While we were out at work it would record any telephone messages or relay any pre-recorded messages to others; control the heating; and if our evening meal was required and prepared by us (although house-trained robots may do this in the more distant future), it would have the meal ready on our arrival back home. It would open the door in response to valid voices only and greet us with a friendly word together with information about any callers or telephone messages during our absence. In the evening, it could entertain the children, hopefully with more stimulating "games" than those currently available for the domestic television sets. It could set homework or produce additional tuition in certain subjects. Later on before going to bed, the adults could play cards or draughts or even fairly good chess with it, discuss tomorrow's menu, inform it about the bills paid or unpaid and the presents we "forgot" to buy, and make a plea to remind us first thing in the morning about them; and so on. Such a system is all technically possible today and is not the science fiction fantasy that it may seem.

In contrast to the image of the computer as a family pet, it could equally take on the spectre of an ogre and become a Big Brother figure. We have already discussed how easy it would be to build up a complete record from birth to death for every person and how this could be open to mis-use by an unscrupulous government. Widespread use of computer-assisted learning, in which the computer would generate students' lessons to teach only what is held in its storage system, as well as monitoring the performance and progress, could well be used by an undesirable régime to "brainwash" youth into a rigid social and philosophical pattern. Again, a system like this is technically possible and a government bent upon the mis-use of computer technology would not have too far to go to force a society into the "the big brother era".

Apart from these good and bad images, there are other aspects to mention. It was not uncommon a few years ago, when time-sharing systems were becoming commonplace and the cost of computer terminals was decreasing rapidly, to be swept along by predictions put forward by some computer experts that every home would have its own computer terminal. Naturally, people began to talk about the possibility of staying at home and contacting the office via the terminal; of no longer going out to work in an office but of performing all work at home because the information held at the office could be relayed via a time-sharing system to the home. A similar situation was envisaged for students with computer-assisted learning. All teaching and monitoring of progress would be done by the computer. School would become the computer installation, and contact made with the "school" via the home terminal. Furthermore, if the domestic terminals could be linked to shopping centres, then the shopper could also stay at home and order food and clothes over the terminal. The VDU could be used to display the goods offered to the customer.

People today are talking about the *electronic office* as a result of the cheaper computing power of micro-electronics. In such an office there would be no filing cabinets and very little paper to write on since all the "paperwork" would be stored in the electronic storage system. When information was required the office personnel would no longer go to the filing cabinets but request the information to be displayed on VDU screens. If the information had to be sent to another office in the same building or to some outside office, it would be sent in much the same way that users of a time-sharing system send and receive information. This is called *electronic mail* and is almost certain to become a reality in the not too distant future. It will mean a change in our present method of posting letters and have serious repercussions on the Post Office in the UK (and elsewhere), which is the nation's largest employer.

Certainly some of the predictions are likely to happen because technically they are all possible. However, other factors do play an important role in shaping society. For example, it is part of human nature to be sociable, to meet other people. For this reason, the technical vision of staying at home instead of "going to the office or school" or of "going shopping" to see and handle the actual goods on display might not come about. Instead, human nature could well have a more direct influence on what will really happen. Could the Big Brother image become a reality? We cannot tell, of course, and can only pose another question in turn. Would Hitler have hesitated in using computer information if he had the opportunity? Here we must underline an important point. The future does not depend so much on computers but upon our use of computers.

If the current shortage of efficient secretarial staff continues, as well as an increase in the high salaries which they demand, then the electronic office could well be very tempting. The present interest in *word processing machines* is no coincidence and the present secretary could find herself replaced by such machines or at least find some of her secretarial/typist skills performed by these machines.

Even education is not free from side effects. The pocket calculator is a prime example of how the low cost of micro-electronics can dramatically reduce the cost of a device and influence its widespread use. Undoubtedly, they are a tremendous boon to everyone who has to calculate. Yet, in time, will we rely too much on them and forget how to perform the simple skills of arithmetic, let alone the more difficult skills of square roots, logarithms and other common mathematical functions? What effect will word processing machines have on the use of our native language? Stereotyped letters will become commonplace and many of us could easily forget how to compose letters and how to express our own personalities through our own use of English. Some educationalists claim that the English language has already been massacred by the appalling standard set by television. Word processing machines with pre-written stored letters can only make matters worse.

Finally, let us predict one virtual certainty, namely the marrying together of two developments: the computer's ability to access and manipulate information on the one hand, and the importance of telecommunications, on the other, to disseminate relevant information on a scale previously undreamt of by the "man-in-the-street". These two parallel activities are destined to unite. When they do, society will be faced with the problem of how to adjust. How it does will be largely in the hands of you now reading this chapter, the future generation, the inheritors of the computerised society.

Exercises 7

1 *a*) State briefly three problem areas and three benefit areas that have arisen with the introduction of computers.

b) Describe the problem and benefit areas that you think might arise in the future from the continuous and increasingly wider use of computers. (*WJEC* 1977)

2 Computer data storage banks hold more information about people's personal affairs every year. Discuss the possible dangers and benefits of this fact and suggest safeguards to limit the danger. (*SWEB* 1977)

3 The Post Office makes use of a computer system.

a) For what purposes does the P.O. use a computer?

b) Summarise the advantages and disadvantages of using the computer:

    i) to the Post Office itself,

    ii) to the customer.

4 Discuss the future influence of micro technology upon society stating reasons why this influence may be for the good of society or otherwise.

5 Laws have recently been introduced which require commercial banks to be licensed. Discuss the reasons which made this more desirable and comment on any further potential threats to society caused by the misuse of the computer. (*UCLES* 1976)

6 "Computers are both an asset and a danger to mankind."

Discuss this statement giving reasons why each point of view might be held. Refer to the effect of computers on employment, availability of employment, the rights of the individual, privacy of the individual. (*JMB* spec).

7 The following paragraph appeared in a newspaper:

"During the last few years computers have been gradually taking over the world. The power which they have over people is very great. Information about everyone in the country is stored on computers. We have no idea whether this information is correct or not, and it cannot be checked. Once the information is put on to a computer it is there for ever, and there is no way of changing it. It is common knowledge that computers are always making mistakes, and no one knows what the computer will do next with this information."

Write a letter to the paper which published the article, saying why you agree or disagree with the points raised. (*YREB* 1977)

8 Development of Computing and Information Processing

Time Chart: a History of Information Processing, Calculating Devices, and Digital Computers

BC

c3700 –3000 Oldest surviving written records—pictographic writing on clay tablets known as cuneiform. Mesopotamia.

c3400 Egyptians introduce symbols for ten, and powers of ten, in recording numbers.

c3000 Cubit rods used as rulers in Egypt. Egyptians discover how to make papyrus and write on it with pen-like implements made from calmus, a reed plant.

c2000 Senkereh tablet on which a list of squares of numbers were depicted in cuneiform. Found near Babylon.

c2000 –1000 Writing in China. Sanskrit writing in India—hymns found.

c1000 First true alphabet. Phoenicia.

c900 First Greek alphabet evolved. Alphabetic writing on "Moabite Stone".

c490 News of invasion by Persians and of victory at Marathon conveyed by runner—Pheidipiddes.

c450 Abacus consisting of beads strung on rods used as a counting device in Greece and Egypt.

c300 Ptolemy I starts the Great Libraries of Alexandria.

c200 Greeks devise a system of written numbers based on ten using alphabetic symbols to represent the numbers. Records kept by the Greeks and Romans on sheets of wood coated in wax. A metal stylus was used to scratch the wax surface.

c150 Use of fire torches for signalling mentioned in the writings of Polybius, a Greek historian.

c100 A form of pocket abacus used by some Romans. Counting with pebbles on a table or counting board still the more common method of calculating and recording.

63 A form of shorthand invented by Tiro and used to record speeches, and also taught in schools. Rome.

AD

c100 Paper invented in China.

136 An earthquake-recording instrument invented in China.

c300 –400 The first codices, parchment manuscripts, made into a book.

c500 Hindu number system, complete with a zero symbol.

767 Block printing in India.

868 First known printed book. China.

876 Use of a zero as a place-holder in written numbers. India.

c900 Arabic number system.

c1000 Spanish number system, a refinement of the Hindu-Arabic system.

1086 Domesday Book.

1150 A pigeon-post established by the Sultan of Baghdad.

c1150 Manufacture of paper originated in Europe by the Moors in Spain.

c1200 Movable type used for printing with separate letters on clay. China. A hand-held abacus known as a "suan pan" introduced in China. Tally sticks used to record transactions. England.

1305	Statute to standardize the lengths of inch, foot, yard, etc. Edward I responsible.
c1400	Number system in use in Italy—a further refinement of the Hindu-Arabic. Symbols very close to our present decimal system. Soon spread into Europe through trade between countries.
c1450	Invention of movable type in Europe. Gutenburg's bible produced using a printing press. Mainz, Germany.
1476	Book printed in English. William Caxton, Bruges, Belgium. A manual on Arithmetic printed. Venice.
1492	Decimal point introduced by Pelazzi. Nice, Italy.
c1500	Chinese abacus introduced in Japan—known as a soroban.
1588	Spanish Armada. News of approach spread across England by fire-beacons.
c1590	Invention of lead pencil.
c1600	Abacus no longer the general computing device in use in Spain and Italy.
1614	John Napier, a Scottish Mathematician, published a paper on logarithms. A method of multiplying and dividing numbers quickly and accurately by performing additions and subtractions.
1617	Napier's bones—a "mechanical" aid to multiplication and division. Ten strips of bone so numbered that when placed next to each other multiplication can be carried out by additions of adjacent numbers.
1618	Briggs introduces logarithms to the base ten.
1620	Gunter's scale introduced. Used with dividers as a slide rule.
1623	Schickard describes a wooden mechanical calculator.
1630	Description of a circular slide rule published.
1632	A slide rule described in the writings of the Rev. W. Oughtred.
1645	Pascal's adding machine—a device with eight counter wheels linked by ratchets for carry-over. Not reliable because parts were not well enough made, but principles sound. Blaise Pascal was a Frenchman.
1654	Bissaker's straight slide rule, similar to modern type.
1694	Von Leibniz's stepped-cylinder reckoner—a calculating device capable of handling the four basic arithmetic operations. Not very accurate as the parts could not be made precisely enough. Many later machines adopted the same principles of design.
1700 –1800	Decline in the use of the abacus in England and Germany.
1714	Typewriter patent taken out by Henry Mill.
1725	Bouchon developed a method of controlling part of the silk weaving process using the positions of holes in a roll of perforated paper. Lyons, France.
1728	Falcon constructed an apparatus making it possible to weave more complex designs in cloth using holes punched in rectangular cards to control part of the process.
c1770	The English developed an efficient system of communicating between ships by signalling with flags.
1794	C. Chappe, France. Optical telegraph—a nationwide system of semaphore towers.
1801	First British national census.
1805	Joseph Jacquard's loom attachment—an advance on Falcon. The device used punched cards strung together and provided automatic control of the warp threads. Each card contained code for part of a design. By stringing cards together a complete pattern was formed and by joining them in a loop the pattern was repeated.

1808 Typewritten letters found dated from this year.

1812 11 000 looms reported in use in France using Jacquard's attachment.

1814 *The Times* produced by steam-operated printing press—Koenig and Bauer.

1817 Planimeter invented to measure area of irregular shapes—Hermann and Lammle, Bavaria.

1820 Charles Thomas' Arithmometer. This was the first really practical application of Leibniz's principles. A firm was set up to manufacture the calculators and 1500 were sold over the following 60 years.

1822 Charles Babbage's model of a "Difference Engine". A calculating machine designed to compute mathematical and statistical tables using the difference theory. Once initial values had been set, the engine could compute the next few thousand values without error. A bigger version was proposed capable of calculating to 20 decimal places but technology at the time was unable to meet the design specifications. Work ceased on the new engine in 1833.

1837 Electric telegraph developed by Cooke and Wheatstone, Britain.
S. Morse demonstrated the electromagnetic telegraph in the U.S.A. Babbage's "Analytical Engine"—a design for a digital computer. The computer was to have had a MILL to perform arithmetic operations, a STORE to retain a thousand 50 digit numbers, INPUT from punched cards, OUTPUT engraved on metal plates for printing, and a CONTROL device based on Jacquard's punched card principle. Engineering of the day was not capable of producing all the parts so the engine was not built. Details of Babbage's plans and ideas are known to us through the writings of Lady Lovelace, Lord Byron's daughter.

1840 Postal reform made it possible for anyone to send letters. First postage stamp—Rowland Hill.

1848 Carrier pigeons extensively used during the French Revolution.

1850 First key-driven adding machine. Patent obtained by D. Paramalee in the U.S.A.

1851 Invention of microfilm by B. Dancer.

1853 A "Difference Engine" based on Babbage's ideas constructed by George and Edward Scheutz, Sweden.

1857 First key-driven, four-process calculating device developed by Thomas Hill in the U.S.A.

1861 Transcontinental telegraph established in the U.S.A.

1864 International Telegraph Union established.

1868 Patent for a typewriter with a QWERTY keyboard—Sholes and Glidden, U.S.A. QWERTY is the sequence of keys in the top row of letters, left-hand side.

1871 Commercial use of microfilm to store information.

1872 A reliable typewriter marketed in Denmark—Hansen.

1873 Remington market the Sholes and Glidden typewriter in the U.S.A.

1874 Universal Postal Union.

1876 Lord Kelvin developed a tide predictor on the planimeter principle and proposed a differential analyser. His brother, James Thomson, produced an integrator on the same principle. Invention of the telephone—Alexander Bell.
Decimal system of classification proposed by M. Dewey in the U.S.A.

1877 Phonograph patented by Thomas Edison in the U.S.A.

1878 Calculator based on the Leibniz stepped-cylinder developed by Willgodt Odhner in Sweden.

1884 First cash register—invented by James Ritty in the U.S.A.

1887 First reliable key-driven multiple-order calculator, known as the "Macaroni Box", developed by Dorr Felt in the U.S.A. This machine was the forerunner of the comptometer.

Machine developed by Léon Bolée, in France, capable of direct multiplication instead of calculation by repeated additions.

Invention of the mimeograph to copy documents.

A wax-cylinder motor-driven sound recorder developed by Edison.

1890 Processing of census data in the U.S.A.—using punched cards and card punch, reader, sorter and tabulating machines designed by Herman Hollerith.

1891 An adding machine, key driven, complete with printing feature developed by William Burroughs in the U.S.A.

1895 Wireless communication over a distance of more than a mile achieved by Marconi in Italy.

1896 Tabulating Machine Company founded by Hollerith. Later to merge with other firms to form IBM.

1897 Cathode ray oscilloscope developed by K. Braun in Strasbourg.

Typewriter developed by Underwood which enabled the operator to see what was being typed.

1900 Office dictating machines available using Edison wax recorder principle.

1901 Marconi sends a wireless signal across the Atlantic.

1908 Punched card developmental work at the Census Bureau continued by James Powers. A different mechanical method of sensing punched holes patented by Powers.

1909 First accounting machine developed by Charles Kettering for the National Cash Register Company in the U.S.A. The machine was capable of sorting data, recording, calculating and summarizing.

1911 Tabulating Machine Company merges with others to form the Computing-Tabulating-Recording (CTR) company. Punch card machines used in the British Census.

1915 The Kardex visual record system. J. H. Rand; New York, U.S.A.

c1920 First electromechanical calculating machines came on the market.

1924 The CTR company changes its name to International Business Machines (IBM) Corporation.

1925 A large-scale analogue computer (a type of calculating machine operating on numbers represented as measurable quantities) developed at the Massachussetts Institute of Technology (MIT) by Dr. Vannevar Bush. The machine was essentially mechanically operated but used some electrical power.

1928 Demonstration of transatlantic television by John Logie Baird, Britain.

1929 Television service using the Baird principle (mechanical scanning) started in Britain.

1931 Integrations performed using adapted Burroughs calculators. L. J. Comrie, Britain.

1933 An electrical analogue machine using coils and transformers developed by R. Mallock.

1935 Commercially successful electric typewriter marketed.

1936 Design proposals for a digital computer made by Alan Turing, Britain.

1938 L. Biro invents a ball-point pen—Hungary.

Z1—the first program-controlled computer, designed by K. Zuse, Germany. Like Babbage's proposed analytical engine, Z1 was purely a mechanical device.

Prototype computing element for an electronic computer built by John Atanasoff and Clifford Berry at Iowa State College, U.S.A.

182

1939 Bell Model 1—a semi-automatic computer which used telephone relays to perform its computations—developed at the Bell Telephone Laboratories in the U.S.A. by Dr. George Stibitz.

1941 Z3 built by Zuse in Berlin. A binary computer with a 64-word store. Relays used for circuit elements, punched tape and keyboard for input, and a lamp display for output.

1943 COLOSSUS—an electronic computer built by Professor M. H. Newman and T. H. Flowers for the British Foreign Office during the 2nd World War to crack German codes. Contained 1500 valves and used a fast photo-electric tape reader for input.

1944 Harvard Mark 1—an electro-mechanical computer built by Howard Aiken at Harvard University in the U.S.A. Approximately $\frac{3}{4}$ million parts including 500 miles of wire. Counter wheels used for storage, punched paper tape for input of instructions, switches for setting data, and a typewriter for output. Addition of two numbers in 0.3 secs and multiplication in 6 secs. In use for 15 years.

1945 Dr. von Neumann's paper on the design principles of the digital computer, notable for the concept of the stored program that would make the computer fully automatic. Philadelphia, U.S.A.

1946 ENIAC—a fully electronic computer designed by Professors Presper Eckert and John Mauchly to carry out research in ballistics and built at the Moore school of Mathematics at Pennsylvania University. Used 18 000 vacuum tubes and performed arithmetic in decimal. Addition of two numbers in 0.2 millisecs and multiplication in 3 millisecs (1 hour of ENIAC operation = 1 week of Mark 1). Programs wired on plug boards. Cathode ray tube developed for storage purposes. Known as the 'Williams Tube' after its inventor, Professor F. C. Williams, Britain.

1947 Magnetic drum storage pioneered by Dr. A. D. Booth of Birkbeck College, London.
Invention of the transistor at the Bell Telephone Laboratory, U.S.A.

1948 Manchester Mark 1—an experimental laboratory model significant as the first computer to use a cathode ray tube (CRT) memory system, and also as the earliest stored-program computer. Built by Professor F. C. Williams and Dr. Kilburn at Manchester.
BINAC—a special-purpose computer built by the newly formed Eckert-Mauchly computer corporation for the Northrop Aircraft Company. Significant for its use of magnetic tape for storage.

1949 EDSAC—the first practical stored-program computer to be completed. Built at Cambridge University under the guidance of Professor Maurice Wilkes. Mercury delay lines used for storage and paper tape for I/O.

1950 ACE—the first computer to use a two address code (one to signify the location of the data to be operated on and the other for the address of the next instruction). Designed and built at the National Physics Laboratory at Teddington.

c1950 Copying machines becoming a standard part of office equipment.

1951 1st GENERATION COMPUTERS
–1958 (see chart on pages 186–87)

1951 UNIVAC 1—the first computer designed for commercial applications, i.e. able to handle alphabetic data as well as numeric. A binary machine with delay line storage and used magnetic tape for I/O. Marked the beginning of the computer industry. 48 UNIVAC 1 systems were ordered and installed.

LEO—Lyons Electronic Office. A computer developed and installed by the caterers, J. Lyons & Co. It was the first machine in Britain used for commercial applications. In the first year, used to calculate payroll and in the following year for stock control.

WHIRLWIND 1—a computer originally installed with a CRT storage system that was changed one year later for the first successful use of magnetic core. Built at MIT by Dr. J. Forrester. Six years to pass before core was widely used.

First software development by UNIVAC—a sortmerge program.

1952 EDVAC—the first stored program computer completed in the U.S.A. A binary machine based on von Neumann's theories. Designed by Eckert and Mauchly.

IAS—a computer developed at the Institute of Advanced Study Princeton University, U.S.A. Successful use of CRT storage.

IBM announce their entry into the computer business with the 701 computer, a scientific machine.

1953 IBM 650, a general purpose computer. The most successful machine of the 1st Generation, placing IBM at the forefront of the computer industry where they have been ever since. Over 1000 650s sold.

1955 Costs of software amount to 5% of total computing costs.

1956 FORTRAN language introduced by IBM.

Significant developments in the reading of holes in cards and paper tape by photoelectric method.

First transatlantic telephone cable.

1957 First integrated circuit produced. 7 years pass before general use.

1958 First ever satellite radio message.

1959 2nd GENERATION COMPUTERS
–1963 (see chart on pages 186–87.)

1960 Invention of the laser by T. Maiman.

1960– Development of on-line computer
onwards peripherals: line printers, plotters, visual display units. Prior to these developments output was to punch cards or paper tape. These were then fed to a printer to provide printed output off-line.

1961 Golf-ball typewriter introduced by IBM.

ANITA—a commercially available electronic calculator.

1962 Launch of Telstar satellite, making transatlantic television available for 2 hours each day or 600 independent telephone circuits.

First genuine mini-computers on the market.

1964 3rd GENERATION COMPUTERS
–1969 (see chart on pages 186–87)

1965 Digital Corporation introduce the PDP8, the first mass-produced mini-computer.

Software costs equal to about 50% of computing costs.

BEA install Beacon, a system for the control and booking of seats on scheduled air flights.

English Electric-Leo-Marconi link with Plessey and ICT Ltd. to form International Computers Ltd. (ICL) to become the largest computer manufacturer outside the U.S.A.

1966 Early use of MICR and OCR equipment.

1969 Introduction of GPO Datel links for terminals.

1970 Late 3rd GENERATION COMPU-
–1980 TERS (see p. 185 and pp. 186–87)

1971 INTEL 4004—the first microprocessor on a single chip.

1972 Sinclair Executive—a popular electronic pocket calculator.

1975 Software costs risen to 75% of total costs (estimate for 1985 is 85%).

1976 CRAY 1—a supercomputer

1977 Development of Teletext and Viewdata information services.

Late 3rd Generation 1970–1980

Computers are classified as belonging to a particular generation by the principal electronic components used in their construction (see chart on pages 186–87). The period after 1970 is generally refered to as late 3rd generation since no fundamentally new component has been introduced to give rise to a 4th generation. Nevertheless the technology has moved forward significantly. Components have become very much smaller and much cheaper with far-reaching consequences.

The ability to create microscopic integrated circuitry with thousands of miniature components combined on a tiny silicon chip has given us the microprocessor. It has also led to the development of semiconductor memories, thus greatly reducing the physical size of main memory, improving speed of performance, and cutting production costs. Semiconductor memories are often referred to as integrated circuits since all the necessary components are integrated together on a single chip. Large scale integration (LSI) is the term used when currently more than 10 000 circuits are fitted on the one chip.

At the other end of the scale to the microcomputer, a number of supercomputers have been developed. A new company called CRAY has emerged to compete at the big end of the market. The CRAY 1 is said to be about five times as powerful as the giant IBM 370/195. There has also been considerable growth of activity in the mini-computer field and in the use of small machines as satellites to larger ones.

Machines now classified as small are as powerful as the large machines of yesteryear. Today you can buy for a few thousand pounds a machine equivalent to the giants of the fifties. But whilst the cost of hardware has decreased, the cost of developing and maintaining software (operating systems, language compilers, program packages, etc.) has increased significantly.

Mini-Computers

Mini-computers first came on the scene in the mid 1960s. Mini means small. As a prefix to the word computer, it refers to a combination of computing power, physical size and cost.

Computing power is judged on such factors as processing capability, speed of access to store and transfer of information, and storage capacity. Storage locations in the memory of a mini are normally smaller in size (i.e. can contain fewer bits) as well as fewer in number compared to medium-scale computers. The design of a mini often incorporates a smaller and more limited set of machine instructions to make the design simpler and to reduce hardware costs.

A mini may be compact enough to fit into a box that sits quite happily on a desk. It may also be relatively cheap to purchase but the computer will require peripheral devices to make it functional, e.g. devices to perform input and output and to provide backing storage. These devices are likely to cost more than the mini-computer itself.

A basic mini-computer system consists of the following devices:

1) Central processing unit.

2) Teletype for both entering data and the output of results in hard-copy form.

3) Magnetic disc drive (cartridge/floppy).

4) One or more tape units (standard/cassette).

A system may also include a card/document reader, a low-speed line printer, additional teletypes, or VDUs. A basic system can usually be expanded by increasing the memory size and adding more backing store. It can also be made more flexible by incorporating different types of input/output methods.

Mini-computers are used as general purpose devices and also as machines dedicated to a particular application area. Their cost makes them attractive to smaller business concerns and for specialist use within larger organizations. Minis may be used to support a number of terminals, facilitate data collection (e.g. point-of-sale use, and for control in a key-to-disc system), or to perform inventory (stock control) on-line. They may also be installed together with appropriate packages as complete and dedicated systems, e.g. business accounting or word processing systems.

	FIRST GENERATION 1951–1958	SECOND GENERATION 1959–1963	THIRD GENERATION 1964–1969	POST THIRD GENERATION 1970–1980
PRINCIPAL ELECTRONIC COMPONENTS	vacuum tubes	transistors and diodes	integrated circuits	microscopic integrated circuits
INTERNAL OPERATING SPEEDS MEASURED IN	milliseconds (10^{-3} sec.)	microseconds (10^{-6} sec.)	nanoseconds (10^{-9} sec.)	approaching picoseconds (10^{-12} sec.)
CENTRAL MEMORY	mercury delay lines, cathode ray tubes, magnetic drum	magnetic core	thin film, LSI (large scale integration)	
SECONDARY STORAGE	punched cards, paper tape; magnetic drum; magnetic disk; magnetic tape	removable packs introduced	ECS (extended core store)	
OPERATING SYSTEMS	batch processing	multi-programming; time-sharing; real-time		networks
INPUT AND OUTPUT MEDIA AND METHODS	punched cards, paper tape; printers —(on line); magnetic tape	teletypewriter terminals; VDUs; OCR & MICR readers	key-to-tape/disk/cassettes	
PROGRAMMING LANGUAGES	machine code; symbolic languages; high-level languages; Fortran, Algol, Cobol		PL/1 — Basic — Pascal	

NOTABLE MODELS AND COMPUTER SERIES			
UNIVAC I & II IBM 701 IBM 650 BURROUGHS E101	IBM 1401 IBM 7090 ATLAS UNIVAC 1004 HONEYWELL 400	IBM System/360 series ICL 1900 series UNIVAC 1100 series CDC 6000 series DEC PDP range HONEYWELL 200 series BURROUGHS 7700	IBM System/370 series ICL 2900 series CDC Cyber 170 range HONEYWELL 6000 series CRAY 1
OTHER DEVELOPMENTS			
		minicomputers	microprocessors and microcomputers
		improved data communication techniques	word processing
		package developments	voice response units
BRIEF NOTES			
…slow and unreliable, and generated so much heat that air-conditioning was a problem. Scientific applications at first, followed by beginnings of data processing in business.	were smaller (but still large), much more reliable, consumed less power, faster in operation, but still relatively expensive. Rapid growth in data processing applications. Introduction of time-sharing, real time systems.	Computers were smaller, still faster, more reliable, and used much less power. More powerful machines were developed and also minicomputers. The overall increased efficiency resulted in greatly reduced computing costs. Significant improvements occurred in the development of software and operating systems.	Yet more powerful and more versatile computers and computing systems; faster, smaller and less expensive. Continued reduction in costs dramatically accelerated by miniaturization (silicon chips). More minicomputers and the coming of the micros (the advent of the 4th generation). Advances in storage techniques.

————→ indicates continuing use

– – – – – → indicates declining use

THANK YOU
WH SMITH
LONDON AIRPORT (10)

```
*   1  ***0.70  +
*   2  ***1.25  +
*   2  ***0.95  +
*   2  ***1.50  +

31MA  6450  *  A  ****4.40  T
```

Companies particularly concerned with the manufacture of mini-computers include Digital Equipment Corporation (DEC), Hewlett-Packard and Data General.

Microprocessors

At the opposite end of the scale from the giant supercomputer is the tiny microprocessor. Essentially, a microprocessor or microprocessing unit (MPU) consists of one or more tiny chips of silicon, each no bigger than a finger nail, on which micro-circuitry has been etched to form one or more of the units of the CPU (i.e. arithmetic logic unit, control unit, and memory). A micro-computer system is formed when microprocessor units or chips, together with input/output and other peripheral devices, are linked to form a complete working system.

Microprocessors are used to carry out functions within mini-computers and in peripheral equipment such as terminals. They are also used as control devices in such familiar commodities as washing machines, heating systems, typewriters, in TV games, and in an increasing range of toys. Because of their small size and low cost, it is anticipated that microprocessors will be increasingly used and that they will gradually take over from conventional electrical and mechanical methods of control in almost all appliances and devices. Their potential is tremendous, both as special-purpose hard-wired controllers in applications not currently associated with computers, and as general-purpose computers replacing mini-computers and increasing the usefulness of larger systems.

The construction of a chip requires several processes. The combinations of circuits required are drawn to a large scale. The drawing is then photographed, reduced, and etched on to a wafer of silicon. Even more tightly packed circuitry is obtained with the aid of electron beam cutters which bombard the chip with electrons.

Silicon is an excellent semiconductor, i.e. it can conduct or reject electricity depending on the way it is formed. A minute area can be deprived of electrons and another given a surplus. When two such areas are separated by a third, they act as an electronic switch or transistor. What is so remarkable is that thousands of such transistors can be formed on a single chip to carry out the functions of the arithmetic logic

Fig. 8.1 A typical microcomputer design. There may be three chips as suggested in the diagram, or the three functions may even be combined on one chip. The CPU itself may be made up of more than one chip.

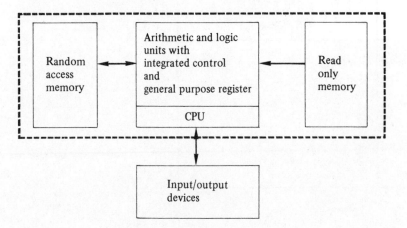

unit and control unit, and that they can also be designed to provide memory.

There are three principal types of memory elements called RAMs, ROMs and PROMs. A RAM chip provides random access memory consistent with the behaviour of normal computer memory, i.e. data can be read from or written into any location.

A ROM chip provides read only memory capability. Data, e.g. a program of instructions, can actually be built or "burnt" into the ROM chip at the time of manufacture. The data is wired in so that it is permanently there and is not lost when power is switched off. It is unalterable and can only be read. A chip of this type is ideal for a single purpose application when the task to be carried out can be exactly defined and in the knowledge that it will never need to be changed.

A PROM chip provides programmable read only memory. The apparent contradiction within the name needs explanation. Fixed information is "wired" into the chip at the time of manufacture but the chip is so constructed that the information can be modified by programming technique. This enables a PROM to be used in the form in which it is built or to be changed to reflect the circumstances in which it is going to be used. In either case, when in use it has read only capability. A PROM cannot normally be re-programmed more than once. Like the ROM, information is not lost when power is switched off.

There is a special type of PROM called an EPROM, an erasable programmable read only memory. The information on this type of chip can be erased to allow re-programming by exposing the chip to ultra violet light. The erasing process can be repeated as often as required. Otherwise an EPROM behaves like a ROM.

The early microprocessors were designed to handle information in 4 bit or 8 bit form. 16 bit is now coming in. Examples of firms manufacturing microprocessors are Intel, Signetics, Texas Instruments Inc., Zilog, and Motorola.

Exercises 8

1 Computers are commonly divided into three generations. What electronic components distinguish the generations? (*WJEC*)

2 Name the inventor of each of the following:
a) 80-column punched card *b*) analytical engine *c*) magnetic drum *d*) Harvard Mark 1 *e*) EDSAC

3 Expand each of the following acronyms:
a) LSI *b*) IBM *c*) BASIC *d*) VDU *e*) ICL

4 Write brief notes on the contribution made to the history of computing by *three* of the following:
a) Dr. von Neumann *b*) Professor F. C. Williams *c*) Charles Babbage *d*) Professor P. Eckert and J. Mauchly *e*) Herman Hollerith

5 Trace the development of central memory from the mercury delay lines of the early 1st generation machines to the large-scale integration used today. What advantages did each stage bring?

6 What is a silicon chip?

7 Briefly describe the difference between RAMs, ROMs and PROMs.

8 What are mini-computers and for what applications are they particularly used.

General Questions

1 List the basic operations of a computer.

2 Modern computers are electronic devices. State three characteristics which distinguish their performance from mechanical calculating machines. (*WJEC* 1977)

3 Describe the function of the CU when control transfer takes place. (*AEB* spec.)

4 *a*) Name two high-level languages, the first of which is particularly suitable for commercial data processing and the second of which is suitable for scientific computation.
b) For one of the languages which you have named, explain one reason for its particular suitability. (*OLE* 1978)

5 Explain the "fetch-decode-execute" cycle. (*EAEB* 1976)

6 What is the difference between a conditional and an unconditional jump? Illustrate with examples in a named high-level language.

7 Which of the following is a peripheral?
a) the arithmetic unit *b*) a program *c*) a graph plotter *d*) an assembler *e*) the immediate access store (*EMREB*)

8 The fastest way to list a permanent copy of a disc file would be to use
a) a teletype *b*) a card punch *c*) a plotter
d) a VDU *e*) a line printer (*EAEB*)

9 Optical character readers are used for
a) visual display unit screens *b*) file protection *c*) output *d*) spooling *e*) input
(*EAEB*)

10 One disadvantage of magnetic tape is that
a) it can only be used for direct access storage
b) it is the most expensive form of storage
c) data can only be accessed by a COBOL program
d) the data on it can only be accessed serially
e) only small amounts of data can be stored (*EAEB*)

11 The following 6-bit codes are to have a parity bit added to make them ODD parity. What would this bit be in each case?
a) 000000 *b*) 111111 *c*) 101010

12 Classify each of the following items as to do with input, output or the CPU:
line printer, ferrite core, magnetic tape, console, punched card, logic circuit, paper tape reader, light pen.

13 What do you understand by the term data preparation?

14 How does a backing store differ from the main store of a computer? (*OLE* 1976)

15 Choose *three* of the following peripherals. For the ones you choose state briefly what the device does, suggest a possible user of the device, and explain what use this user would make of the device.
teletype, graph plotter, VDU, OCR, light pen, MICR, mark sense reader (*SWEB* 1977)

16 Describe the way in which the storage of information is organised on *either* magnetic tape *or* magnetic disc. (*OLE* 1976)

17 Name *one* type of backing store and an application for which it is suitable. (*OLE* 1976)

18 Describe briefly a key-to-disc system and suggest why such systems are now used by business and commerce.

19 List six different areas of modern life in which computer applications are used. Two of these should be named as "real time" applications. Indicate these. (*JMB* 1975)

20 Explain how a computer system, linked to the cash tills, might help in the management of a supermarket. (*UCLES* 1976)

21 Write briefly about how a computer system could be used in two of the following operations. Your answer should include reference to data preparation, hardware used and form of output.

a) Identification of suspected criminals from their description
b) Stock distribution to a chain of supermarkets
c) Keeping a hospital's medical records
d) Handling the payroll for a large factory. (*SWEB* 1977)

22 What steps should be taken within for example a business organization before a particular task is programmed for computer solution?

23 If you applied for a job as a computer operator and were accepted as a trainee, what duties would you expect to be taught to become an operator?

24 Describe in some detail how the computer is used in a field of your own choosing, e.g. in banking, or medicine, or airways, etc. (This will probably mean you having to seek out more information on the subject you choose.)

25 What type of storage media would you use for the following sets of information?
Give reasons for your choice.
a) The details of bookings on an airline company's flight.

b) The monthly salary details of a firm's employees.
c) The operating system used in a large computer installation. (*YREB* 1977)

26 The types of program listed below are often included in the computer software provided for use on a large computer.
　compiler; assembler; operating system; utility program; application package.
　a) Describe the main features of each.
　b) Name the type of software from the list above which you would expect to be used for the following jobs:

i) Copying a program automatically on to a magnetic tape.
ii) Sending a message to the operator that the line printer requires more paper.
iii) Working out the payroll of a company.
iv) Translating a Fortran program into machine code. (*YREB* 1977)

27 *a*) Explain the terms *on-line* and *off-line*.
　b) Name one computer input medium which requires off-line data preparation and one which does not, and for each suggest one suitable application. (*OLE* 1978).

28 A local education authority decides to establish a data bank on the children in its schools. They decide to include the details of:
　1) each student, e.g. height, weight, and their performance in School subjects each year;
　2) the parents, e.g. how old, what work they do;
　3) the home, e.g. what kind of dwelling, what class of area;
　4) medical reports.
As matters of privacy are involved, how would the files be protected and what assurances could be given to the students? What would your reaction be to this news?

29 Describe the main hardware developments which have taken place in electronic computers from the 1st generation to the present day. (*EMAEB*)

Appendix 1 Computer Number Systems

Introduction

For many, binary arithmetic forms part of a general mathematics course at secondary level schools in the UK. This appendix has been included to cover basic principles for those who have not studied this topic before or who are in need of some further coaching. It is necessary to understand the rather simple rules of binary arithmetic in order to grasp fully the content of Chapter 1.

The Idea of a Base

In our everyday arithmetic, we make use of numbers in what is called the *decimal* or the *denary* number system. Any other system could be used but by tradition (i.e. everyday practice) it happens to be the decimal system, probably because we have ten fingers (two of which we call "thumbs"). The word decimal or denary in fact means "ten". In mathematical parlance, every number system has a *radix* (from the Latin meaning *root*) or *base*, i.e. the number of individual digits including zero which that system can use. Because zero must always be included, the actual digits used go up to one less than the base itself. Thus, in the decimal system, the ten digits are 0, 1, 2, 3, 4, 5, 6, 7, 8, 9, i.e. from zero up to one less than the base itself, i.e. $(10-1)$. A base of five then would use only the digits, 0, 1, 2, 3 and 4; a base of eight would use 0, 1, 2, 3, 4, 5, 6 and 7; a base of sixteen would use 1, 2, 3, 4, 5, 6, 7, 8, 9, 10, 11, 12, 13, 14, and 15.

In a base which is higher than ten, there is always a problem with those digits above 9 and it is customary to use letters of the alphabet;

thus, $A = 10$, $B = 11$, $C = 12$, and so on. The base sixteen, called the *hexadecimal* number system (hex being Greek for six), is commonly written with the following digits: 0, 1, 2, 3, 4, 5, 6, 7, 8, 9, A, B, C, D, E, and F.

Binary Number System

Although, as humans, we use the decimal system, this proves to be difficult (but not impossible) for computers. The ten digits of the denary system would have to be represented somehow inside the computer. As pointed out in part A of Chapter 1, a computer being an electronic machine would require to have ten distinct voltage levels. However, it is simpler for electronic engineers to create electronic circuits with only two states. For this reason, the binary number system with only two digits, zero and one, is the ideal number system to represent the two-state electronic circuits and, as a result, people studying computers have to become aware of binary arithmetic.

Each electronic circuit inside the computer can be in either one of two states and, as we have seen in Chapter 1, the circuits are frequently grouped together into sixes or eights (called *bytes*), or sometimes in much larger groups of 12, 16, 32, 36 or even 60. Each circuit of the group can hold or represent a binary one or a binary zero. A grouping of 32 circuits can therefore hold 32 binary digits (*bits*) whereas a group of six can hold six bits. The decimal number 239 means "two hundred and thirty-nine". The digit 9 on the right-hand side is the least significant digit (LSD) and the 2 on the left-hand side is known as the most significant digit (MSD). The same applies to binary numbers, except that we use the word "bit" instead of "digit", thus

$$1001$$

MSB⌐   ⌐LSB

Because the binary number 1001 could so easily be confused with the decimal number "one thousand and one" we shall adopt the usual practice of using a small number after the LSD to signify which base is being referred to; thus, 239_{10} means that the number is in base ten; but 1001_2 would mean base two; 103_8 indicates base eight, etc. Where the base number is omitted, the base ten is assumed, so that 1001 implies "one thousand and one" in base ten.

Conversion of Binary Numbers into Decimal Numbers

Although programmers can use a binary representation for the computer's internal electronic states, that does not mean that every number they input to the computer must be in binary. If the decimal number 109 has to be input, then it can be written in decimal and it will be converted to binary by a pre-written set of routines without the programmer being aware of what is happening to his decimal number. If a computer is used to produce salary slips in a payroll application, employees would not be pleased to have all the information in binary. Another set of routines, therefore, convert binary back into our everyday characters, so that we can read with ease our salary slips or whatever else is produced by the computer.

However, as students of computing we should know how to handle some binary numbers and especially how to convert a binary number into decimal. Let us take the number 1001_2 and convert this to our everyday base of ten. One simple way of doing this is to give each digit, starting from the right-hand side, a particular weighting as shown in Figure A1.1. Figure A1.2 shows more binary numbers.

How did we arrive at this weighting? If we have a decimal number, say 2139, the weighting of each digit is:

$$2 \quad\quad 1 \quad\quad 3 \quad\quad 9$$
$$= 2 \times 10^3 + 1 \times 10^2 + 3 \times 10^1 + 9 \times 10^0$$
$$= 2000 \quad + 100 \quad + 30 \quad + 9$$
$$= 2139_{10}$$

Each digit has a position. Thus digit 3 is *not* the unit 3 but by its position is really 30 (3×10^1). The 2 by its position is *not* the unit 2 but stands for 2000 (2×10^3). The same applies to *any* base, thus $nnnn_b$, where b stands for any base, can be generalised as follows:

$$n \times b^3 + n \times b^2 + n \times b^1 + n \times b^0$$

In the case of the base two, 1111_2 will become

$$1 \times 2^3 + 1 \times 2^2 + 1 \times 2^1 + 1 \times 2^0 = 15_{10}$$

Fig. A1.1

	bit 4	bit 3	bit 2	bit 1
Decimal weighting	8	4	2	1
Binary number	1	0	0	1
Decimal equivalent	8 +	0 +	0 +	1 = 9_{10}

Decimal weighting	8	4	2	1		
Binary number	1	0	0	1	=	8 + 0 + 0 + 1 = 9_{10}
	0	1	1	0	=	0 + 4 + 2 + 0 = 6_{10}
	0	0	0	0	=	0 + 0 + 0 + 0 = 0_{10}
	1	1	1	1	=	8 + 4 + 2 + 1 = 15_{10}
	1	1	0	1	=	8 + 4 + 0 + 1 = 13_{10}

Fig. A1.2

2^0	= 1	=	1
2^1	= 2	=	10
2^2	= 4	=	100
2^3	= 8	=	1000
2^4	= 16	=	10000
2^5	= 32	=	100000
2^6	= 64	=	1000000
2^7	= 128	=	10000000

	bit 3	bit 2	bit 1		
Decimal weighting	4	2	1		
Binary number	0	0	0	=	0
	0	0	1	=	1
	0	1	0	=	2
	0	1	1	=	3
	1	0	0	=	4
	1	0	1	=	5
	1	1	0	=	6
	1	1	1	=	7

Fig. A1.4

Figure A1.3 shows the decimal weighting for the powers of two. Note especially how each succeeding power is double that of the previous power. Thus $2^8 = 2^7 + 2^7 = 128 + 128 = 256$. The six-digit binary number 101010 can now be easily converted into decimal in one of two ways.

First Method

	bit 6	bit 5	bit 4	bit 3	bit 2	bit 1	
	1	0	1	0	1	0	
Dec. wtng.	32	0	8	0	2	0	
Result	32 +	0 +	8 +	0 +	2 +	0	$= 42_{10}$

Second Method

	bit 6	bit 5	bit 4	bit 3	bit 2	bit 1	
Binary number	1	0	1	0	1	0	
Power of 2	1×2^5	0×2^4	1×2^3	0×2^2	1×2^1	0×2^0	
Decimal result	32 +	0 +	8 +	0 +	2 +	0	$= 42_{10}$

Octal and Hexadecimal Number Systems

Two other number systems are frequently used in computing as a result of the binary system. If you recall, the octal base can only use the digits 0 to 7. There is now an interesting result if binary digits are grouped into threes, namely that with three bits the entire range of octal digits can be covered, as illustrated in Figure A1.4. Thus, any pattern of 3 bits will represent one octal digit. For example, if a six-digit binary number is divided into two groups of three, and each group converted to its octal digit, the result will be the octal equivalent of the binary number.

$$1\ 0\ 1 : 0\ 1\ 0 = 101010_2$$
$$5_8 : 2_8 = 52_8$$

The octal number can now be converted to decimal by using the generalised base conversion formula on page 193, thus:

$$\begin{aligned} & \quad 5 \quad\quad\quad 2 \\ = & \ 5 \times 8^1 + 2 \times 8^0 \\ = & \ 40_{10} + 2_{10} = 42_{10} \end{aligned}$$

Groups of *four* binary digits cover all sixteen digits $(0 - F)$ of the hexadecimal number system (see Figure A1.5). Thus the binary number 11101010 can be converted to hexadecimal by splitting the binary number into groups of four (starting from the LSB) and converting each group into the hexadecimal digit:

$$1110\ 1010 = 11101010_2$$
$$E_{16} \quad A_{16} = EA_{16}$$
$$= 234_{10}$$

NB: convert the binary number direct to decimal and compare this with the above result.

These other two number systems are frequently used to reduce the number of binary bits the

Binary bits	5	4	3	2	1	Base		
						16	10	8
Decimal weighting:	16	8	4	2	1			
Binary number:		0	0	0	0	0	0	0
		0	0	0	1	1	1	1
		0	0	1	0	2	2	2
		0	0	1	1	3	3	3
		0	1	0	0	4	4	4
		0	1	0	1	5	5	5
		0	1	1	0	6	6	6
		0	1	1	1	7	7	7
		1	0	0	0	8	8	10
		1	0	0	1	9	9	11
		1	0	1	0	A	10	12
		1	0	1	1	B	11	13
		1	1	0	0	C	12	14
		1	1	0	1	D	13	15
		1	1	1	0	E	14	16
		1	1	1	1	F	15	17
	1	0	0	0	0	10	16	20

$$E_{16} \qquad A_{16}$$
$$= E \times 16^1 + A \times 16^0$$
$$= 14 \times 16^1 + 10 \times 16^0$$
$$= 224_{10} + 10_{10}$$
$$= 234_{10}$$

Conversion of EA_{16} to decimal

Fig. A1.5

human mind has to remember. Which number would you prefer to remember?

$$1111010100011011_2$$

or the octal equivalent

$$001\ 111\ 010\ 100\ 011\ 011$$
$$\ \ 1\quad 7\quad 2\quad 4\quad 3\quad 3$$
$$= 001111010100011011_2$$
$$172433_8$$

or even the hexadecimal equivalent

$$1111\ 0101\ 0001\ 1011 = 1111010100011011_2$$
$$\text{F}\quad 5\quad 1\quad\ \text{B}\ = \text{F51B}_{16}$$

Note that in order to keep to groups of three for the octal number, two leading zeros were introduced. These do not affect the binary number itself. A simpler example can demonstrate this. The binary number 1101111 in groups of 3 for octal conversion becomes:

$$001\ 101\ 111$$
$$\ 1\quad 5\quad 7\ = 157_8$$
$$= 1 \times 8^2 + 5 \times 8^1 + 7 \times 8^0$$
$$= 1 \times 64 + 5 \times 8 + 7 \times 1$$
$$= 64 + 40 + 7$$
$$= 111_{10}$$

and in groups of 4 for hexadecimal it becomes

$$0110\ 1111$$
$$6\qquad \text{F}\ = 6\text{F}_{16} = 6 \times 16^1 + \text{F} \times 16^0$$
$$= 6 \times 16 + \text{F} \times 1 \quad (\text{i.e. } 15 \times 1)$$
$$= 96 + 15$$
$$= 111_{10}$$

Binary Arithmetic

Let us consider each of the four basic arithmetical processes using binary; addition, subtraction, multiplication and division.

Addition

This becomes extremely simple because only two digits can be used, and the rules for addition are very few as shown in Figure A1.6.

Example 1

$$0101 = 5_{10}$$
$$+0110 = 6_{10}$$
$$\overline{}$$
$$10^11 1 = 11_{10}$$
$$\uparrow carry$$

$$
\begin{array}{rcrcr}
0 & + & 0 & = & 0 \\
0 & + & 1 & = & 1 \\
1 & + & 0 & = & 1 \\
1 & + & 1 & = & 0 \text{ and a carry of 1}
\end{array}
$$

Fig. A1.6

Example 2

$$
\begin{array}{rl}
1101 = & 13_{10} \\
+0110 = & 6_{10} \\
\hline
10^10^111 = & 19_{10}
\end{array}
$$

Example 3

$$
\begin{array}{rl}
101 = & 5_{10} \\
111 = & 7_{10} \\
+010 = & 2_{10} \\
\hline
11^11^10^1 = & 14_{10}
\end{array}
$$

Multiplication

Again the rules here are much simpler than for the decimal system. Figure A1.7 shows the rules.

$$
\begin{array}{rcrcr}
0 & \times & 0 & = & 0 \\
0 & \times & 1 & = & 0 \\
1 & \times & 0 & = & 0 \\
1 & \times & 1 & = & 1
\end{array}
$$

Fig. A1.7

Example 4

$$
\begin{array}{ll}
010 = 2_{10} & \text{multiplicand (MD)} \\
\times 101 = 5_{10} & \text{multiplier (MP)}
\end{array}
$$

$$
\begin{array}{ll}
010 \quad 10_{10} & \text{product} \\
000 & \\
\underline{010} & \\
01010 \quad & \text{product}
\end{array}
$$

Notice that when a 1 bit appears in the MP, we simply have to write down the MD and, when a zero appears in the MP, we simply write down a series of noughts, remembering to shift one place to the *right* with each digit of the MP. Then the rows of the partial products are added together following the rules of binary addition. Some people are used to multiplying first by the LSB of the MP rather than with the MSB as in Example 4. Example 5 illustrates this case but the shift now is one place to the *left*.

Example 5

Starting with LSB:

Binary number   Decimal number

$$
\begin{array}{rl}
10101 = & 21 \text{ MD} \\
100100 = & \times 36 \text{ MP} \\
\hline
00000 & \left.\rule{0pt}{0.8em}\right\} 756 \text{ prod.} \\
00000 & \\
10101 & \left.\rule{0pt}{2em}\right\} \text{ partial products} \\
00000 & \quad \text{ one shift to left} \\
00000 & \\
10101 & \\
\hline
\end{array}
$$

1011110100 product

Fig. A1.8

Product bits	10	9	8	7	6	5	4	3	2	1
Decimal weighting	512	256	128	64	32	16	8	4	2	1
Binary product	1	0	1	1	1	1	0	1	0	0
Converted to base ten	512 +	0	+ 128 +	64 +	32 +	16 +	0 +	4 +	0 +	0

Division

Division can be performed by the conventional "long division" method.

Example 6

$$
\begin{array}{r}
11 \\
1010\overline{)11110} \\
1010 \\
\hline
01010 \\
1010 \\
\hline
00000
\end{array}
\quad
\begin{array}{l}
\text{i.e. } 11_2 = 3_{10} \\
\\
\\
1010_2 = 10_{10} \\
11110_2 = 30_{10}
\end{array}
$$

Subtraction

Subtraction does not prove to be quite so simple as the other three arithmetical processes. Let us first see the rules in Figure A1.9.

		Result	Borrow
0 − 0 =		0	0
1 − 0 =		1	0
1 − 1 =		0	0
0 − 1 =		1	1

Fig. A1.9

Example 7

$$101 = \ 5_{10} \quad \text{minuend}$$
$$-100 = -4_{10} \quad \text{subtrahend}$$
$$\overline{001 = \ 1_{10}}$$

Example 8

$$1111 = \ 15_{10} \quad \text{minuend}$$
$$-0101 = \ -5_{10} \quad \text{subtrahend}$$
$$\overline{1010 \quad 10_{10}}$$

The only real problem comes with the borrow as in the following example.

Example 9

$$\lfloor 101 = \ 5_{10}$$
$$-0\lfloor 10 = -2_{10}$$
$$\overline{011 = \ 3_{10}}$$

The borrow works as follows. When we come to the second digit in the subtrahend, we have to borrow a 1 from the next highest column of the minuend, as shown by the lines. But this will now reduce that column by 1, effectively reducing it to zero. This is, of course, the normal procedure for subtraction in any base. But it does introduce two stages. For example, if we subtract the binary number 01 from 10, we can see how this works:

Step 1

$$\lfloor 10$$
$$-0\lfloor 1$$
$$\overline{\quad}$$
$$\quad 1 \qquad \text{1 is borrowed from the next column so that 1 is left in the result}$$

Step 2

$$00$$
$$-01$$
$$\overline{\quad}$$
$$\quad 01 \qquad \text{the borrowed 1 leaves zero in the "borrowed" column so that we are subtracting nought from nought.}$$

Thus, Example 9 can be written in two stages:

Step 1

$$101$$
$$-010$$
$$\overline{\quad}$$
$$\quad 11 \qquad \text{the borrowed 1 leaves the minuend as 001 for step two}$$

Step 2

$$001$$
$$-010$$
$$\overline{\quad}$$
$$\quad 011$$

Fortunately, we can forget about this method of subtraction now and also the more complex problems when the subtrahend is larger than the minuend, since computers perform subtraction by a form of complementation which we discuss below. But for those who would like to continue with binary subtraction see if this example will deter you!

$$0101 = \ 5_{10}$$
$$-1011 = -11_{10}$$
$$\overline{-01110 = \ -6_{10}}$$

One way of doing this is to reverse the two numbers, subtract in the normal way, and then append a negative sign to the result:

$$1011$$
$$-0101$$
$$\overline{\quad}$$
$$0110 \quad \text{negate to } -0110$$

Apart from addition and complementation, performing the other arithmetical processes of multiplication, division and subtraction in binary provides no real practical value for the majority of computer users and so we need not dwell any longer on these processes. However, on occasions it may be necessary to convert a decimal number into binary, octal or hexadecimal, or vice versa. We have already seen how to convert from binary into decimal, octal and hexadecimal, and so we shall now concentrate on converting from decimal into binary.

Conversion of Decimal into Binary

A decimal number may be converted into binary in one of two ways. A *straightforward method* is to see which two binary powers the given decimal number lies between. For example, the decimal number 99, lies between the two binary powers 2^7 and 2^6, i.e. 128_{10} and 64_{10}. The lower power is always taken first and that power subtracted from the decimal number. In our case this leaves a remainder of 35_{10} ($99 - 64 = 35$). A 1 bit is marked in the 2^6 position, and then we repeat the process for the remainder. 35 lies between 2^6 (64) and 2^5 (32). The lower is again taken and a 1 bit marked in position 2^5. The subtraction results in a remainder of 3 ($35 - 32 = 3$). This lies between the powers 2^2(4) and 2^1(2). Again the process is repeated until we have exhausted the powers. Figure A1.10 illustrates this more clearly.

The *second method* can be simpler if we repeatedly divide the decimal number by 2 until zero is reached. Each division will result in either a 1 or a zero remainder. These form the bits of the eventual binary number.

Conversion of 98_{10} into binary

$$98 \div 2 = 49 \text{ remainder } 0 \quad \text{(LSB)}$$
$$49 \div 2 = 24 \text{ remainder } 1$$
$$24 \div 2 = 12 \text{ remainder } 0$$
$$12 \div 2 = 6 \text{ remainder } 0$$
$$6 \div 2 = 3 \text{ remainder } 0$$
$$3 \div 2 = 1 \text{ remainder } 1$$
$$1 \div 2 = 0 \text{ remainder } 1 \quad \text{(MSB)}$$
$$1\ 1\ 0\ 0\ 0\ 1\ 0$$

The conversion of a decimal number into octal or hexadecimal is best performed by converting to binary, and then grouping the binary bits into threes (for octal) or fours (for hexadecimal) as previously shown.

The Idea of Complementation

Subtraction is performed in computers by a form of complementary arithmetic. In the decimal number system there are two types of complementation, the *nines complement* and the *tens complement*.

Tens Complement

The tens complement (10C) of a decimal number is that number which when added to it will give a power of ten. Thus, the 10C of 56 is the number 44 since $56 + 44 = 100$ which is the power of ten for a two digit decimal number (10^2). Figure A1.11 gives a list of the 10C of various numbers.

Fig. A1.10

Binary powers	2^8	2^7	2^6	2^5	2^4	2^3	2^2	2^1	2^0
Decimal weighting:	256	128	64	32	16	8	4	2	1
Decimal number			99	35			3	1	
Binary ones:			1	1			1	1	
Fill in with zeros	0	0	1	1	0	0	0	1	1

$64 + 32 + 2 + 1 = 99_{10}$

Number	Tens complement		
1	9	= 10	= 10^1
4	6	= 10	= 10^1
21	79	= 100	= 10^2
37	63	= 100	= 10^2
101	899	= 1000	= 10^3
1456	8544	= 10 000	= 10^4

Fig. A1.11

Nines Complement

The nines complement (9C) of a number is the value which when added will give one less than a power of ten (Figure A1.12).

Number	Nines complement	
1	8	= 9
4	5	= 9
21	78	= 99
37	62	= 99
101	898	= 999
1456	8543	= 9999

Fig. A1.12

Usually, we do not bother with complements in the decimal system because there is no real value in doing so, with the exception of the shopkeeper. A shopkeeper being given £1 (100p) for an article worth 73 pence does not bother to subtract 73 from 100 to calculate the change. Instead he will select coins from his till starting with the lowest ones and add up from the price of 73 until he reaches 100. Thus, he will select a 2p piece from the till to make 75p, a 5p piece to make 80p, and then two 10p pieces to make the 100p. Thus the change to the customer will be $2p + 5p + 10p + 10p = 27p$. This is a faster method in practice for the shopkeeper than the more usual subtraction.

In computers, complementation in binary also proves to be a much faster method of subtraction. Binary complements take the form

of the *twos complement* (2C) and the *ones complement* (1C) and these correspond to the tens and the nines complements respectively.

Twos Complement

The twos complement of 1011_2 is that binary number which when added to it will produce 10000_2. Thus, the 2C of 1011_2 is 0101_2.

$$\begin{array}{ll} 1011 & \text{original number} \\ +0101 & \text{2C} \\ \hline 10000_2 \end{array}$$

Ones Complement

The ones complement of 1011_2 is that binary number which when added to it will produce all ones.

$$\begin{array}{ll} 1011 & \text{original number} \\ +0100 & \text{1C} \\ \hline 1111 \end{array}$$

This is equivalent to the nines complement in the decimal system where the value to be added must result in all nines. The twos complement is similar to the tens complement since the twos complement, when added, results in one more than the ones complement. Figure A1.13 shows the ones and twos complements of various binary numbers.

Binary number		2C	Power	1C	
10	+	10	= 100	01	= 11
101	+	011	= 1000	010	= 111
111	+	001	= 1000	000	= 111
1001	+	0111	= 10000	0110	= 1111
101010	+	010110	= 1000000	010101	= 111111

Fig. A1.13

But how do we find the complement of a binary number? It is here that the usefulness of binary complementation becomes clear. Look at the ones complement in Figure A1.13 and see if you can notice anything about it. In every case, the ones complement is the exact reverse of the original number, i.e. every 1 bit in the original number becomes a 0, and every 0 bit becomes a 1!

In other words to get the ones complement of any binary number, we simply reverse the bits. Nothing could be simpler!

The twos complement of a number is the ones complement plus 1 added at the LSB.

The Use of Complementary Arithmetic

In the decimal system if we wish to subtract 98 from 132 we can use the traditional method or we can *add* to the minuend (132) the 10C of 98 and ignore the MSD of the result.

Traditional method

```
  132   minuend
−  98   subtrahend
 ____
   34
```

Tens complement method

```
  132   minuend
+   2   the 10C of 98
 ____
  134   ignore MSD to obtain result
```

Nines complement method

```
  132   minuend
+   1   9C of 98
 ____
  133   add the MSD to the LSD


   33
+   1   the MSD of previous result
 ____
   34
```

Binary System

With binary numbers, computers use complementation to perform subtraction by the use of the ones or twos complement. Thus to subtract 101_2 from 111_2 we can add the twos complement to the minuend and ignore the MSB.

```
  111   minuend
+ 011   2C of 101
 ____
 1010   ignore MSB
```

If the ones complement is used, then the ones complement of the subtrahend is added to the minuend and the MSB is added to the LSB of the result. This process of adding the MSB in the case of ones complement is called the *end around carry*. Figure A1.14 shows the two cases and includes the traditional method of binary subtraction.

Traditional method		1s complement		2s complement	
111	minuend	111	minuend	111	minuend
−101	subtrahend	+010	1C of 101	+011	2C of 101
010	result	1001		1010	MSB ignored
		+ 1	MSB end around carry		
		010			

Fig. A1.14

200

Example 10

$$1101 = 13_{10}$$
$$-1001 = -9_{10}$$
$$0100 = 4_{10}$$

1101	1101
+0110 1 C of 1001	+0111 2C of 1001
̶10011	̶10100
+ 1	
0100	

Notice how the subtrahend *must* be filled out with leading zeros if the subtrahend has less digits than the minuend (as in the following example), otherwise the method will not work.

Example 11

$$
\begin{array}{ll}
1010011 & \text{minuend} \\
-\quad 10111 & \text{subtrahend} \\
\hline
0111100 &
\end{array}
$$

$$
\begin{array}{ll}
1010011 & \\
+1101000 & \text{1C of } \underline{0010111} \\
\hline
̶10111011 & \\
+\qquad 1 & \\
\hline
0111100 &
\end{array}
$$

$$
\begin{array}{ll}
1010011 & \\
+1101001 & \text{2C of } \underline{0010111} \\
\hline
̶10111100 &
\end{array}
$$

Both forms of complementation are used to perform subtraction in present-day computers but an advantage of the twos complement is that there is one less step involved and therefore it can be performed much faster.

Binary number		1	1	1	1 • 1	1	1	1	1	1
Decimal weighting		8	4	2	1 • 2	4	8	16	32	64
Decimal equivalent		$8 + 4 + 2 + 1 + \frac{1}{2} + \frac{1}{4} + \frac{1}{8} + \frac{1}{16} + \frac{1}{32} + \frac{1}{64}$								

Fig. A1.15

Binary Fractions

To complete this appendix we shall look briefly at binary fractions. In our denary number system, fractions can be expressed as digits to the right of the decimal point. Thus, 23.526 is not an integer number where increases (or decreases) in the number go up (or down) in steps of one. In binary, all digits to the right of the binary point indicate and express a fraction. They have a positional weighting which decreases in powers of two (Figure A1.15).

Binary fraction	Decimal equivalent				
.1	.5	=	$\frac{1}{2}$	=	2^{-1}
.01	.25	=	$\frac{1}{4}$	=	2^{-2}
.001	.125	=	$\frac{1}{8}$	=	2^{-3}
.0001	.0625	=	$\frac{1}{16}$	=	2^{-4}
.00001	.03125	=	$\frac{1}{32}$	=	2^{-5}
.000001	.015625	=	$\frac{1}{64}$	=	2^{-6}

Fig. A1.16

Figure A1.16 shows some binary fractions together with their decimal equivalent and the power of 2. One interesting feature of decimal fractions using decimal points is that certain pure fractions such as $\frac{1}{3}$ cannot be precisely expressed. Thus 0.33333333 recurring can get ever nearer to the exact $\frac{1}{3}$ but never quite so. The same occurs in binary fractions. For example, 0.2 cannot be precisely expressed as a *binary* fraction. Try it and see! Again, $\frac{1}{3}$ cannot be precisely contained as a binary fraction. This may appear daunting since computers are supposed to be highly efficient calculators. In practice, programmers who are aware of this can accept the situation (as mathematicians do in the case of representing $\frac{1}{3}$ in decimal fractions) and arrange their programs to cater for the situation. In the more expensive computers and calculators, sophisticated rounding procedures overcome this problem.

Exercises

1 Multiply the following two positive binary numbers, leaving your answer in binary: 01110×0101. (*OLE* 1977)

2 Write down the complement of 0011011100. (*OLE* 1977)

3 Convert the positive decimal integer 395 to binary. Calculate as a binary number the product $01101_2 \times 01011_2$. (*OLE* 1978)

4 How many different character codes can be made with six bits? Only one of the following is correct.
a) 63 *b*) 6 *c*) 12 *d*) 36 *e*) 64.
(*SWEB* 1977)

5 Convert the following base-two numbers to base ten:
a) 101 *b*) 10000 *c*) 11111
Convert the following base ten numbers to base two numbers.
a) 3 *b*) 18 *c*) 39 (*SWEB* 1977)

6 State briefly why an allocation of four bits would not be adequate for storing the representation of each alphabetical character. (*UCLES* 1977)

7 For the groupings given by the brackets write the octal representation and the hexadecimal representation of the twelve bit word:

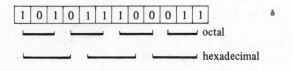

8 Convert +13 (base ten) and −13 (base ten) to binary using a six-bit word and employing twos complement for the negative number.

9 *a*) Interpret the following 8-bit words as denary integers:
i) 00101011
ii) 11111111
(Assume the MSB bit represents the sign bit of the number.)
b) What is the largest positive integer the 8-bit word can hold? (*JMB* spec. 1978)

10 Explain the terms sign-and-magnitude (sign-and-modulus) and twos complement. Use examples to illustrate.

11 For an eight-bit word, what is the range of positive and negative numbers which can be held by the sign-and-magnitude and the twos complement method?

12 In a computer, integers are held in signed twos complement binary. Non-integer numbers are held in floating point form.
   i) What is the value (base 10) of the integer in Figure (i).
   ii) What is the value (base 10) of the positive number in Figure (ii). (*EAEB* 1977)

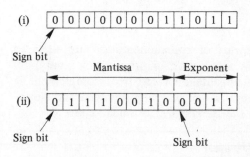

13 Convert the octal number 35 to binary and to hexadecimal.

14 *a*) The octal (base eight) number 216 when written in binary (base two) is

i) 101110 ii) 010001110 iii) 001000010110 iv) 27 v) 20

b) The denary (base ten) number 67 when written in octal is

i) 55   ii) 83   iii) 89   iv) 103   v) none of these

c) The binary number 1010101 when written in denary is

i) −21   ii) 25   iii) 85   iv) 170   v) none of these   (*WMEB* 1976).

15 *a*) Base 8 is often used in computing because

A   8 is a power of 2

B   8 is a lucky number.

C   Electronic circuits can be made to work in base 8.

D   There are 8 bits in a byte.

E   Some computers use an 8 bit word.

b) $111010 + 11010 =$ (numbers and answer in binary)

A   112020.

B   1010100

C   1000100

D   111010.

E   100100.

c) $10000 - 1 =$ (numbers and answer in binary)

A   1001.

B   10011.

C   1000.

D   00000.

E   1111.

d) The twos complement of the binary number 001010 is

A   001010.

B   110101.

C   010100.

D   110110.

E   10.

(*SWEB* 1977).

Appendix 2 Hints and Answers to Selected Exercises

Introduction

1

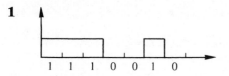

1 1 1 0 0 1 0

2 The electronic circuitry used in computers has only two states: on or off, conducting or nonconducting. It is because all the states of a digital circuit are confined to these two values that the logic, arithmetic and storage functions of a computer can be expressed in terms of the two binary numbers zero and one, i.e. base two.

3 *b*).

4 Analogue computers: continuous, physical information such as temperatures and pressures used as input data.

Digital computers: discrete, individual electrical pulses in one of two states used as input data.

5 An information processor.

6 *b*).

7 Speed, accuracy, automatic, tirelessness, storage ability (any three to be described).

8 *a*) Input device; *b*) output device; *c*) CPU; *d*) auxiliary storage—to extend the limited main memory.

9 Fortran—mathematical, scientific problems.

Cobol—commercial problems.

Basic—used in the mathematical and commercial problems but also a useful teaching language.

10 To drive the hardware units and turn them into a functioning computer system.

Chapter 1

2 $16K \times 32 \text{bits} = (16 \times 1024)(32) = 16\,384 \times 32 = 524\,288$ bits.

$32K \times 16 \text{ bits} = (32 \times 1024)(16) = 32\,768 \times 16 = 524\,288$ bits.

4 Different names for the main memory unit of the CPU.

5 $2^6 = 64$, $2^5 = 32$. Therefore, 2^6 required, i.e. six bits per word (or byte).

6 As groups of electrical pulses (represented by bits), arranged into either bytes of six or eight bits, or as words of 12 or more bits. At least six bits are required to represent the 26 letters of the alphabet, the ten digits, 0 to 9 and some of the special symbols such as comma, full-stop, open and closed brackets, etc.

7 *d*).

8 Storage of data and/or instructions in the main memory; performing arithmetic and comparison operations in the ALU; decoding instructions and controlling flow of data to and from main memory and the ALU, and, input/output devices and auxiliary storage, by the CU.

10 Large word lengths, 32 bits per word at least; very fast arithmetic/logic unit; compilers for mathematical programming languages, such as Fortran, Algol.

14 Real and integer numbers. (See Chapter 1 for how they are stored.)

17 *a*).

18 *Hint*: always add in outputs from the gates (*C* and *D* below), then draw a truth table. Note that *D* is the final output from the circuit.

A	B	C	D
0	1	1	0
1	0	0	1

a)

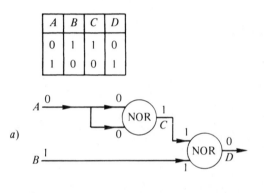

b)

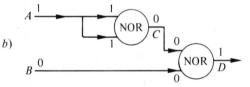

19 Inclusive-OR gate.

20 $A = 1,\ B = 0,\ C = 1$
$A = 0,\ B = 1,\ C = 0$
$A = 1,\ B = 1,\ C = 0$

A	B	X A OR B	Y NOT B	C X AND Y
1	0	1	1	1
0	1	1	0	0
1	1	1	0	0

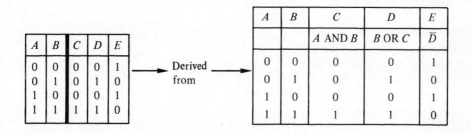

A	B	C	D	E
0	0	0	0	1
0	1	0	1	0
1	0	0	0	1
1	1	1	1	0

Derived from →

A	B	C	D	E
		A AND B	B OR C	$\bar{D}$
0	0	0	0	1
0	1	0	1	0
1	0	0	0	1
1	1	1	1	0

22 NB: Redraw the truth table as shown in larger table, then fill in column D in smaller table. Also note that with three inputs (A, B and C) there are eight possible inputs (2^3).

Inputs			$\bar{A}$ OR B	C	X AND C	D
A	B	C	X	C	Y	$\bar{Y}$
0	0	0	1	0	0	1
0	0	1	1	1	1	0
0	1	0	1	0	0	1
0	1	1	1	1	1	0
1	0	0	0	0	0	1
1	0	1	0	1	0	1
1	1	0	1	0	0	1
1	1	1	1	1	1	0

A	B	C	D
0	0	0	1
0	0	1	0
0	1	0	1
0	1	1	0
1	0	0	1
1	0	1	1
1	1	0	1
1	1	1	0

24 "Overflow" means that the result of a calculation cannot be contained in a given word length. Thus, if multiplying two integer numbers results in 14 bits, but the accumulator contains only 12 bits, then two bits are lost. Overflow with two real numbers occurs if the result of a computation exceeds the number of bits reserved for the exponent.

Chapter 2

1 Cobol

2 "Diagnostics are the AIDS available to help a programmer DEBUG a program. Error messages are produced if there are faults at COMPILE time. Run time errors may occur if the program LOGIC is faulty."

3 *a*).

5 The source program as written by the programmer in a high-level language is input to the compiler.

The compiler outputs object code in the machine language of a given computer.

7 One high-level language statement will be translated into several machine code instructions. For example,

LET M = A + B * C becomes

	LDA	B
	MULT	C
	ADD	A
	STO	M

(Note that this is an assembly version of the machine code.)

8 One assembly instruction will be translated into one machine code instruction.

13 *a*) 2^3 i.e. allows for eight different function codes.

b) 2^{11} i.e. allows for 2048 directly addressable locations of central memory from 0 (zero) to 2047.

16 *e*).

17 Here are two different solutions to the same problem. Note well that the main difference between the two flowcharts is the position of the decision box to determine the end of reading in any more numbers.

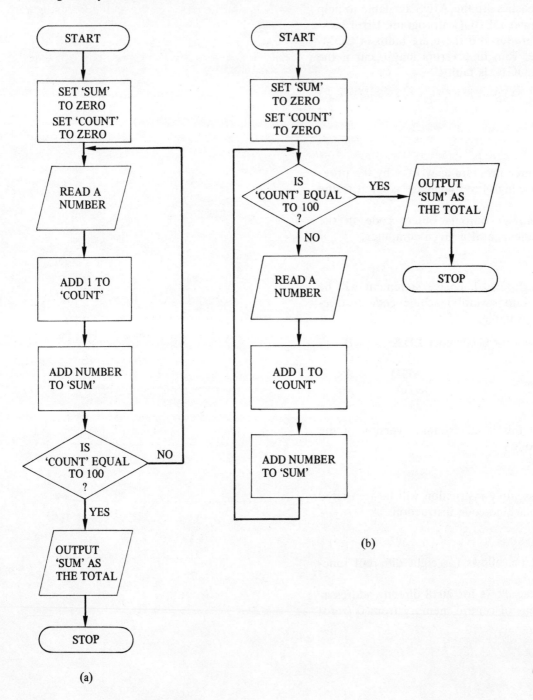

(a)

(b)

18 *Compiler-found errors* (NB. the language used ought to be named)

   i) A syntactical error, i.e. misuse of the programming language's grammar, e.g. in Basic, 00100 LET MM = X (misuse of variable names, MM not a valid name)

   ii) No statement number on a Basic statement, LET X = M.

Non-compiler-found error

A logical error such as jumping/going to the wrong instruction. Discovered (hopefully) by checking program output.

(Or a data input error, found by checking results of program; or system hardware error such as wrong information being transferred from magnetic tape to central memory, found by operating system message indicating a parity error.)

19 The program executes as follows:

+7 found in location 100 is placed in the accumulator

+29 is added to accumulator (7 + 29 = 36)

   this result is placed in address 102

+149 is subtracted from accumulator contents (−113)

   this result is placed in location 104

   stop execution by repeatedly jumping to same instruction.

22 *a*) binary digit

   b) i) 0101 (i.e. 5_{10}, because it is the next in sequence) is MULTIPLY code

      0110 (i.e. 6_{10}, because it is the next in sequence) is DIVIDE code.

      ii) see below.

Binary Instruction		Instruction		Accumulator and Data Word Contents				
Op. Code	Address	Op. Code	Address	Accumulator	Word 13	Word 14	Word 15	Word 16
				0	+4	+2	−1	+10
0001	00001110	LOAD	14	+2	+4	+2	−1	+10
0011	00001111	ADD	15	+1	+4	+2	−1	+10
0100	00001101	SUBTRACT	13	−3	+4	+2	−1	+10
0010	00001111	STORE	15	−3	+4	+2	−3	+10
0001	00010000	LOAD	16	+10	+4	+2	−3	+10
0011	00001111	ADD	15	+7	+4	+2	−3	+10

Chapter 3

13 In blocks—interrecord gaps. Speed of tape—stopping and starting—reading, writing, skipping, winding—slack needed for take up—lessens tension.

14 Teletype—hard copy print-out, but slow; VDU—fast display of information but no record.

15 Transfer of data check based on number of 1 bits. Some systems even parity, some odd; check performed automatically.

16 Data prepared by typing/printing; readable by man and machine; expensive equipment to obtain accuracy and reasonable input speed.

17 Random access: data items retrievable in any order from addressable location. Serial access: data items arranged in sequence and only accessible in order.

18 Economy of space—speed of retrieval—cheapness of consumables.

21 Punched card: 1 character per column, 80 per card, character represented by 1, 2, or 3 holes, zone and numeric punches.

Paper tape: tracks/channels (5 or 7), character per row (width of tape)/frame, 1 or more holes per character, 10 ch/in.

Chapter 4

2 1) Validation refers to checking input data by a validation program run. For example, if a sex code forms part of the data, the program will check that only one of two possible codes is present; also that alphabetic fields contain only alphabetic information, that numeric fields contain only numeric information, that the contents of a field are within reasonable limits (e.g. ages are within the limits of the application, that invoices for £0.0 are not sent out, etc.).

2) Verification refers to checking input data at source, e.g. information punched on cards or entered at a keyboard is correct before being passed to the computer.

NB: Both may take place at the same time if data is entered at a keyboard. The validation program can display the entered data for visual verification by the operator, whilst the program can verify the data and pass any comment to the keyboard operator if data is not valid.

3 *a*) Think out problem from first idea.

b) Produce flowchart or other visual representation of program.

c) Check logic of flowchart—using test data.

d) If flowchart correct, then code into programming language.

e) Dry run (i.e. desk check) program using test data.

f) If correct, run program for compilation errors.

g) If correct, run program with full test data and check results.

h) If results are correct, allow program to be used with "live" data.

5 *a*) Interpretation means the printing above the punched holes of a punch card.

Data on punched cards is verified by a second person keying in the same information at a verifier. If the two match, the data is said to be correct. If the two do not match, the verifier locks, and the data preparation operator has to check for the error.

d) Sorting is necessary for information stored on magnetic tape because the individual records can only be accessed sequentially. Therefore, any re-ordering of the file must be done by sorting. (See also answer to Exercise 15.)

7 *a)* Expense incurred for systems analyst feasibility study.

b) New computer personnel to be employed.

c) Operating system software to be purchased to drive the hardware.

d) Application packages to be purchased.

e) Room space for computer installation, and air conditioning unit if required.

f) Maintenance contract for computer hardware.

10 Job description: analyse existing system and produce feasibility study; design new system giving details of all input data files, output data files; resources required (hardware, type of computer system, any special input devices); description of all program files for the programming department and system charts.

Information:

1) Details of books (author, title, publisher, whether book is fiction or non-fiction, the category, i.e. whether SF, love story, adventure, etc., and for non-fiction whether belonging to music, history, cookery sections, etc.)

2) How the files are organised—use above record fields as example of "book-details-file". Perhaps use the International Standard Book Number (ISBN which is unique to every new book published) as the numerical key field.

3) Output lists could include all books in library, output under categories; those out on loan, list of overdue books (needed for stock control); list of users' names and addresses; reminder letters for overdue books.

4) VDUs for fast display of information; keyboard devices for input; perhaps bar-code reader for details of books when lent to users. Magnetic disc for backing stores.

15 *a)* System B.

b) Transaction file must match the order of the master file tape, otherwise there will be great inefficiency in going up and down the file. System B has no such problem since discs (random access) are available

d) System A because of generations. System B improved by duplicating disc copies or generating magnetic tape copies.

e) System B because of direct random access.

Chapter 5

1 Processing information crucial to a business or organization by computer or with computer assistance, e.g. payroll, billing, accounting, etc., processing information for management. Complete organization required for handling DP—staff structure indicates activities.

6 *Computer-aided design*: creativity, graphs, drawings, designs, animation—view from different angles, easy modification; creation of models to test design; special VDUs, plotters, microfilm. Examples.

Process control: industrial process, control without human intervention, improved efficiency, maybe safer. Give examples of processes controlled.

Word processing: computer-assisted production of text; typing of draft, text stored, easy editing, automatic formatting and printing of finished copy, use of different typefaces. Office use and environment where articles, pamphlets, etc. are written and produced.

Simulation: computing model of real situation, valuable for experiments and testing, saving in time and costs, maybe safer, educational use.

Information retrieval: storage and retrieval, some editing and updating of files but no complicated processing, use of large amounts of backing stores, normally random access; information speedily found. Examples.

Machine intelligence: "thinking" machines, learning by experience, imitating human actions/behaviour, robotics.

7 Collection of related programs, common purpose; user does not have to program, only adds data; may have to be adapted to fit local requirements.

8 *Medicine*: administrative functions, health records, aid to diagnosis, intensive care, teaching, research.

Education: administrative, CAL, CAI, CML, simulation.

Science and engineering: design, controlling processes, research. Give examples, e.g. constructional engineering.

Commerce: processing information—billing, invoicing, accounting, staff files, payroll etc. Give examples, e.g. banks.

Chapter 6

1 *e*).

3 *c*).

4 There must be room for the data and the operating system supervisor.

7 Monoprogramming is the name given to a system whereby only one user program is in main memory at one time.

Multiprogramming is the name given to the system whereby two or more user programs are in main memory at the same time. However, only one user program is executed at any given moment.

9 *Batch processing*: many programs batched together and read on to magnetic tape. Central memory can then accept each program at the full speed of the magnetic tape (or, indeed, disc) rather than at the slower speed of the main input peripheral such as the card reader. Same for output. Mention of overlapping batches would be desirable if time permits.

Multi-access: each program allowed a time slice (typically 10 milliseconds) on a round robin basis. The next program can be read into memory whilst the current program is being executed. Note also that the operating system controls this function and can do so at the internal speed of the processor.

Multiprogramming: several programs are in main memory at the same time. When one becomes occupied in an input/output operation, the supervisor can switch the CU to execute one of the other programs. Again, this is achieved at the internal speeds of the CPU.

Chapter 7

1 *a*) *Benefits* (only three of the following required)

1) Knowledge gained which would have been impossible without use of computers, e.g. satellites in weather prediction and the space programme.

2) Ability to handle and retrieve information on a vast scale.

3) Many jobs created by the computer industry itself; computer personnel required for computer installations; creation of new job areas, e.g. systems analysis.

4) More reliable and up-to-date information available to users, e.g. to company management so that the companies are run more efficiently; to doctors to help in diagnosing medical conditions faster and more accurately.

5) Certain workers freed from repetitive work to undertake more creative and interesting work.

Problem areas:

1) Misuse of stored information.

2) People have become sensitive about the information stored in computer files; is it correct? what is stored?; etc.

3) Employment problems especially for the unskilled workers and assembly line workers.

b) *The future benefits*

1) More computer power available at lower costs, e.g. a medium-scale minicomputer could cost as little as £100 by 1985 whereas today it would cost about £10 000.

2) This would mean a vast increase in the amount of information which could be processed, resulting in an intellectual revolution for society.

3) Further advances in micro-technology will extend the use of computing power into many more areas.

The future problem areas

1) If fewer people work, how much tax will they have to pay to maintain the Welfare State?

2) Will crime and common vandalism increase due to more people idle as a result of fewer jobs? (or will micro-technology actually increase the number of jobs?)

3) Will there be a danger of people "forgetting" how to perform even simple arithmetic and how to write letters?

4) Society will have to become aware of the inherent dangers of computer-based societies and order its own future, hence the need for computer education.

NB: Answers to any questions on the social implications of computers are very much a personal matter, and therefore not easy questions to set or to mark. The above should not be taken as "correct" answers in any way, but as possible answers.

Appendix 1

1   01110
    $\times$ 0101

    01110
    00000
    01110
    00000

01000110

2   1100100011 (ones complement) or
1100100011 + 1 = 1100100100 (twos complement). NB: do not forget to mention which complement you use.

3   110001011   256 128 64 32 16 8 4 2 1
                  1   1   1   1 1
i.e. $256 + 128 + 8 + 2 + 1 = 395$

    10001111 NB: always show your working as in Exercise 1.

4   *e*)

5   *a*) 5   *b*) 16   *c*) 31.
    a) 011   *b*) 10010   *c*) 100111.

6 $2^4 = 16$ but the alphabet has 26 characters, therefore $2^5 = 32$ required, i.e. five bits.

7   101 011 100 011 = 5343 in octal
    1010 1110 0011 = AE3 in hexadecimal

8   +13 using 6 bits = 001101.
    -13 using 6 bits and twos complement = 110010 + 1 = 110011.

11   The leftmost bit will be zero for positive numbers giving a range of 0 to 127 (s and m); and 0 to 127 (2C).

The leftmost bit will be one for negative numbers giving a range of -1 to -127 (s and m); and -1 to -128 (2C).

12   i) +27
    ii) Mantissa is +114. Exponent is +3, i.e. $0.114 \times 10^{+3} = 114.0$

13   35 in octal is 100 011 in binary
    35 in octal is 23 in hexadecimal

15   *a*) A   *b*) B   *c*) E   *d*) D.

General Questions

1   *a*) input/output operations; *b*) arithmetic operations; *c*) logical/comparison operations; *d*) movement of data or structuring data within the CPU.

2   1) Uses electronic circuitry not mechanical gears and wheels.

2) Can operate at the speed of electronics.

3) With stored program concept, the computer becomes automatic.

4) No need for computer programmer to operate machine.

5) Can process information as well as performing calculations.

3 Control transfer is the same as GOTO or jump instructions. The purpose of these types of instructions is to replace the automatically incremented instruction address in the program counter (PC) with the address of the instruction which the programmer wishes to be executed next.

4 *a*) i) Cobol—Common Business Oriented Language—commercial

  ii) Algol—Algorithmic Language—scientific

b) Cobol is particularly suitable for a commercial environment since it allows for files, records and items to be constructed easily in Cobol statements.

(Algol is particularly suitable for a scientific environment since it permits mathematical and scientific formulae to be easily constructed in Algol statements.)

5 Before a program can be executed it must reside in main memory. Each instruction is obeyed/executed/decoded in the CU. Thus, an instruction must be "fetched" from main memory and placed in the control unit; then, it can be "decoded" by the circuitry in the CU; and, finally, as a result of being decoded the instruction is "executed". Hence the "fetch-decode-execute" cycle. Sometimes the cycle is called a "fetch-execute cycle" since the act of decoding an instruction results in its execution.

13 In readiness for input to computer—from raw form to machine understandable; data onto various media—ranging from punched card to discs. Need for accuracy—verification. Heavy staff commitment.

14 Main memory has immediate access; area of computer for program in execution—not permanent; core, LSI. Backing store random or serial access—slower; permanent and large amounts of information; magnetic tape, disc, floppy disc.

16 Magnetic tape: reels, tracks (7 or 9), magnetized spots, character per frame in coded form, blocks of data and interrecord gaps, up to 1600 ch/in density.

Magnetic disc: surfaces, magnetized spots, character as a string of bits, tracks arranged as concentric circles, sectors, addressable locations, high density.

18 Keying-in stations (8 to 64), VDU for visual check, mini to control checking, editing, storage arrangement. Direct data entry, collection at source, ease of verification and modification.

20 Stock control, automatic accounting, information on popular and unpopular lines, automatic ordering of replacement stock, shelves to fill.

21 *a*) Rapid match of information with computer files, check made without a chance of human error; policeman on beat can ask for check. Keyed-in data, stored on disc, displayed visually, printed copy when required.

b) Ordering prompted by details of sales captured at the point-of-sale, stocks fall below a certain level automatic ordering, printing of delivery notes, control of stock at central warehouse, management information. Terminals, printer, disc.

c) Up-to-date files on backing store, probably disc. Updated by keying-in or card/document input. On-line enquiry, display and/or printed output.

d) Retention of up-to-date files for each employee, preparation and input of current information collected from work dockets, etc. Various input forms, magnetic tape or disc storage, output on pre-printed payslips.

22 Feasibility investigation, examination of existing procedures, changes in organization necessary, design of new system.

23 How to operate the various peripheral devices, getting the system ready for operation, monitoring system behaviour, preventative maintenance.

25 *a*) Magnetic discs or drums because of the need for very fast and direct access to answer queries.
b) Magnetic tape useful because of sequential processing required by application.
c) Only magnetic discs or drums because of speed and direct access requirements.

26 *b*) i) utility program as part of general operating system.
ii) operating system.
iii) application package.
iv) compiler.

27 *a*) A device is on-line if it is directly controlled by the control unit of the CPU. A device is off-line if it is controlled by a device other than the CPU, e.g. a human operator or a card punch.
b) Punching of cards is off-line data preparation. It takes place before the cards are read on to a card reader which may be on-line to the CPU. Similarly for paper tape.

Glossary of Terms

absolute address
An address which permanently identifies a unique, physical location in main memory.

access speed
data is called from storage (main or secondary) and the instant at which that data can be used.

accumulator
A special storage register associated with the arithmetic/logic unit for storing the results of steps in a calculation or data transfer.

address field
That part of a machine code instruction which supplies the address of the data in main memory for the operation (function) code to work upon.

address modification
One method of increasing or decreasing the contents of the address field of an instruction by the use of the modification (index) register.

analogue computer
A computer in which data is represented by a continuously variable physical quantity such as voltage or angular position.

ancestral file system
Grandfather, father, son files are the three most recent versions of a file that is periodically updated. These are retained for security purposes.

arithmetic/logic unit
(ALU) The part of the CPU where arithmetic and logic operations are performed. Sometimes called the arithmetic unit.

arithmetic operator
The arithmetical signs of addition, subtraction, division and multiplication as used by a given programming language.

assembler program
A program, usually provided by the computer manufacturer, to translate a program written in assembly language to machine code. In general, each assembly language instruction is changed into one machine code instruction.

assembly language
A low-level programming language, generally using symbolic addresses, which is translated into machine code by an assembler.

auxiliary store
(also backing store, secondary storage) A means of storing large amounts of data outside the main memory.

batch processing
A technique in which computer processing does not begin until all input (data and/or programs) has been collected together (i.e. "batched").

binary
(also base two) The binary number system which uses only the two digits one and zero.

binary coded decimal
(BCD) A numeric coding system in which each decimal numeral is represented by a four-bit group.

216

bit	Shortened term for binary digit. A bit can only have the value one or zero (1, 0).
byte	A set of eight (or six in some computers) bits often grouped together to form one character. Sometimes, a byte may be a sub-division of a larger group of bits.
central processing unit	(CPU) The main part of the computer, consisting of the immediate access store (central memory), arithmetic unit, and control unit. Also called the central processor.
character	One of a set of symbols which can be represented in a computer. These can be letters, digits, punctuation marks, etc.
character set	The total number of characters which can be used in a programming language, or which a computer system can recognise and reproduce.
compiler program	The program which translates a high-level language program into a computer's machine code. Each high-level language instruction is changed into several machine code instructions.
conditional instruction	Causes a departure from the normal sequential execution of program steps. Sometimes called a "jump" or "branch" instruction.
control unit	That part of the computer which accesses instructions in sequence, interprets them and, then, directs their implementation.
data	Information coded in a form acceptable for input to, and processing by, a computer system.
data bank	A collection (bank) of databases.
database	A file of structured data. The use of the data is independent of any particular application.
data processing	The complete operation of collecting data, processing it, and presenting results. The term Data Processing is normally applied to business tasks where the use of a computer is involved. Sometimes called electronic data processing (EDP).
data processing manager	The person responsible for the overall running of the computer department.
desk check	The use of test data to check the paths through a program or flowchart without the use of a computer. Sometimes called a "dry run".
diagnostic	An error message that attempts to indicate the type of fault.
digital computer	A computer where data is represented by a combination of discrete (individual) pulses denoted by 0s and 1s.
documentation	A complete description of a program, usually including helpful notes, flowcharts, program listing and test data.
execution error	An error in a program that only occurs during the execution of that program.
feasibility study	An investigation process which collects information

	enabling systems analysts to establish whether a computer system should be used in solving some particular problem.
fetch-execute cycle	Refers to the process whereby the control unit must first fetch an instruction from main memory before it can execute (interpret) that instruction.
field	Part of a record containing predetermined data. (Do not confuse the field with the data it contains.)
file	An organised collection of records which are related.
fixed length records	A record in which the data cannot exceed a predetermined maximum number of characters.
flowchart	A diagrammatic representation of a sequence of operations necessary to solve a problem.
hard copy	Usually refers to a printed copy (of characters and/or graphs or diagrams) which can be kept and re-read at any time as opposed to a cathode ray tube (CRT) version which can only be viewed at the time it is being generated by the VDU.
hardware	The physical units which make up a computer system.
high-level language	A problem-oriented programming language in which instructions may be equivalent to or generate several machine code instructions and which can be used on different computers by using an appropriate compiler.
indirect addressing	A programming technique in which the address part of an instruction refers to another location which contains the desired address.
information retrieval	The name given to the process of recovering specific information from stored data.
input data file	A file of records containing data for input to a computer program.
instruction decoder	Complex circuitry in the CU designed to decode (interpret) any instruction in the computer's machine code repertoire.
instruction register	(IR) The register used to contain the address of the next instruction to be expected. Also referred to as the Next Instruction Register, Control Register, Sequence Control Register, Program Counter, Instruction Address Register (IAR).
item	A unit of data contained in the field of a record.
key field	A particular field in a record whose contents can be used to locate or identify individual records in a file.
keying in	Typing characters at a terminal input device for input to a computer system.
label	A group of characters used to identify a given low-level instruction.
library routine	A pre-written and stored "program" contained in a library of such programs and held in secondary storage on a computer system.

logical operator	Name given to the logical symbols for "greater than", "less than", etc, as used by a particular high-level language. Also called "relational operators".
loop	A sequence of instructions that is executed repeatedly until some specified condition is satisfied.
low-level language	A machine oriented language in which each program instruction is similar in representation to a single machine code instruction.
machine code	The entire instruction repertoire adopted in the design of a particular computer. Any one instruction may be executed by the machine without further translation.
master file	A file of data used for reference purposes by an applications program.
memory unit	Part of the computer where data and instructions are held. (Also known as main memory, store, core store, immediate access memory, central memory.)
microfiche	A rectangle of film on which a standard 30 or 60 frames are recorded.
mnemonic	Greek word for "memory". Letters used to represent the decimal (or binary, or octal, or hexadecimal) numbers representing machine code instructions.
modification register	(MR) Register used to modify (change) the contents of the address field of a machine code instruction. Sometimes called an "index register".
multi-programming	A method of benefitting from the speed of a CPU compared to slower peripheral devices, by allowing two or more programs to be processed apparently simultaneously, but actually in short bursts, controlled by an operating system. For example, while one program is waiting for an input/output operation to be performed (say), another may have access to the CPU.
object program	The translated version of a program which has been processed by the assembler or compiler.
off-line processing	Processing carried out by devices not under the control of the central processor.
on-line processing	Processing performed on equipment directly under the control of the central processor, whilst the user remains in communication with the computer.
operator	A person responsible for operating the computer system on a day-to-day basis.
operation code	Part of a machine code instruction specifying the operation to be performed.
package	A generalised program designed to perform a particular task (e.g. payroll, invoicing) for more than one user.
parity check	A test applied to binary data to check for even or odd parity, as appropriate.
even parity	is present in any group of binary bits in which the number of 1s is even;

odd parity	is present in any group of binary bits in which the number of 1s is odd;
parity bit	is a binary digit appended to binary data. The state of the bit is such as to ensure even parity or odd parity as used by the computer system in question.
program	A complete set of program statements to perform a specified task.
programmer	A person responsible for writing computer programs. Can be either a systems programmer (i.e. one who writes programs which control a computer system) or an applications programmer (i.e. one who writes programs to be processed by a computer system).
program listing	A list of a program's instructions, often containing additional material supplied by the computer system, such as compiler diagnostic messages.
random access	The process of storing or retrieving an item of data directly without the necessity of reading any other stored data first. Also known as "direct access".
real time system	A system which is able to receive continuously changing data from outside sources, and which is able to process that data sufficiently rapidly to be capable of controlling or influencing the sources of data (e.g. air-traffic control, air line bookings).
record	A collection of related items of data, treated as a unit (e.g. one line of an invoice may form a record and a collection of such records form an invoicefile).
register	A location, which is sometimes protected, used for specific purposes only, e.g. accumulator, control register.
reserved words	Particular words in a programming language or an operating system command language which have a set meaning and purpose and which can only be used within that context.
serial access	The process of storing or retrieving an item of data in such a way that all previous items must be read first. For example, to store a tenth record will necessitate reading all previous nine records before coming to the tenth storage area for that record.
software	The term used for any type of program whatever its purpose.
source program	A program written by the programmer in a programming language. A source program must be assembled or compiled and then interpreted before it can be run.
store location	The basic unit within a computer store capable of holding a single unit of data.
syntax error	An error which occurs when the rules governing the structure of a language are wrongly applied.
systems analysis	The art of analysing the methods of performing a task.
systems analyst	The person responsible for the analysis of a business

	system to assess its suitability for computer application. He may also design the necessary computer system.
test data	Data used to test a program.
time sharing system	A means of providing multi-access to a computer system. Each user is, in turn, allowed a time slice of the system's resources, although each appears to have continuous use of the system.
track	A channel or path along a storage medium on which data is recorded. For example, the tracks of a magnetic disc, magnetic tape or paper tape.
transaction file	A file of records used to update the master file.
truth table	A Boolean operation table in which the result is tabulated for all possible combinations of the variables.
updating	A process of altering information held on records in a file to bring it up-to-date. This may involve deleting and/or adding records in a file, and/or changing items in existing records.
validation	A process of checking the validity of information held in a file.
variable length records	Records whose length (i.e. the number of characters in each field) may vary from record to record.
verification	The process of checking data which has been keyed onto some medium or memory, usually by keying in the information a second time and comparing the results.
word	In computer terminology, denotes the collection of bits which is treated by the central processor as a single unit.
word length	The number of bits normally used in a word in a particular computer. The number of bits varies from 4, 8, 12, 16, 32, etc, up to 64. Some modern computers allow a variable number of bits to constitute a word in order to provide flexibility of storage; instructions are then provided to manipulate differing number of bits (as a word). This is known as "variable word length".

Index